Back to the Soil

BACK TO THE SOIL

The Jewish Farmers of Clarion, Utah, and Their World

ROBERT ALAN GOLDBERG

THE UNIVERSITY OF UTAH PRESS I *Salt Lake City*

The Defiance House Man colophon is a registered trademark
of The University of Utah Press. It is based upon a four-foot-tall,
Ancient Puebloan pictograph (late PIII) near Glen Canyon, Utah.

Library of Congress Cataloging-in-Publication Data

Goldberg, Robert Alan, 1949
Back to the soil.

Bibliography: p.
Includes index.

ISBN 978-1-60781-155-8

1. Jews—Utah—Clarion Colony.
2. Farmers, Jewish—Utah—Clarion Colony.
3. Jews—Colonization—Utah—Clarion Colony.
4. Clarion Colony (Utah) I. Title.

F834.C48G65 1986   979.2 86-13185

Maps by Gene Ockinga

To my Parents, for Instilling a Jewish Essence
my Wife, for Nurturing It
my Sons, Who Will Carry It Forward

Contents

TABLES

MAPS

ILLUSTRATIONS

Let us now sing the praises of famous men,
the heroes of our nation's history, . . .
Some there are who have left a name behind them
to be commemorated in story.
There are others who are unremembered;
they are dead, and it is as though they had never
existed,
as though they had never been born
or left children to succeed them.
Not so our forefathers; they were men of loyalty,
Whose good deeds have never been forgotten.
Their prosperity is handed on to their descendants,
and their inheritance to future generations. . . .
Their line will endure for all time,
and their fame will never be blotted out.
Their bodies are buried in peace,
but their names live for ever.
                    Ecclesiasticus 44:1, 8–11, 13–14

We came to build the land and be built by it.
                    Hebrew folk song

Preface

Between 1880 and 1920, two million Jews left their homes in Eastern Europe for the urban centers of America. Their migration and subsequent settlement have attracted historians and sociologists who, in turn, have generated studies concerning all facets of the urban Jewish experience. Researchers have traced the emergence of the Jewish community and the proliferation of its social, economic, and cultural institutions in the big-city ghetto. They have followed the immigrants and their children to the suburbs. The Jewish rise from peddler and factory worker to middle-class professional and business entrepreneur has been well documented. Several works have appeared dealing with Jewish generational change and conflict in the urban setting. The Jewish impact upon the political, economic, and social life of the wider urban community has similarly been surveyed. This concentrated focus has created an image for the academic community and the general public of Jews solely as urbanites with the Lower East Side of New York City their home. The promised land of America thus became in the title of an eminent historian's book *The Promised City.*

The urban complexion of American Jewry disguises, even from itself, a people rooted in the soil. Although forgotten and ignored, biblical Jews were herders and farmers. The Five Books of Moses, the words of the Prophets, and the Psalms are replete with agricultural allusions and allegories. Isaiah spoke to farmer-warriors when he prophesied, "And they shall beat their swords into plowshares, and their spears into pruning hooks." Micah's words were reassuring to a people bound to the land: "They shall sit every man under his vine and under his fig tree; and none shall make them afraid." Few Jews reflect upon the agrarian foundation of their identity even as they construct booths for *Succoth,* the Feast of Tabernacles celebrating the final gathering of the harvest in ancient Israel. In the biblical land of milk and honey, it was the Canaanite whose nationality was synonymous with trading or peddling.

The urban concentration also fosters an amnesia about the Jewish effort to return to the soil in America. Immigrants from Eastern Europe joined their resources with the philanthropy of American Jews to create agricultural colonies in New Jersey, North and South Dakota, Louisiana, Oregon, Colorado, and Kansas. Between 1881 and 1915, approximately forty such farming settlements were planted in the United States. The American effort was part of an international back-to-the-soil movement that saw Jewish colonies established in Argentina, Canada, and Israel. Although forgotten, Jewish farmers could be found tilling soil and raising livestock closer than the nearest Israeli *kibbutz* or *moshav.*

The Jewish colony of Clarion in Utah was a product of this attempt to revive the agrarian life. In 1911, 200 immigrant Jewish families living in New York City, Philadelphia, and Baltimore subscribed funds to return to the land. They created this cooperative experiment to kindle a movement to the countryside among Jews crowded in the urban slums of the East. Farm ownership, the colonists believed, would destroy the opprobrious image of Jews as *luftmenshn* (those who live without visible means of support) and demonstrate to the Christian world the Jewish stake in the new homeland. Eighty-one families moved west and farmed the Clarion tract. Although the governor of Utah encouraged the colony and the Mormon Church provided financial aid, Clarion survived as an organizational entity only until 1916. A dozen Jewish families remained on the land following the colony's demise, the last leaving Utah in the mid-1920s.

Clarion was not an isolated or eccentric moment in Jewish time. The colonists' story is central to Jewish life in the modern period and touches the wider historical context in several ways. Clarion's ideological and cultural roots grew in the soil of the Russian Pale. From the pogroms, discriminatory laws, and economic hardships of the Pale captivity came the Jewish response that birthed the socialists, anarchists, and Zionists who peopled the Utah colony. The Clarion Jews shared, too, in the migration to America, a passage of faith and pain that deeply etched the immigrant generation. In urban America the newcomers attempted amid tenements and sweatshops to rebuild their lives. For the Clarion Jews, the urban land forged not the promise of a better world for themselves and their coreligionists, but chains that enslaved a people to the caricatures of the past. The escape to the soil carried Clarion's men and women into the midst of a national and international Jewish experiment.

Clarion was the last of the major attempts to colonize Jews on the land in the United States. It was, moreover, the largest in population and land area and had the longest temporal existence of any Jewish colony west of the Appalachian Mountains. Its representative nature allows a generalization of the Clarion experience to the other attempts at Jewish-American colonization. Clarion offers insights, as well, into the worldwide effort to establish Jewish agricultural colonies. In Clarion are visible the factors that operated to affect the economic and ethnic success or failure of these diverse settlements. The recovered Clarion fragment thus becomes a crucial part of the larger mosaic of Jewish history.

A lack of information and records has hampered in-depth research of the Jewish agricultural movement. Clarion's farmers, perhaps aware of the significance of their efforts, have left an abundance of source materials. I discovered the Clarion Colony in a tourist book about Utah ghost towns given to me by a friend for the purpose of entertaining out-of-state visitors. My curiosity led me to a short article about the colony based upon research in the papers of a Utah governor and the records of the state land board. Among the land board's papers were the names of the Jews who had participated in the project. Because of the few materials available, I planned only to publish a collective biography of the colonists fashioned from data gathered for the 1910 United States Census.

Wanting to do more, I placed a small ad in a Salt Lake City Jewish community newsletter seeking information about the colony. There were two responses to my inquiry. One person gave me the name of a Utah man who he believed had been born in the colony. A telephone call and subsequent interview uncovered my first Clarion family and yielded a tape recording made a decade earlier of the experiences of a Clarion colonist. The second response was from a local Jewish history buff who provided me with Clarion materials that he had collected. These included the memoirs of the colony's founder, a taped interview with a Clarion colonist, and the names of four colonist families. These families, in turn, put me in contact with four more Clarion descendants. I then placed ads in the *New York Review of Books* (which attracts a middle-class Jewish audience) and in Yiddish newspapers in New York City and Los Angeles. These ads produced letters and telephone calls from eleven additional Clarion families.

When the ad campaign had run its course, I reviewed the land board's list of names to isolate the more unusual ones. Fifty-six uncommon surnames such as Nilva, Binder, Radding, Okune, and Geronemus were selected from the more numerous Cohens, Goldbergs, and Horowitzs. Based upon the heavily urban character of the American Jewish population, I asked research assistants to scan the current telephone directories of the nation's twenty largest metropolitan areas for the chosen names. If they found ten or fewer entries for a particular name in a given directory, they recorded telephone numbers and addresses and letters were sent seeking information. The great majority of letters missed their marks. Still, this part of the search uncovered eleven Clarion families.

These recovered thirty-one families provided information about colonists' place and date of birth, occupation, educational and political backgrounds, marital status, organizational ties, and memories of experiences in Europe and America. This enabled me to construct family biographies tracing the colonists from their birthplaces in Russia through the eastern cities of America to Utah and beyond, and to subsequent generations. In addition, I asked each family about other Clarion people. Their continuing relationships brought me to another twenty-two colonist families. Reaching this group allowed me to find families that otherwise would have been lost because of marriage, a common name, or a name change (i.e., Brownstein, to Brownie, Levitsky to Levit, and Chatsky to Chat).

Biographical information and second-generation memories were not the most important items these families shared. They also possessed nine colonist journals and reminiscences varying in length from 15 to 200 pages. Photographs of the families and life in Clarion surfaced, adding a visual dimension to the story. The first generation spoke as well through two taped recordings made a decade ago and an interview recently conducted with the last surviving adult member of the colony. I have donated these materials to the Department of Special Collections at the Marriott Library at the University of Utah and they are open to researchers.

Thus, the Clarion Colony is no longer beyond reach. Formerly perceived only through government documents, the colony has now lost its faceless anonymity and emerged as the human drama that it was. The varied sources provide the opportunity to explore the immigrant experience and the communal process within a framework of family history. The values and ideals of the colonists, the daily rhythm of life, the personalities of the settlers, and the struggle for and eventual collapse of their dreams are now open to examination.

The University of Utah Press asked me about reprinting *Back to the Soil* to mark the twenty-fifth anniversary of its publication and the one hundredth anniversary of the Clarion Colony's founding. I was only too glad to cooperate. This book began for me as a curiosity. Aware of the urban roots of America's Jews, the agricultural colony in the Utah outback was something out of place. I initiated *Back to the Soil* as a scholarly project. This microhistory would spotlight a little known piece of Jewish history. It would focus on men and women seeking a better life for themselves and their children. It would manifest the Jewish ideal of *tikkun olam*—Hebrew for repair of the world. Coming from diverse ideological positions and human motives, these Jews were not simply fixed on the present or their personal ends. They looked outward to change a people. Their story revealed patterns that escaped the confines of Clarion and shaped a larger Jewish world.

I realized early on that this was much more than an academic exercise. I had recently moved to the state and a position in the Department of History at the University of Utah. The economic, political, and cultural influence of the Church of Jesus Christ of Latter-day Saints and its members demands of others a firm grounding in their own religion's theology and history. Clarion, then, became very personal, a means to secure my Jewish moorings and to lay claim to my new home. Reinforcing this was the support of the Clarion families. Their heartfelt letters, brimming with information, insisted that something significant had happened on the land. As Harry Bernstein, son of colonists David and Sara, wrote: "The three years our family lived there seem to have had a deep and enduring influence, perhaps more than any other before or since. Apart from the expected nostalgic memories, [we recalled] the striking contrasts between our earlier life in the city and the pleasant, peaceful setting of the Clarion environment, the sense of 'belonging,' of pride and independence it brought, and the cooperative atmosphere we found...."[1] Or as colonist Samuel Sack's daughter Sarah described her father even many years after Clarion: "Deep down in his heart, he was still a farmer."[2] Frequently,

---

1. Harry Bernstein to the author, June 22, 1984.
2. Sarah Sack Bober to the author, August 10, 1982.

Clarion families contacted me when they planned "pilgrimages" to visit the colony's ruins. These contacts have continued in the twenty-five years since publication. So, too, have my efforts to find new information about Clarion to make the story complete. I have added new material to this book to insure its accuracy. I feel privileged to be part of the Clarion story and to help in its telling.

This sense of connection, I quickly learned, extended beyond the Clarion circle. Groups in the Utah Jewish community repeatedly asked me to lecture about the colony. I had not kindled an interest, I responded to a need. I felt this hunger also in the young and I took my Hebrew School classes of sixteen- and seventeen-year-olds on field trips to Clarion to witness and be moved by the reminders of Jews on the land.

Clarion's call has been heard beyond the Jewish community. If Clarion is a Jewish space, it also occupies Mormon minds. This began when Mormons welcomed Jews in 1911 and offered assistance to the colonists. Later, Mormon neighbors gathered and protected Clarion artifacts and records and kept the history alive. They still help Jews navigate the site and locate landmarks. Local Mormons built a protective fence around the Clarion cemetery's two Hebrew-inscribed gravestones to shield them from grazing cattle. I was particularly moved when a history textbook used in Utah middle schools added several paragraphs on Clarion to the story of Jews in the state. Sharing a history of persecution and pioneering, Jews and Mormons have found common ground in Clarion.

Now, a century after the colony's founding, Mormons have joined with Jews to celebrate the event. For the one hundredth anniversary of the Jewish settlement, Mormon teenagers in Gunnison, near Clarion, are practicing their roles in a play recalling the colony while their elders prepare a welcome for Jewish visitors from Salt Lake City and Clarion family members from around the United States. Not since Clarion's zenith have so many family and friends gathered to share its history. The land of the Clarion colony has remained a constant these many years. So, too, has the dream. It touches us even now.

This book is the work of many minds, hands, and hearts. I have accumulated heavy debts, both personal and academic, in its research and writing. Edward Eisen's generous gift of source materials and continuous prodding helped convince me to devote three years of my life to this study. The Clarion families willingly opened their lives and shared both sweet and tragic memories. They bestowed an honor in allowing me to remember with them their fathers, mothers, sisters, and brothers. Particularly important to my research were Abraham and Alex Bassin; Harry and Michael Bernstein; Sivan Hamburger; Albert Isgur; Ben Kristol; Louis Levit; Joseph Levitsky; Daniel Malamed; Benjamin Paul; Beckie Mastrow Pullman; Beryl, Jeffrey, Susanah, and Julia Rosenstock; Carol Smith; and Sara Binder Steinberg. David Green and Michael Walton fired my efforts with their enthusiasm and support. "Our" book would not have been completed without their friendship. Everett Cooley, Lamont Nielsen, and the Zucker family graciously permitted me access to their Clarion materials.

I have benefited from the aid and advice of Morris Schappes, Maia Gregory, Max Rosenfeld, Adah Fogel, L. A. Munsey, Phyllis Dee, Miriam Deutsch, and Kathleen Albrycht. Ann Chambers, a graduate student at the University of Utah, gave far more than the maximum expected of any research assistant. Clarion became her story as well as mine. I have learned much from the critical yet gently tendered suggestions of Claire and June Outsen, Dean May, Harris Lenowitz, Floyd O'Neil, Gordon Irving, Gregory Thompson, and Moses Rischin. I hope that I have shaped the manuscript sufficiently to fit their perceptive suggestions. To thank Karen Lauridsen, Tony Scott, and Joan Larscheid for typing and processing this study would far understate their contributions. Their constant excitement, support, and above all, patience with repeated demands have enshrined them in my heart. The American Philosophical Society; the University of Utah, College of Humanities; and the Jewish Studies Program of the Middle East Center, also of the University of Utah, provided grants of time or money to facilitate research and manuscript preparation.[3]

This book has done much to strengthen my sense of family solidarity. In rallying to my prodigious personal and scholarly needs, each of those close to me has earned coauthorship. My father, perhaps retouching his own past, has given of himself in every way possible to make this study a success. With this book, my aunt and uncle reemerged as significant figures in my life. They gave their time and energy accomplishing all tasks requested and more. In addition to his usual strong support, my brother performed interview, research, and critiquing assignments. There are few in whom I have such confidence. My sons, Davy and Josh, yet too young to read this book, pledged what they could—patience, diversion, and love.

---

3. Parts of this preface are reprinted by permission of the editor of *Historical Methods*

Finally, the reprinting of *Back to the Soil* gives me a unique opportunity to honor my wife, Annie. Intellectually and emotionally I have found my intended, my soul mate. Sharing this seals her deeper into my heart.

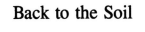

Back to the Soil

1

The Pale Roots

Tsum lebn tsu veynik,
tsum shtarbn tsu fil.*

Yiddish proverb

When will the time come finally
when we Russians will not
have to blush before you Jews?

Deputy of the First Duma,
1906

In September 1911, on a barren hill in south central Utah, twelve Jewish farmers hoisted an American flag to signal the transformation of a dream into reality. A Jewish agricultural colony had arisen from the desert. The creation of Clarion was not an escape to isolation nor an act of estrangement. Rather, this cooperative effort was born of a sense of Jewish nationalism and infused with a concern for the larger group. Clarion was to be the beginning of a crusade that would reclaim the pride, honor, and future of a people. Jewish social and economic revival would occur through the soil and in the restora-

---

*"Too little to live, too much to die."

tion of the calling of their ancestors. While these Jewish farmers looked to the future, they acted and dreamed in response to their past. The meaning of Clarion to its creators and the wider Jewish society of the early twentieth century is impossible to comprehend without reference to the political, social, and cultural environment which spawned the people and their experiment. The Russian experience was Clarion's prologue. It molded their personalities, abilities, interactions, beliefs, and hopes. From the Pale came the human ingredients and ideological currents which envisioned a Clarion, fashioned it, and directed its development. Without grounding in this Jewish past, Clarion would be nothing more than an isolated desert outpost lacking significance to all but a handful.

I

During the nineteenth century approximately one-half of the world's ten million Jews lived under the rule of the Russian tsars. Ironically, history's movement had located Judaism's center within the bastion of Greek Orthodoxy. Religion, history, folklore, tradition, dress, diet, and even language were barriers dividing the two peoples. Animosity was generated, as well, economically. The Jewish merchant and the Christian peasant were rivals in a struggle for subsistence which grew fiercer because of the religious cast of the competition. Governmental and religious leaders, both creators and creatures of public opinion, further inflamed relations with words and deeds. The chasm between Jewish society and Christian Russia was immense with few bridges existing to foster understanding or cooperation. Thus, although counted as Russian subjects, the Jews existed apart, almost a nation within a nation.[1]

Settlement patterns exacerbated the situation. To control the "alien" people and to avoid contamination of the Christian population, the tsars ordered all Jews to live in a social and economic Siberia known as the Pale of Settlement. This massive ghetto with invisible walls consisted of fifteen western provinces extending from the Gulf of Riga in the north to the Black Sea in the south. Even within these borders there were restrictions, for no Jew was permitted to reside in the cities of Kiev, Nikolaev, Sevastopol, and Yalta. Ninety-five percent of all Russian Jews settled in the Pale, residence outside forbidden except for military service or by special permit. While Jews constituted only 12 percent of the Pale's population, they had little interaction with their Christian countrymen. By choice and outside pressure, Jews insulated themselves physically in tight protective clusters either in the large cities or in regional market centers called *shtetlach*. Some *shtetlach* were composed

THE JEWISH PALE OF SETTLEMENT

BALTIC SEA

GERMANY

•Riga

KOVNO

Kovno•

•Vilna

VILNA

•Minsk

•Bialystock

GRODNO

Warsaw•

POLAND

MINSK

VITEBSK

•Vitebsk

•Mogilev

MOGILEV

•Gomel

•Moscow

CHERNIGOV

VOLYNIA

Zhitomir•

POLTAVA

KIEV

Poltava•

GALICIA

AUSTRIA-HUNGARY

PODOLIA

•Ekaterinoslav

EKATERINOSLAV

KHERSON

Kishinev•

•Odessa

TAURIDA

BESSARABIA

RUMANIA

BLACK SEA

BULGARIA

MAP 1

almost entirely of Jews. Shocks from the outside, however, repeatedly re-
minded Jews of their precarious place in the Russian empire.[2]

In an atmosphere precluding personal contact and community interaction, centuries old suspicion and distrust festered. To Christians the Jews
were *inordsy* (those of another race), lecherous for gold, and cursed for the
murder of their Savior. In the eyes of the Jews the peasants were inferior culturally, religiously, and intellectually. Thus, Chaim Weizmann, who would
later become Israel's first president, dismissed them: "Non-Jews were for me
something peripheral."[3] Jewish nationalist Chaim Zhitlovsky was more blunt:
"As for the Russian masses, we regarded them as brute animals."[4] Still, fear
overshadowed this contempt. Without warning or reason came accusations of
blood libel, the violence of the pogrom, and police harassment. Jewish
awareness of the tenuousness of existence was pervasive and instilled as a primary part of the socialization process. Mary Antin, an immigrant to America
in the 1890s, wrote:

> I do not know when I became old enough to understand. . . . My
> grandmother told me about it when she put me to bed at night. My
> parents told me about it when they gave me presents on holidays.
> My playmates told me, when they drew back into a corner of the
> gateway, to let a policeman pass. . . . And sometimes, waking in the
> night, I heard my parents whisper in the dark. There was no time in
> my life when I did not hear and see and feel the truth. . . .[5]

II

The Jewish presence was an accomplished fact that the Russian government
felt compelled to confront. Not only were Jews religiously, ethnically, and
culturally distinct, but their concentration along the defensively vulnerable
western border required policies designed to crack the "foreign" menace. To
achieve this end the tsars pursued a solution of assimilation through segrega-
tion. While confined to the Pale ghetto, Jews would be stripped of their religious and cultural identities. To attain this goal, inducements would be
offered Jews who sought assimilation and sanctions levied upon those who
clung to their beliefs. In the end the Jewish population would be winnowed
through death, departure, and conversion so that an empire of one faith, one
culture, and one people would emerge. Only in means and rate of speed did
tsarist policies differ.[6]

The tsars issued hundreds of decrees restricting Jewish rights and making the practice of Judaism more onerous. Jews were forbidden to keep inns
or taverns, and special taxes were placed upon Sabbath candles and Kosher

meat. Thousands of Jews were uprooted from the rural areas of Moghilev, Vitebsk, Grodno, and Kiev provinces and ordered into crowded cities. All Jews were expelled from a thirty-mile-wide strip along the western border. The tsars barred the wearing of traditional Jewish dress and abolished communal government institutions. Imperial edict obligated all Jewish males, ages eighteen to twenty-five, to serve twenty-five years as soldiers. Removed from the support of family and synagogue and afflicted with mental and physical tortures, many were lost through death or conversion to Christianity. Sometimes boys as young as eight or nine were caught in the conscription net.[7]

Rewards designed to facilitate Russification partially balanced these punishments. The tsars granted Jewish schoolchildren free access to Russian schools and universities in hope of weaning them from traditional Jewish education. Jews were permitted to own land and, by exemption from taxation, encouraged to farm. Jews served upon municipal councils in the Pale, and children were spared conversion without parental consent. The government bestowed residential privileges outside of the Pale upon wealthy Jewish merchants and Jews with university degrees. At the same time, the escape to equality was available to all who bowed before the Greek cross.[8]

After nearly a century of manipulation the Jew remained fixed in a tenuous position between citizen and alien, assigned all of the responsibilities and obligations required of a subject, yet few of the rights. Piecemeal changes in status the tsars offered were designed to break down Jewish exclusiveness and generate a gradual fusion with the majority. Jews thus remained pawns unable through their own efforts to effect change in their condition. Whether benign or harsh, gradual or rapid, the Russians sought to extinguish the essence of the Jewish presence.[9]

Official inertia and bureaucratic clumsiness, to some degree, insulated Jews and muffled the severity of tsarist policy. Even more important in protecting Jewish self-worth and identity was a physical, emotional, and mental huddling against the hostile world. Yet, by the 1860s tsarist assimilation efforts had generated cracks in Jewish society. If conversion was an unviable option for most Jews, social and intellectual conformity was not. At first, a small minority among the elite took hold of the educational benefits the tsars offered and enrolled its children in Russian schools. Other classes followed the elite's lead so that during the last quarter of the nineteenth century, one in four Jewish children was studying in a Russian school. By 1911, the *cheder,* or religious elementary school, educated a minority of Jewish children of school age. The universities also experienced a rising Jewish student population. Jews with sufficient wealth or the proper educational credentials began to move outside the Pale and into the larger Russian cities. There they spoke and dressed like their Christian countrymen and tasted of the political, social, and cultural currents of secularization which were reaching into Russia after sweeping over the rest of Europe. The tsarist honey of assimilation, with its privileges and opportunities, had begun to attract the top echelons of Jewish society and effect their Russification.[10]

III

Economic forces were at work as well, gradually eroding the unity and self-containment of the Jewish world. In the 1860s, the emancipation of the serfs economically dislodged Jews who had administered rural estates and served as middlemen in marketing surplus produce. With these roles now eliminated or assumed directly by peasant or noble, the Jew's stake in the feudal system became untenable and forced removal to the *shtetl* or city. Relief, however, was unavailable in the urban centers of the Pale, for the emerging factory system economically suffocated Jewish living standards. The industrialization of Russia, beginning in the last decades of the nineteenth century, offered little to Jewish workers. Employer anti-Semitism, conflicts, real or imagined, between Jewish and Christian workers, proclivity to strike, and refusal to work on the Sabbath led to exclusion from the factory labor force. If Jews found industrial places, they were in the smaller, less-modern, unmechanized plants. Jewish artisans remained locked in the prefactory household or putting-out system of production. Entrepreneurs distributed raw materials to individual craftsmen who performed part of the production process for a piece rate. The businessman saw the good through to its finished state and then sold it. In sharp competition with fellow sellers, he reduced every kopeck of waste, demanding of his employees fourteen- to sixteen-hour days while paying them as little as possible. Class antagonism between worker and employer grew in this soil and overshadowed religious affinity. With work seasonal, unemployment was a constant specter. "From ten weeks of work," complained a Minsk worker, "we must live fifty-two weeks."[11] The Jewish artisan, held in the past economically, lost ground to those around him.[12]

Exacerbating this situation were edicts restricting Jews from governmental service and many professions and forbidding most from moving out of Pale communities. With the Jewish population tripling in the second half of the nineteenth century and showing a marked trend (forced and natural) toward urbanization, the result was physical and economic overcrowding and a further pauperization of Jewish society. An 1898 survey of Jewish families indicated that half had annual incomes of $130 and under. With 300 rubles ($154.40) estimated as necessary to maintain a decent standard of living, the majority of Jewish families were below or just hovering above the poverty line. Most of the Jews, observed the American minister to St. Petersburg, "are in poverty and a very considerable part in misery—just on the border of starvation."[13] By the end of the nineteenth century, nearly one in five Russian Jews was unable to celebrate Passover without charitable assistance. A society of *luftmenshn* had arisen. Unemployed, unskilled, they peddled or worked at whatever job they could to earn bread for themselves and their families. These were superfluous men who led a hand-to-mouth existence without visible means of support. Class divisions had begun to splinter the traditional Jewish world.[14]

Jews farmed in Russia, but agriculture did not offer a solution to the economic impasse. Early, the tsars welcomed Jews as farmers by providing land and incentives for the organization of colonies. In 1806, seven settlements were established in Kherson province with others formed later in Ekaterinoslav and Bessarabia. By 1865, some 33,000 Jewish farmers were in the Russian countryside. Further expansion, however, was minimal as marginal soil, drought, insufficient capital, and the reversal of official policy regarding Jewish land tenure eliminated the farm as a significant alternative to the city. Moreover, crude conditions and primitive technology did not nurture in Jewish minds a myth of a Ukrainian pastoral paradise. At the turn of the twentieth century, 40,000 Jewish farmers with 150,000 family members remained on the land accounting for 3.5 percent of the Jewish population. Threequarters of the Russian people, at the same time, were rooted in the soil.[15]

Poet Shalom Jacob Abramovitz described the Russian Jew's existence: "It is an ugly life without pleasure or satisfaction, without splendor, without light."[16] Dark and difficult, the Pale was also far from stable. It shook internally and had begun to dissolve into intellectual, social, and economic pieces. External blows, sometimes warded off, other times painfully absorbed, accelerated fragmentation. Yet, the changes so far considered were gradual, "normal," allowing adjustment and a resumption of balance no matter how precarious. The agents of change, in addition, were unseen, unreasoning, and invulnerable. The hardness of life could be dismissed as fate or divine will, for misery always seemed to be a Jew's lot. More was needed to loosen Jews from their complacency or, perhaps, fatalism. Threats had to be reified, personally felt and unprovoked. Only such dangers could kindle a sense of efficacy that would dispel the numbness and force escape. The shocks came in two waves, the first in 1881-82, and the second in 1903-06.

Events in these two periods made a painful situation intolerable and stirred Jews to reevaluate their present and future courses of action.

IV

On March 1, 1881, a bomb-wielding revolutionary assassinated Tsar Alexander II. With official prodding, the Jewish presence in the movement was generalized to the larger Pale population. The result was an outburst of brutality and violence that consumed 225 communities, left 20,000 Jews homeless, and untold thousands maimed, raped, and murdered. Local police and army units either watched passively or openly participated in the bloodletting. Rarely did they intervene to halt the destruction of life and property. The pogroms' toll may appear insignificant to the post-Holocaust generation; however, at the time the massacres in a seemingly civilized nation shocked the world and elicited outpourings of indignation from Jews and Christians. For the Russian Jew, a dead neighbor, a raped daughter, a burned home brought direct confrontation with the tragedy that was his existence. His environment had become a hostile reality, his life of little value.[17]

Government words and deeds in the aftermath of the pogroms confirmed the fears of the most pessimistic. Tsar Alexander III (1881-1894) believed initially that the pogroms were the acts of revolutionaries seeking to overturn the monarchy. Later, ignoring the evidence of official connivance in the violence, he fastened upon Jewish exploitation of the peasants as the cause of the disorders. His acceptance of this rationale is not surprising in light of his long-standing anti-Semitism. As crown prince he had ordered a financial award for the author of a pamphlet titled, "Concerning the Use of Christian Blood by the Jews." As for the pogroms, he said, "The sad part about these disturbances is the necessity of the government to defend the Jews."[18] The few rioters jailed during the violence were freed or sentenced to minimum terms. The tsar rejected appeals for financial aid to pogrom victims and even the solicitation of funds to aid Jewish survivors. In May 1882, "Temporary Rules" (which remained in effect until 1917) were promulgated to prevent future outbreaks and punish the Jews for provoking attack. The May Laws prohibited new Jewish settlement outside of towns and cities. In some localities overzealous officials interpreted this as sanctioning the expulsion of Jews from farms and villages regardless of their length of residence. Sometimes, Jews returning from trips were declared "new" settlers and forced from their homes. In addition, the Temporary Rules forbad Jews from acquiring village or farm property, and new agricultural opportunities thus closed to Jewish farmers. Jews were also ordered to close businesses on Sundays thereby weakening their competitive positions with Christian counterparts.[19]

Added to previous restrictions, these new decrees further constricted the living and economic space of Russia's Jews. It also fit the broader design of tsarist policy. To Count Konstantin Petrovich Pobyedonostzev, Procurator of the Holy Synod and tutor to Alexander III, "The Jew is a parasite. Remove him from the living organism in which and on which he exists and put this parasite on a rock and he will die."[20] Minister of Interior Count Nicholas Pavlovich Ignatyev was equally direct: "The western borders are open to you Jews."[21]

The Jewish response to the physical and psychic shock of the pogroms assumed several shapes. Some shed their religious burdens and converted to Christianity. While conveying all the rights and privileges of Russian citizenship, the path to Christianity was not heavily trodden, an average of 1,000 converts following it annually during the 1890s. Despair and insecurity led greater numbers to flee the country without plan, resources, or destination. Between 1881 and 1890, 135,000 Jewish refugees heeded Count Ignatyev's words and illegally crossed the border seeking asylum in Austria-Hungary, most eventually finding their way to America. In a more organized fashion, the German-Jewish philanthropist Baron Maurice de Hirsch attempted in the 1890s to ransom 25,000 Jews per year and transport them to farm colonies in the western hemisphere, particularly to Argentina. The plan, while lacking in long-range practicality, went unrealized due to immediate Russian intransigence.[22]

The pogroms silenced those who advocated the means of Russification and assimilation to equality. Men and women who had shed the outer symbols of their heritage—dress, speech, or name—realized that Jewish stigmata could not be expunged in Russian eyes. Hebrew poet Yehuda Leib Gordin's advice, "Be a human being outside and a Jew at home," had proven unreliable.[23] Only as a Christian Russian was a future assured. Moreover, they became thoroughly disillusioned when neither liberal nor conservative Russians came to their defense and censured the government and its agents.[24]

Emancipation, then, could not await Christian mercy nor be gained through Jewish dissimulation. Rather, it required a regeneration from within which trumpeted Jewish pride, honor, and identity. Beyond spiritual renewal it was necessary to "normalize" Jewish economic life and cure it of the paralysis of poverty. This Jewish quest for autonomy moved in several directions. Some traveled the road of Zionism to *Eretz Israel*. The Jewish future lay not in Russia nor in any nation where Jews did not constitute a majority. Strong in cultural heritage and socially cohesive, they would always be economic and political victims in Christian lands. A return to Israel and the recreation of a state would allow Jews to rid themselves of prejudice and discrimination and to build a society mentally and physically free of the ghetto. In such a country, the *luftmenshn* of the Pale would have the strength to transform themselves into productive farmers, workers, businessmen, and professionals. The first agricultural colony was established in Palestine in 1882. By 1900, twenty-five farm settlements with 5,000 colonists dotted the land. With Jerusalem and Zion in the prayers of pious Jews three times daily and metal charity boxes for the Holy Land's righteous in each home, Zionists and the Jewish masses found themselves on common ground.[25]

Zionism as a means of self-emancipation was far from universally accepted. Unwilling to reject the nation of their birth, others sought redemption in revolution. They joined the secret cells of the revolutionary movement believing that the overthrow of the tsar and the creation of a classless peoples' republic would resolve all problems, Jewish and otherwise. Among those rejecting emphasis upon "special" ethnic-religious questions because they distracted attention from the class struggle were such prominent revolutionaries as Leon Trotsky, Jules Marton, and Lev Kamenev.[26]

Most Jewish radicals agitated along different lines. From their perspective within the Pale, these men and women realized that Jewish workers bore a double yoke of class and religion. According to Karl Kautsky:

> If the Russian people suffer more than other peoples, if the Russian proletariat is more exploited than any other proletariat, there exists yet another class of workers who are still more oppressed, exploited, and ill-treated than all the others; this pariah among pariahs is the Jewish proletariat in Russia.[27]

Twice oppressed, Jewish workers had to mobilize not only as a class, but as nationality-conscious radicals to assure their rights in the post-tsarist state. The overthrow of the tsar, then, became a preliminary stage to the creation of a federation of nationalities each with autonomy over education, language, press, and art. In such a pluralistic, socialist state with each nationality enjoying cultural and religious self-rule would anti-Semitism be vanquished and Jews achieve equality. The Jewish radicals' vehicle was the General Jewish Workers' League, or Bund, which was organized in Vilna in 1897 just one month after the adjournment of the first Zionist Congress in Vienna. Coalescing from a collection of workers' discussion groups and activist strike committees, the Bund appealed in Yiddish to the inhabitants of the Pale proclaiming a dual message of anti-tsarism and Jewish worth. As underground revolutionaries, Bundists met in secret, constantly on the watch for the police. Esther Radding, a seamstress and later a member of the Clarion colony, remembered meetings on the move—small groups conspiring while walking the streets to avoid surveillance. She was also amazed by the naivete of her fellow radicals:

> It seemed to me that they are talking the impossible. I visioned [sic] the scene of an elephant and a fly. I thought, what are they talking about, they have no idea with what this is connected. A system which is based on brutality and murder and those youngsters are talking about it as if to eat up something that they don't like.[28]

Despite the danger, by 1905 the Bund counted a membership of 30,000. Among them was Nathan Ayeroff. Born in 1883 into an orthodox family, Ayeroff received a traditional religious education from the *malamed* (teacher) of one of his *shtetl's cheders*. His father deserted the family early, forcing his mother to work to support him and his sister. As an apprentice plumber, Ayeroff endured low wages, long hours, and employer exploitation which pushed him into the Bund. Although he abandoned religion and "if anything challenged it" he saw in the Bund a reaffirmation of Jewish ethnicity and identity.[29] The wounding of Ayeroff's sister by tsarist police during a raid on an illegal meeting further heightened his sense of solidarity with his Jewish socialist comrades.[30]

The Bundist philosophy also drew Morris Bassin. Bassin had been born in 1883 in the Rogatchov *shtetl* on the Dniepper River. He attended the *cheder* only briefly and was apprenticed as a bricklayer. Rejecting Zionism as impractical, he joined the Bund believing its program offered the most effective blueprint for transforming the history of the Jewish people. He was, recalled one of his sons, "an idealist who dreamed of the future."[31] In addition to Radding, Ayeroff, and Bassin's younger brother, Abraham, four other future Clarion colonists were Bundists.[32]

The Bundist prescription not only went further than revolutionary, political change, it also looked beyond its Russian base. Bundists advocated the formation of cohesive Jewish nationality and cultural groupings in other countries. The cultivation of a secular culture rooted in Yiddish and the creation of a diverse economic structure along socialist lines would bring Jewish regeneration and strength. Only from this perspective would the formation of a farm colony in the Utah desert have meaning for a Bundist.

Much hostility existed between Bundists and Zionists. The Bundists accused Zionists of being the tools of capitalism because they cooperated with the economic elite and deflected workers from their genuine class interests. Zionists were, in addition, ridiculed as escapists who failed to consider the reality of Palestine—primitive conditions, marginal soil, and Turkish overlords. Finally, Bundists judged the Zionist solution incomplete, addressing only the needs of a small minority while leaving the mass of Jews confined to their Russian prison. Zionists responded that the Bundist conception of nationalism was stillborn without a territorial dimension. Zionists also pinned a visionary label on them for failing to understand the tenacity of Russian anti-Semitism. The two groups were antagonistic for more practical reasons. Both appealed to some of the same constituencies for resources and recruits. This enmity would continue to surface in future decades and in places far from Russia.[33]

A significant offshoot of both Zionism and Bundism was Labor Zionism. Fusing the two ideologies, this group saw the Jewish future in a socialist Palestine. Founded in Ekaterinoslav in 1900 it recruited an estimated 16,000 members by 1905. David Ben-Gurion, Itzchak Ben-Zvi (a future president of Israel), and ten Clarion colonists joined the organization. Among them was Joseph Furman, born January 5, 1885, in the *shtetl* of Tarascha near Kiev. Following a *cheder* education culminating in *bar mitzvah* in 1898, Furman's father apprenticed him to a carpenter. The five-foot, eight-inch, one-hundred-and-eighty-pound young man turned from carpentry work after a few years and became active in socialist politics. He harangued crowds of Jewish workers from street corners, calling for strikes to hasten the tsar's downfall. Revolution in Russia, however, was not Furman's ultimate dream for he looked toward the rebirth of a Jewish nation he would help build. A socialist Palestine also attracted Barney Sokolov. Born in Krementchug, Sokolov was fifteen years old when Labor Zionism was established. Sokolov received both a traditional Jewish elementary education and advanced training in secular Russian schools. A bookbinder by trade, his solution to anti-Semitism was a nation where a Jewish majority could nurture its political, cultural, and social values and institutions without restriction.[34]

When these ten men believed so strongly in a Jewish Palestine, why did they eventually depart for America and later settle in the Clarion colony? Personal circumstances and family allegiances and responsibilities were crucial in shaping life choices and deferring ideological expectations. Yet, even as the physical distance from *Eretz Israel* increased, they still cultivated hope of eventual migration. Distant Clarion, with its climate similar to Palestine, became to some a way station where agricultural experience could be gained and stored for the future. If they would never live to turn a spade of Palestine's soil, their ideals yet remained driving and real.

The vast majority of Jews, meanwhile, responded to the pogroms with fasts and prayers hoping that through such means the Russian Hamans would be turned from their course. Clinging to the traditional, to the familiar, provided for many the strength to survive. The urgent words of Zionist speakers and the demands of Bundist agitators filling the Pale air failed to move them. Neither Palestine nor revolution impinged upon an existence absorbed with the immediate needs of food, shelter, and clothing, or obedience to God's laws. Gradually, their pain subsided and their fears dissipated in the daily routine. Life thus continued in an atmosphere where persecution and humiliation had become "normal" and expected. The Jews adapted to their alien status, living, working, praying, and dying in the narrow space accorded them. The anti-Jewish restrictions of Tsar Nicholas II, who assumed power in 1894, generated little surprise. Professional opportunities were further curtailed, Jewish residence more tightly defined, and economic conditions in the Pale made more desperate. When asked to chart the Jewish course in the twentieth century, Count Pobyedonostzev allegedly predicted: "One-third will die out, one-third will leave the country, and one-third will be completely dissolved in the surrounding population."[35] Tsarist policy toward the Jews had shown a cold consistency during the past century.[36]

V

Three convulsions occurring between 1903 and 1906 shattered the relative calm in Russian-Jewish society. In April 1903, the body of a Christian boy was found outside the city of Kishinev, the capital of the province of Bessarabia. The local newspaper, which had often in the past padded its pages with anti-Semitic invectives, asserted that the child had been stabbed repeatedly by Jews and drained of his blood to satisfy the Jewish Passover ritual. As the newspaper waged its blood libel campaign, handbills appeared in the city falsely announcing an imperial decree granting permission to punish the Jews. Local authorities did nothing to quench the rumors and in fact fanned fears and hostility. On the eve of Easter, the city erupted with mobs sacking the Jewish quarter, carrying off what they could and burning what remained. Under the gaze of police officials, who dispersed Jewish defense forces, men and women were beaten to death with fists and sticks, women were raped and sexually mutilated, and children were thrown to their deaths from windows and roof tops. Not satisfied with merely killing their victims, the rioters pounded nails into skulls and gouged eyes from their sockets. In its wake, the Kishinev pogrom left forty-five dead, more than 500 raped and injured, and 1,500 homes destroyed. An imperial amnesty freed those rioters foolish enough to be caught.[37]

As in 1881, the pogrom assumed the shape of a mass movement and infected the entire Pale. During the years of intense pogrom violence, 284 towns were drenched in blood. Some Jewish communities were ravaged more than once—Gomel suffered six times; Ekaterinoslav, four times; and Kishinev, six times. In the Dubossar *shtetl*, mobs overran the Jewish section leaving the dead and wounded amid the rubble. Eight-year-old Maurice Warshaw, a future Clarion colonist, surfaced from hiding to witness a horror he could never forget: "I ran to the open door and peered through. Lying in grotesque positions, like so many rag dolls, were [my friend's] mother, father, and all the children. All their throats had been cut."[38] On escaping from the village he remembered "a cart with four bodies on it. There was a big sign painted in white . . . saying 'Kill the Jews.' "[39] During the Odessa pogrom in 1905, police joined the rioters and fought pitched battles with Jewish defense groups. Despite defense efforts, the Odessa disorders left more than 800 Jews dead and 5,000 injured. Esther Radding was in Bialystok in 1905 when a pogrom claimed 200 Jewish lives and maimed 700 more: The rioters "were running like wild animals in each corner to get their victims. It was an atmosphere of blood and murder; and we lay helpless in our hiding places almost breathless waiting for our next [breath]."[40] Emerging from cellars or behind street barricades the Jews counted the human storm's casualties, more than 2,500 dead and 6,500 wounded.[41]

Labor Zionist Moishe Zilberfarb's reaction to the Kishinev massacre could be generalized to the entire period and to the majority of Jews: The pogrom "tore open our eyes and forced us to look around at what was happening in the world."[42] In distant New York City, the Yiddish newspaper *Di Arbayter Shtimme (The Worker's Voice)* likened it to "a clap of thunder" which "left no doubt in any heart."[43] Closer to the devastation, Esther Radding packed a small suitcase and left for America two weeks after the Bialystok pogrom. Barney Sokolov, Celia Yigdoll, Harry Alimansky, and Samuel Alper chose the same course following pogroms in Krementchug, Zhitomir, Makariev, and Vilna respectively. And tens of thousands joined them.[44]

The economic and religious nature of pogrom violence fused with the needs of government officials intent upon undermining those seeking the tsar's overthrow. By the turn of the century, social, political, and economic grievances had generated sufficient fuel to ignite a revolutionary movement uniting intellectuals, workers, and peasants. Dissatisfaction with the status quo rippled through Russia, taking shape in street demonstrations, rural riots, and terrorism that culminated finally in 1905 in massive strikes crippling the economy. As noted, Jewish radicals in socialist groups, the Bund, and Labor Zionist organizations played prominent roles in the agitation. The tsar bowed before the popular outcry and yielded in his October Manifesto to demands for freedom of speech and press and the election of a Duma, a representative assembly. The revolution of 1905, however, proved short-lived as the tsar quickly outmaneuvered his opponents, dissolved the Duma, and began a crackdown on dissidents. With the revolution's collapse, many radicals fled fearing arrest. Among them were Bundist David Cohen and Labor Zionists Joseph Furman and Solomon Steinfeld.[45]

Imperialistic ambitions and an attempt to stifle revolutionary sentiment in foreign adventures created a third tributary to the human flow westward. In 1904-05 draft calls were heard throughout the Pale for service in the tsar's army against the Japanese. Few Jews were interested in fighting in far-off Manchuria for a tsar who despised them. Rather than be sent eastward, young men such as Abraham Bassin, Samuel Chatsky, Nathan Ayeroff, and Samuel Grishkam gathered their belongings and looked toward America.[46]

VI

In every *shtetl*, in every Jewish quarter of the large cities, families calculated the migration equation. To the layers of civil and religious restrictions had been added pogroms, political reaction, and war. Unemployment and poverty stunted many lives as well. Even more debilitating was the realization that there was no hope that tomorrow would be any different than today or yesterday. The push from Russia met the pull of America. Letters from America portrayed a golden land with the promise of dignity, freedom, and jobs. Mary Antin, who had left Russia in the 1890s described the hold America had on the Pale's Jews:

> America was in everybody's mouth. Businessmen talked of it over their accounts; the market women gave up their quarrels that they might discuss it from stall to stall. . . . Children played at emigrating. . . . All talked of it, but scarcely anybody knew one true fact about this magic land.[47]

Maurice Warshaw of Dubossar remembered a similar feeling in 1906: "All who were going to America thought they were going to heaven."[48] Very personal motives supplemented the more general reasons for migration: a wife's death, a family quarrel, mere boredom and a thirst for adventure. Many Jews, then, found their choice of futures clear. Still, the migrating population was hardly random. Jewish immigrants were the less established, less traditional members of the community. The wealthy, the more educated, and the devoutly orthodox generally sought their safety in the familiar. Those who left had not only found conditions intolerable, but were willing to take a chance, to step into the unknown. They were men like Moshe Malamed who knew that "everything was so in the dark."[49]

In 1902, 38,000 Russian Jews departed for America. By 1904, the migration swelled to 77,000 and in 1906 to 125,000. Nearly one-half of all Russian Jews bound for America would leave between 1902 and 1907. Almost three-quarters of the future colonists of Clarion whose dates of departure are known would as well make their new homes in America during that period. The disproportionate percentage of Clarion Jews arriving during these years probably reflects heavy involvement in left-wing political activities and their young ages which made them susceptible to service in the war against Japan. In all, two million, or one-third, of the Jews of Eastern Europe would escape between 1881 and 1914 for a new world.[50]

Jewish refugees made for the border by train, cart, and on foot. With immigration illegal, secrecy and bribery were the means out of Russia. Guided by peasants or the agents of steamship companies, the Jews "stole the border" into Germany and Austria-Hungary. Some crossings were quite dramatic. Anarchist Isaac Isgur, wanted by tsarist police for political activities, left the country dressed as a woman. Sam Kristol, running from the authorities after striking a Jew-baiting Polish landowner, hid covered with straw in the back of a wagon. Actually, border guards were under orders not to stop the Jews as the exodus was consistent with government policy. U.S. Consul Clarence Rice stationed in Polish Russia reported on October 21, 1904, that in government circles, "the emigration of the Hebrew is rather a source of congratulations than otherwise."[51] Border guards, then, were entrepreneurs collecting bribe money to supplement their army pay rather than obstacles to migration. Thus, the only thing surprising about the experience of socialists Herse and Sonia Airoff who heard guards shouting "*Idi! Idi!*" ("Go! Go!") was the failure to exchange rubles.[52]

From the Ukraine, Jews crossed into Austria-Hungary and traveled by train to the ports of embarkation — Hamburg, Bremen, Rotterdam, Amsterdam, and Antwerp. From the northwest the path led either through the Baltic Sea or across Polish Russia to Germany and the ports. In the south, the escape route took Jews across the Mediterranean Sea, a handful heading toward

TABLE 1

Arrival Dates of Clarion Jews Compared with the Arrival Dates of Russian-Jewish Immigrants, 1881-1910, by Percent

Years	Clarion Jews Percent	Russian Jews	
		N	Percent
1881-1883	1	19,758	1.8
1884-1886	0	32,607	3.0
1887-1889	1	61,657	5.5
1890-1892	2	128,691	11.5
1893-1895	4	62,635	5.6
1896-1898	5	48,180	4.0
1899-1901	7	98,946	9.0
1902-1904	30	163,079	14.6
1905-1907	42	332,559	30.0
1908-1910	8	170,952	15.0
Born in United States	1	—	—
Total Number	108	1,119,064	

Source: Clarion biographical data; Samuel Joseph, *Jewish Immigration to the United States from 1881 to 1910* (New York, 1914), 93.

Palestine. From Europe the great majority headed for America, with smaller contingents bound for Canada, South America, and Australia. Migration often occurred in chains, male family members departing first, saving money, and then bringing relatives to America over time. Thus, the Plonsky family from a *shtetl* near the Polish-German border sent eldest brother Ben to America in 1897. He worked and saved money for brother Philip's passage in 1899. Adam followed in 1901, Louis in 1904, and Max in 1905. The chain was completed in 1906 with the arrival of the rest of the family. Family ties also played a crucial role in determining destination, initial residence in New York City, Philadelphia, or Baltimore often binding those coming after. Such links were so strong for Labor Zionist Joseph Furman that they turned him from Palestine toward Harlem. *Landsmen,* former residents of the home *shtetl* who had already journeyed to America, often substituted for family by determining destination and providing support in the new land.[53]

The ports of embarkation or rather the steamship companies acted as funnels collecting the human streams for transport overseas. The companies were not passive recipients of the flow, having dispatched agents to the Pale to encourage and expedite departure. The agents not only provided travel information but sold tickets, arranged border crossings, and planned the immigrant's trip across Germany to their respective company's site of operations. The processing procedures of the American Line of Hamburg, which transported tens of thousands of Russian Jews, were representative of steamship company activities at other ports. One of those Jews was Clarion colonist Samuel Grishkam of the Lutzier *shtetl*, a refugee from the tsar's army. His experience was typical of the great majority of Jewish immigrants. The American Line established a holding village on the outskirts of Hamburg where it could house as many as 4,000 immigrants until departure. The complex was divided according to nationality, with Grishkam placed in the Russian-Jewish section in a men's dormitory which slept ten to a room. The company provided a synagogue, hospital, and dining hall for the immigrants' use. Upon arrival in the village and on the day of departure, Grishkam underwent medical examinations, for those denied admission to the United States were returned to Europe at company expense. In addition, his clothes were deloused and he faced a compulsory bath. Then, orderlies applied a shampoo made of soap, carbolic acid, creotin, and petroleum with a stiff-bristle brush. Women were spared the regulatory shearing of hair performed on men. Like Grishkam, the great majority of Jews held steerage tickets costing approximately $30. The ticket allowed Grishkam to board the SS *Haverford,* bound for America, where he arrived on November 27, 1904, with just $7.50 in his pocket. Others such as Aaron Binder and Sam Levitsky could afford to go only as far as Liverpool, England. There they found jobs, saved, and eventually booked passage to America on the SS *New England* and the SS *Friesland* respectively.[54]

A steerage ticket entitled a passenger to accommodations in the cargo hold of the steamship where every vibration from the engines could be heard and every pitch of the sea felt. Between 1,500 and 2,000 immigrants were crammed below deck, divided into groups of 300 and separated by sex and family status. Overcrowding meant added discomfort and danger to passengers but increased profits for shipowners. Each person was allotted a metal-framed berth two feet by six feet set in tiers from deck to ceiling for living space. Mattresses and pillows stuffed with seaweed were provided for each immigrant. Because there were no storage compartments, baggage remained in the berth. No privacy was possible under these conditions so people slept in their clothes. Food for those who could stomach it was non-Kosher and eaten in the passageways between the tiers of bunks. Washing facilities consisted of faucets giving cold salt water, and one toilet was provided for every

forty-seven people. Poorly ventilated, without portholes, and with no provi-
sion for the sick except sawdust spread upon the deck, steerage would be the
immigrants' home for ten days to two weeks. A female investigator for the
U.S. Immigration Commission, disguised as an immigrant, described conditions: "There was no sight before which the eye did not prefer to close.
Everything was dirty, sticky, and disagreeable to the touch. Every impression
was offensive."[55] Physical relief was possible when immigrants went above
deck to breathe the sea air; but here, too, they faced humiliation as cabin
passengers threw candies and pennies toward the "amusing" source of distrac-
tion. This practice, wrote an observer, "holds all the pleasures of a slumming
expedition with none of the hazards of contamination."[56] Although reforms
were legislated enclosing berths and improving washing and toilet facilities,
nearly all of the Jews coming to America would experience the more debilitating and degrading rite of passage.[57]

VII

As the ship drew nearer to America, immigrants' thoughts strayed from the
physical discomforts of steerage to the last obstacle blocking entrance into the
new land: the processing center of Ellis Island. The subject of discussions,
coaching, and rumors, it was known among immigrants as the Island of
Tears, for its door swung two ways—open to a new life and closed for rejection. In 1890, Congress had set aside the three-acre, flat island in New York
harbor to serve as a sieve to filter out undesirables among the immigrants.
The list of those ineligible to enter America had increased over the years to
include prostitutes, criminals, polygamists, the insane, anarchists, and those
liable to become public charges. In addition to economic and personal qualifications, there were medical requirements for admission. Immigrants diag-
nosed as suffering from tuberculosis, venereal disease, or any "loathesome or
contagious disease" were returned to Europe.[58]

The immigrants disembarked from their steamship at Hudson River
piers on the west side of New York City and were ferried to Ellis Island.
Blue-coated officials then shuttled the immigrants into the processing complex, a large red brick building with cupola-topped towers, the largest building that many of the immigrants had ever entered. Directed up a long flight of
stairs, the immigrants entered an enormous hall and were sorted into a series
of corridors formed by long, iron guardrails. The first test was a cursory
medical examination weeding out those with obvious deformities. Next, a
more rigorous physical checked eyes, ears, heart, lungs, and limbs. Immigrants suspected of disease received a chalk mark on their coats. Marks of

"E" for eyes, "H" for heart, "G" for goitre, and "X" for mental illness meant more thorough examination later. The most dreaded part of the doctor's inspection was the examination for trachoma, a highly contagious disease of the eyelids which untreated could result in blindness. To inspect under the eyelids the physician inserted a glove button hook which he subsequently wiped upon a towel to ready for the next immigrant. The procedure caused momentary, acute pain and exposed immigrants coming after to possible contagion. The immigrant next proceeded to the registration clerk who asked approximately twenty questions: What is your nationality? How old are you? Are you married? What is your occupation? Accustomed to old-world patterns, some immigrants prepared money packets to bribe the clerk and facilitate the process. With as many as 5,000 immigrants passing through the island daily, the questioning could easily become perfunctory. Perhaps that is how anarchist Isaac Isgur easily escaped the net. At the registration desk many family legends concerning name changes originated. Misunderstanding or a desire by clerk or immigrant to Americanize a name produced the transformation. Once a healthy immigrant had answered all the questions satisfactorily, he received an "admit" card from the clerk. Two-thirds of the immigrants then caught the ferry to New York City with the rest buying railroad tickets to their destinations. The entire procedure, depending upon the number of immigrants processed, lasted from forty-five minutes to four hours.[59]

Russia was the past. The specifics of tsarist legal restrictions, pogrom violence, and *shtetl* life were memories gradually fading, salient only because of family and friends left behind. In time, such memories would lose even these pillars of meaning and reality. Years and decades, people and places blended and were forgotten in a world so different and far away. America now absorbed all energy, demanding accommodation and speedily effecting it. Yet, the experience of America was not written upon a blank slate. Rather, it was interpreted and redefined according to the attitudes and values cultivated in the Pale. The migration had thus transplanted the Jews' Russian roots into American soil. Survival in the new environment would require all of the skills, new and old, mental and physical, that the immigrants could conjure.

2

Cities of Steel

We wore cheap clothes, lived in cheap
tenements, ate cheap food. There was
nothing to look forward to, nothing to
expect the next day to be better. . . .
You stayed and you survived, that's all.

Garment worker
Triangle Shirtwaist Company

. . . the whole thing looks like a dream, a
utopia, but didn't every big movement
start as a dream?

Barney Silverman
Clarion colonist

If Russia was the lost hope, America was the open possibility. Immigrants
conceived America in many ways: a religious refuge, an economic pot of
gold, a political haven, and a social ladder. The American promise, sought in
dreams and struggled for in life, caused expectations to soar. The immigrants'
first impressions were frightening, yet at the same time reassuring and vali-
dating. The ferry ride from Ellis Island to Manhattan revealed an America

larger and busier than any *shtetl* or city in Russia. This was simply life on a different scale.

With expectations so very high and opportunities seemingly within easy reach, disappointments caused profound disillusionment and frustration. Life and work in the golden land could be harsh, existence a daily bout with pain and fear. Most interpreted their lives from a solitary perspective and pursued an individual response without reference to the larger Jewish community. But, some of those lost in the American whirlwind looked toward certain collective experiences for remedies. Life in old and new world alike had fostered solutions stressing group consciousness and fortifying a sense of personal responsibility to the Jewish whole. This did not mean self-sacrifice, for individual growth and achievement could occur in a context of Jewish solidarity. A concern for justice mixed with ethnicity to color the Jewish frame of reference. A history of persecution, a religious tradition emphasizing fairness to all regardless of circumstance, and the emergence of a radical subculture in Russia cultivated this regard for equity. Change could be effected, the human condition politically, socially, and economically ameliorated through collective action. From this sense of ethnicity and the search for a better world came the collective response that was the Clarion experiment.

I

The Lower East Side of New York City was the geographic and cultural core of Eastern European Jewry. Bounded by imaginary borders running east from the Bowery almost to the East River and south from Fourteenth Street to the Brooklyn Bridge, the Jewish quarter encompassed more than two hundred city blocks. By 1910, over one-half million Jews had settled on the Lower East Side making it the largest Jewish city in the world. One hundred thousand more Jews, lured by low rents and extended transportation lines, found homes to the north in Harlem. Others established residential footholds in the boroughs of Brooklyn and the Bronx. In New York City as a whole, by 1915, one in five citizens was Jewish.[1]

The manuscript sheets of the 1910 U.S. Census testify to the compactness of Jewish settlement. Census takers assigned to the Lower East Side recorded tenement floor after tenement floor, building after building, and block after block of solidly Jewish composition. Rarely is the list of Cohens, Greenbergs, and Goldmans broken by a Rinaldi or an O'Malley. This was a Jewish world where English was a second language and Yiddish held sway on the storefronts and in the air. The Lower East Side offered its residents a rich Jewish cultural life with Yiddish newspapers and theater, educational institu-

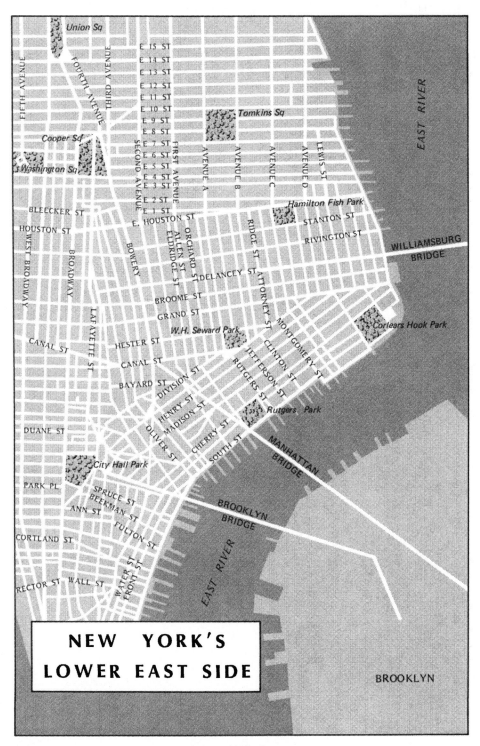

Union Sq

FIFTH AVENUE

FOURTH AVENUE

THIRD AVENUE

E 15 ST
E 14 ST
E 13 ST
E 12 ST
E 11 ST
E 10 ST
E 9 ST
E 8 ST
E 7 ST
E 6 ST
E 5 ST
E 4 ST
E 3 ST
E 2 ST
E 1 ST

Tomkins Sq

Cooper Sq

Washington Sq

SECOND AVENUE

FIRST AVENUE

AVENUE A

AVENUE B

AVENUE C

AVENUE D

LEWIS ST

EAST RIVER

BLEECKER ST

HOUSTON ST

WEST BROADWAY

BROADWAY

BROADWAY

E. HOUSTON ST

BOWERY

ORCHARD ST

ALLEN ST

ELDRIDGE ST

Hamilton Fish Park

STANTON ST

RIVINGTON ST

RIDGE ST

WILLIAMSBURG
BRIDGE

DELANCEY ST

BROOME ST

GRAND ST

ATTORNEY ST

LAFAYETTE ST

HESTER ST

W.H. Seward Park

Corlears Hook Park

CANAL ST

CANAL ST

BAYARD ST

DIVISION ST

MONTGOMERY ST

CLINTON ST

JEFFERSON ST

RUTGERS ST

Rutgers Park

HENRY ST

MADISON ST

DUANE ST

OLIVER ST

CHERRY ST

SOUTH ST

MANHATTAN
BRIDGE

City Hall Park

PARK PL

SPRUCE ST

BEEKMAN ST

ANN ST

FULTON ST

BROOKLYN
BRIDGE

CORTLAND ST

EAST RIVER

RECTOR ST

WALL ST

WATER ST

FRONT ST

BROOKLYN

NEW YORK'S
LOWER EAST SIDE

MAP 2

tions, lectures, and cafe discussion groups. *Landmanshaften,* organizations formed by immigrants from the same *shtetl,* handled social and financial needs. Religiously, the community was a prism with a multitude of synagogues divided as to nationality, custom, and interpretation. Freedom extended to politics also, opinions and organizations covering the entire spectrum from Anarchism and Marxism to Republicanism.[2]

The street activity on the Lower East Side never failed to draw the attention of observers. The sidewalks were crowded spaces filled with people buying, socializing, arguing, or merely lounging. What playwright Anzia Yezierska called "the raucous orchestra of voices" emanated from hastily convened street-corner meeting places and well-established tenement-stair rendezvous.[3] Few strangers, however, connected the rich street life with the need residents felt to escape their tenement homes. Most New York City Jews lived in tenement houses narrowed at the center and constructed in the shape of a dumbbell (see page 28). This architectural blueprint had been submitted in 1879 for a prize competition seeking a design best utilizing the standard twenty-five-by-one-hundred-foot city lot. The winning dumbbell apartment house format was mass-produced in the city until outlawed in 1901. The building was a brick structure five to seven stories in height, twenty-five feet wide, and ninety feet deep. Each floor contained four apartments of either three or four rooms each and was bisected by a long hallway. The largest room in each apartment was the front parlor measuring ten feet by eleven feet. Bedrooms, at seven feet by eight feet, were "hardly more than closets."[4] Only four of the fourteen rooms received direct sunlight, with the rest dependent upon an air shaft twenty-eight inches wide and fifty to sixty feet in height for light and ventilation. It was, said a young girl, "a place so dark it seemed as if there weren't no sky."[5] The shaft quickly became a trash receptacle while conveying odors and noises throughout the building. According to a housing investigator, the shaft was "a culture tube on a gigantic scale."[6] The fire danger was acute in the tenements, for the air shaft functioned as an effective flue feeding the blaze and carrying it throughout the apartment house. Fire escapes often did not exist or if present directed residents into the backyards of the tenements where they found themselves trapped by fences and other buildings. Inspectors even found escapes attached to the walls of the air shaft. Of the 250 recorded deaths in Manhattan's fires between 1902 and 1909, one in three was a Lower East Side victim of a tenement inferno. In the better tenements two water closets were provided for each floor. Many, however, had only a sink in the hallway for washing, bathing, and drinking. Backyard privies, often neglected and filthy, constituted a significant health hazard. In addition, many of the houses were plagued with broken stairs, falling plaster, rats, and plugged plumbing pipes. The Tenement House Department of New York City summed up the situation:

> Tenement conditions in many instances have been found to be so bad as to be indescribable in print; vile privies and privy sinks; foul cellars full of rubbish, in many cases of garbage and decomposing fecal matter; dilapidated and dangerous stairs; plumbing pipes containing large holes and emitting sewer gas throughout the houses; rooms so dark that one cannot see the people in them; . . . dangerous old fire traps without fire escapes.[7]

Overcrowding worsened the existing low standards of life. The tenements housed poor families with many children who supplemented their incomes by renting living space to lodgers. Approximately one-third of the Russian-Jewish families on the Lower East Side took in an average of two boarders each. People doubled up in the bedrooms and at night, living rooms and even kitchens resembled dormitories. A 1900 survey of a typical block in the Jewish tenth ward counted thirty-nine tenements, divided into 605 apartments, and inhabited by 2,781 people. There was an average density in 1910 of 600 persons per acre on the Lower East Side with some areas registering as many as 1,000 inhabitants per acre. Jewish sections ranked second, third, fourth, and fifth in population density among Manhattan's twenty-two wards. Of the fifty-one most congested blocks in New York City, not less than thirty-seven were located in the Jewish wards. "The architecture," said Arnold Bennett of a typical street of the Lower East Side, "seemed to sweat humanity at every window and door."[8] This situation surely took a personal toll. Such heavy population pressure restricted privacy and could only exacerbate interpersonal tensions, thus tearing at the fabric of family life. The relationships between husband and wife, parents and children, already strained by the circumstances of immigrant life, suffered still more under the press of people. In light of the realities of tenement life, it is hardly surprising that men and women would look to the farm and countryside for escape.[9]

Philadelphia, which sheltered the second largest Jewish community in America, offered different living arrangements yet problems of a similar sort. Fifty-five thousand Jews lived in the city, with the heaviest concentrations in the southeastern sector bounded by Broad, Spruce, and Mifflin streets on the west, north, and south, and the Delaware River on the east. Within these borders the most defined pockets of Jewish settlement were centered between Second and Sixth and Lombard and Catharine streets, in a modified triangular area south of Moyamensing Prison, and along South, Bainbridge,

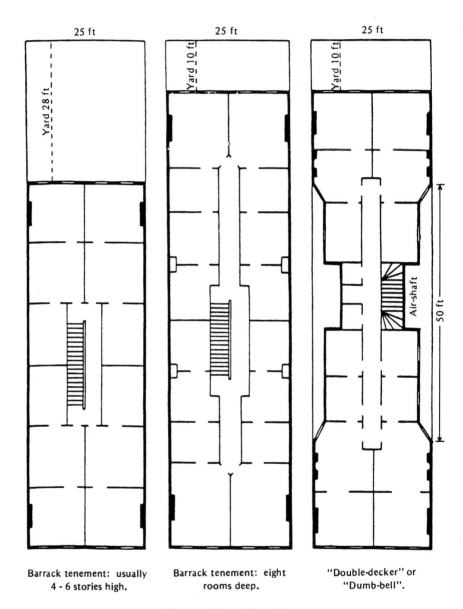

Barrack tenement: usually   Barrack tenement: eight   "Double-decker" or
      4 - 6 stories high.   rooms deep.   "Dumb-bell".

Tenement house floor plans.

Fitzwater, Spruce, and Pine streets. Unlike the compact Lower East Side, Philadelphia's Jewish neighborhoods were heterogeneous, with large, inter-mixed Slavic, Polish, Italian, and black populations creating a human mosaic. Philadelphia had relatively few tenements, housing its poor instead in small, single-family, two-story dwellings containing three or four rooms. Yet, the disease of poverty infected the area and brought forth familiar symptoms: overcrowding when families doubled up or took in boarders, health hazards resulting from poor drainage and improper sewage treatment, and inadequate bathing and toilet facilities. The golden dreams immigrants long cherished were hammered quickly to dross in the slums of New York City and Philadel-phia. The impact of the Back to the Soil call would be measured not only in the relief it promised from overcrowding, unsanitary conditions, and low standard of life. It promised, as well, to revive the American dream.[10]

II

Further complicating the New York City and Philadelphia housing situations was the intimate relationship between home and work. The massive influx of immigrants to America coincided with the transformation of clothing manu-facturing to a mass production and distribution industry. Custom tailoring was more and more reserved for the wealthy while family production became less viable as inexpensive, ready-made clothing was made available in a growing array of colors and styles. The mechanization and routinization of garment production and the industry's concentration in the eastern cities opened an economic niche which the new immigrants quickly filled. There were other factors making the garment industry a Jewish enclave. Employers took advantage of tailoring experience that Jews had gained in the Russian Pale where they dominated the craft. Observant Jews found that industry business could be conducted without interfering with religious practices. Family integrity could be maintained because work was performed in the ten-ement apartment. Finally, the business placed few language demands on its employees, for Yiddish was the medium of exchange. Thus, the garment in-dustry employed nearly two-thirds of New York City's and 20 percent of Phil-adelphia's Jewish wage earners.[11]

There were several systems of clothing production. As in Russia, con-tractors put out bundles of cloth material to people in their homes and for a piece rate they produced pants, vests, and coats. Tenement apartments be-came workshops, with father in the front room treading the sewing machine, the children around him basting and finishing, and mother pressing the com-pleted garment in the kitchen. Some businessmen assumed greater control

PHILADELPHIA'S
SOUTHEASTERN SECTION

MAP 3

over production by assembling workers in one or more apartments. Such operations were small, with 78 percent of the city's tailoring establishments employing five or less workers. At the pinnacle of the sweatshop system were the relatively few factories which occupied several floors or an entire apartment building.[12]

Workers bore the burden of their employers' greed and their industry's cutthroat competition. Production costs were lowered on the backs of employees who were expected to work long hours for as little return as possible. Over one-half of the garment workers averaged nine- to ten-hour days in weeks that included Saturdays and sometimes Sundays. In season, workdays could last sixteen to eighteen hours with no overtime pay. Male employees earned an average of $13.30 per week while women workers were paid just over $8.00. Regardless of industry, over one-half of those employed on the Lower East Side brought home $18.00 or less in weekly wages. With $18.00 set by *Der Yiddisher Emigrant* in 1911 as necessary "for a more or less respectable living," many found it difficult to pay for rent, clothing, and food.[13] Another 30 percent of the Lower East Side's work force earned between $18.00 and $22.00 per week and hovered precariously above this poverty line. Illness or layoff could thus prove disastrous for a family's economic well-being. In fact, unemployment was a real and constant fear in the garment industry for it ran on a five-season year: winter, spring, summer, fall, and slack. In 1913, less than 20 percent of New York City's garment workers were employed continuously throughout the year. To make ends meet, homes were opened to boarders, second jobs were found, and children who could earn $1.50 for a six-day week were sent into the sweatshops.[14]

Deplorable and humiliating working conditions accompanied low wages and long hours. Garment employees encountered all of the abuses of tenement life in their workplaces: noise, overcrowding, inadequate light, vermin, and poor ventilation. Pot-bellied stoves, the only source of heat during the winter, proved insufficient. Employees were docked for toilet visits and fined if supervisors believed they wasted time. Water was available from a single tap located in the halls, and lunch was eaten quickly at the machines. Talking was forbidden and workers fined for lateness, staring out windows, and laughing. In addition, workers paid fees for lockers, stools, needles, and for the electricity to power their sewing machines. Less obvious but more exploitative was the speed-up which demanded increased output without matching pay raises. The contractor

> would tell his men that there was not much work and he was obligated to take it cheaper, and since he did not want to reduce their

wages and pay them less per day, all they would have to do would be to make another coat in the task. That is, if they were accustomed to making 9 coats in the task, they would be required to make 10, and then 11, and so on. The wages were always reduced on the theory that they were not reduced at all but the amount of labor was increased. In this way intense speed was developed. The men who had been accustomed to making 9 coats in a task would make 10, and so on, up to 15, 18, and even 20, as is the customary task at the present time [1901]. The hours began to be increased, in order to make the task in a day.[15]

Religious affinity did not restrain employers from controlling their work force with blacklists, scabs, lockouts, and company spies. The law stood behind the owners and their efforts to keep workers powerless. During a 1909 garment industry strike, a judge sentenced two women to scrub floors at the Blackwell Island workhouse in New York with these words: "You are on strike against God and Nature; whose primary law it is that man should earn his bread in the sweat of his brow."[16] Employers also aggravated firetrap conditions by boarding up windows to eliminate distractions and locking doors to prevent absenteeism. Such practices led to tragedy, the most infamous occurring on Saturday, March 25, 1911, when the middle floor of the Triangle Shirtwaist Company caught fire. Fueled by bolts of fabric, the blaze spread rapidly, catching the company's 600 workers unprepared. Many who tried to escape found the doors bolted from the outside and the windows nailed shut. In eighteen minutes the fire claimed 146 lives, mostly Jewish and Italian women between the ages of thirteen and twenty-three years. Some were found only as charred skeletons hunched over their sewing machines. It was a disaster the entire East Side community felt, the *Jewish Daily Forward* running the banner headline: "THE MORGUE IS FULL OF OUR DEAD."[17]

Conditions in other Jewish-dominated industries were less publicized but no better. Tobacco workers and cigar makers were, as well, exposed to wage and hour abuse, employer harassment, and the deleterious effects of a tenement workplace. The New York State Factory Investigation Commission described the situation in the baking industry in 1912:

The bakers worked in deep and dark subcellars, without ventilation or hygenic conditions. The walls and ceilings were moist and moldy. The shops were infested with rats and reeked with dirt. The air was pestilential. The bake ovens were primitive. No machinery was used. The work was all done by hand.[18]

Living and working amid such surroundings combined with improper nutrition and inadequate health care to debilitate men, women, and children. It is hardly surprising that public health surveys of Jewish workers between 1911 and 1913 uncovered a variety of physical complaints. Two-thirds of New York City's Jewish bakers were reported ill, suffering from such ailments as anemia (28 percent), bronchitis (23 percent), eye infections (16 percent), and cardiac trouble (7 percent). Tuberculosis was so common in the garment industry that it was known as the "tailor's disease." A study of 3,000 garment workers indicated that large numbers complained of rhinitis, some degree of spinal curvature (50 percent of the men and 20 percent of the women), and defective vision and hearing. The sweatshop maimed its inmates physically as well as psychologically.[19]

The men and women of Clarion profoundly felt the pain of "sweatshop slavery," and the vivid stories of fact and legend passed on to their children reflect the weight of their experience. Sam Levitsky of Philadelphia worked as a furrier twelve hours a day, six days a week "when he could get it."[20] Stripped to his waist in the hot, unventilated shop, he stretched and dried hides that would eventually adorn the wealthy. Despite his efforts, he could not support his family, so eldest son, Louis, at age thirteen, labored sixty hours weekly for a wage of $5.00. Philip Plonsky and his brothers each took home $8.00 per week for making paper boxes in a Lower East Side factory. Isadore Mastrow sewed shirtwaists for $2.50 per day to maintain his wife and three young children. Twenty-one-year-old Celia Yigdoll was a seamstress in a sweatshop near her East Harlem home. To realize her aspirations, she attended night school to learn to read and write after working long hours. The pace became too much and one day she fell asleep at her sewing machine. Her Jewish boss felt no empathy and demanded she decide between her job and her schooling. Yigdoll quit night classes and forever ended her formal education; however, the incident did lead her into the newly organized International Ladies Garment Workers Union. The "monotonous work" of sewing buttons on coats all day, every day, made Esther Radding weary and caused her to fall asleep at her workplace.[21] Her boss fired her immediately. Julia Warshaw Grishkam, who like her brother Maurice had witnessed the Dubossar pogrom, worked a six-day, sixty-hour week in a poorly lit, ill-ventilated sweatshop. A fire that nearly took her life proved sufficient when added to wage and hour complaints to push her to union activity. Repairman David Bernstein was dismissed from his $15.00 a week job when he defended a garment worker whose defective sewing machine had caused him to fall behind during a speed-up. The slack season and unemployment took their toll

The David Bernstein family in New York City on the eve of departure for Clarion. Courtesy of Michael Bernstein.

in emotional and financial resources among Clarion's people: silk weaver Harry Benskofsky was without work for nine weeks in 1909; furrier Harry Tucker, twelve weeks; and tailor Meyer Peltz, twenty-four weeks. These men and women would risk much because they saw Clarion as the only alternative to the sweatshop for themselves and their children.[22]

Many Jewish immigrants avoided the sweatshops and factories and tried peddling. Requiring little money, a smattering of English, and much persuasive ability, the immigrant peddlers pleaded their trade door to door or from behind pushcarts. Their dream was to build sufficient capital to move from street to store and eventually away from the Lower East Side. The large number of Jewish commercial establishments, big and small, testified to their success. So do the many family histories which trace their beginnings in America to a grandfather who peddled. Often forgotten are the many more who tried and failed. They lived a life of denial, filled with risk, without even the meager security of low wages. "The peddler's life," wrote Clarion colonist Isaac Friedlander, "was one of pressure, anxiety, living from hand to mouth."[23] The *luftmenshn* had come to America. By wit, wile, and sheer tenacity they lived on the edge, with only the fortunate gaining an economic foothold.[24]

The large Jewish migration to America, its urban concentration, and its dependence upon a few economic pillars forged a hard life. Theirs was a physical poverty of cold and cramped rooms, labor-induced exhaustion, and untreated medical complaints. Psychologically it exacted a heavy burden for it was so unexpected; America was the dreamed-of golden land where life was supposedly comfortable and work rewarding. Poet Elyakum Zunser articulated the disillusionment of his fellow immigrants when he asked in 1894, "For Whom Is the Gold Country?":

> I came to the land, saw it and Lo!
> Tears and suffering and tales of woe.
> In its narrow streets, on square and place,
> Darkness, poverty, writ on each face
> Stand from morn till night
> Huddled masses, a frightful sight.
> One would sacrifice his child for a cent,
> Or drive a man from his rooms for rent.
> Here a greenhorn hung'ring for bread
> Falls in the street, starved, dead!
> Poverty, misery, darkness, cold—
> Everywhere in this land of Gold!

Of toil and sweat, and sweat and toil
The worker has no lack
Weary when the season's "busy"
Hungry when it's "slack."
The boss is his worker's keeper
Until a machine can do it cheaper.
What a man is, and what he's been
Is sacrificed to the machine.
And more and more the streets are filled
With wandering men whom fate has willed
To be a brother to the horse
Who pulls the streetcar down the course.
The machine has done its job—
See that broken crippled mob.
One loses his sight, another his hand
To the machine, in this Golden Land.[25]

III

These difficult times are often forgotten in the wake of American Jewry's success. The immigrant past has become for many Jews a transitory stage towards a better life, a necessary and instructive rule of thumb to measure mobility from then to now. If this past is conjured up on its own merits, it usually appears as the golden age of Yiddish literature and theater. Yet, here too, the past fades and seems anachronistic. Remembering the immigrant years in terms of the present is ahistorical for it fails to consider those who come before from their own perspectives, from their own locations in time and space. It is necessary to discover the past world through the eyes of those who lived it when the future was far more uncertain.

The Jewish response to twentieth-century America's challenge assumed several shapes. A few, especially among the very religious, were unable to adjust to the secularized *treyfe medineh* (unholy land) and returned to Eastern Europe. A small stream of Jewish radicals who correctly sensed that revolutionary potential was higher in Europe than America joined them. The vast majority of Jews remained in their new homeland and pursued solutions along both individualist and collectivist lines with the distinction often blurred. Many mired in sweatshop and tenement life perceived their circumstances as temporary and assailable through hard work and belt-tightening. Vigorous efforts and underconsumption now would be rewarded later with escape from the ethnic ghetto and the working class. Spurred by their aspirations, the opportunities afforded by an expanding economy, and the examples of friends' and relatives' mobility, they or their children eventually secured middle-class berths in American society.[26]

A variety of organizations supported these individual and familial efforts. The *landmanshaften,* mutual benefit associations founded by former neighbors in the old country, aided needy members and their families during times of unemployment, illness, and death. Labor unions mobilized workers to pressure employers to raise wages, reduce hours, and improve working conditions. Their achievements went beyond formal membership to touch the lives of all workers. Meanwhile, the settlement houses and schools taught immigrants to read and write while they inculcated American customs and traditions, skills necessary to emerge into the wider society. The combination of self-help and collective action enhanced the socioeconomic and residential mobility of the Jewish people in America. Their rise was visible to some by the beginning of World War I and a demographic fact by the 1920s.[27]

The large number of Socialist voters in Jewish immigrant communities testifies for the view that adaption within the capitalist system was a far from unanimous choice. Rejecting piecemeal and gradual progress, the Socialists campaigned for a democratic revolution transferring the means of production—factories, farms, and mines—from private hands to the state. This redistribution of wealth and power would eliminate corporate and industrial abuses and provide all the opportunity to attain their maximum potential. The people of the Lower East Side responded to the Socialist call electing Meyer London to represent them in the House of Representatives in 1914. But, the softening of capitalism's crust combined with the immigrant generation's social and economic mobility blunted the Socialist thrust.[28]

Another alternative, now nearly forgotten, was also promoted. To solve the problems of urban clustering and economic congestion, spokesmen across the spectrum of Jewish opinion encouraged the immigrant to go back to the soil. The farm would, as well, remake the Jew physically and spiritually and free him from the past. Agriculture offered Jews the path to economic and social independence as it allowed the immigrants the most efficient and effective means to equality.

The rationale for a Back to the Soil movement was many-sided and appealed to a diverse constituency. Farming would decentralize the Jewish mass, making immigrants more responsive to Americanization and speeding the conversion from alien to native. Rooted and working in the soil, Jews would demonstrate to Christians a commitment to their adopted land, an option not as readily available in the urban ghetto. As a neighbor, the Jew could

gain an acceptance which would forever elude him as a distant urban stereo-
type. The long-popular agrarian ideal which extolled agriculture and farm
life influenced Jews as well. In farming, Jews as individuals and as a group
would find the key to a needed restructuring of their lives. Agriculture
offered to "productivize" the Jew by removing him from the artificial and less
worthy sectors of urban commerce and industry while providing him with a
measure of dignity and self-worth. The Jew would claim the power of decision making and initiative along with the sense of fulfillment generated by
hard work and land ownership while contributing in a real sense to the well-
being of his fellow countrymen. Further, a return to the land promised an end
to dependence upon the sweatshop and the peddler's pushcart and the creation of a balanced economic structure, the absence of which had plagued the
Jewish world in the Diaspora. No longer would anti-Semites be able to smear
Jews as commercial parasites who fed upon the sweat of the producing members of society. Jews, in turn, would be cleansed of the debilitating self-
hatred produced when such slurs were internalized. "The damning marks,"
editorialized Philadelphia's *Jewish Exponent* in 1889, "of the middleman or
the three balls man will no longer cling to their largely regenerated physi-
ognomies or poison the very vitals of their capable natures."*[29] A new Jewish
type would emerge from the farm—muscular, self-confident, and vigorous—
to replace the round-shouldered, pale-complected caricature of the ghetto. In
addition, farming would effect a decrease in the oversupply of hands in the
labor markets of the eastern cities thus improving life for those who remained
behind. The country would also save the children. The farm, devoid of the
congestion, unsanitary conditions, and vices which infected the tenements,
was a proper environment for childrearing. Finally, the agricultural solution
drew adherents because it preached self-help and work rather than charity or
a perpetual ward status.[30]

   Back to the Soil, then, translated into a sweeping cure for many Jewish
ills—unemployment, poverty, slum living, disease, crime, prejudice, and discrimination. There seemed no fruit the soil could not bear. Self-interest had
merged with idealism as a varied constituency rallied to the cause. German

---

*It is interesting to note how ingrained these anti-Semitic accusations had become in
the Jewish mind. Many Jews, regardless of class or ideology, appeared to take for
granted charges that the occupational niches they occupied were contemptible. Few
questioned the ill-conceived assumption that a Jewish transformation would eradicate
prejudice. Perhaps, on some level, Christian hatred was perceived as legitimate. Such
attitudes of self-abasement and doubt made Jews psychic prisoners of the Christian
world in which they lived.

and Eastern European Jews, rich and poor, conservatives, radicals, and the apolitical coalesced in support of the agricultural remedy.

Many influential German and American-born Jews, *Yahudim,* viewed the Eastern European influx with deep concern and disgust. The Eastern Europeans appeared their antithesis: superstitious, uncivilized, poor, and radical. Would not their presence in America, so obvious in its compactness, ignite a campaign of hate that was to that time unknown in the new land? Could not such an anti-Semitic reaction generalize to the *Yahudim* and erode their hard-won gains and precarious status? The German Jews' initial response, reflecting their fears, was to reject the newcomers. In 1882, Augustus S. Levey of the New York Hebrew Aid Society wrote: "We as a society and as American citizens cannot and will not be parties to the infliction upon our communities of a class of emigrants whose only destiny is the hospital, the infirmary, or perhaps the workhouse."[31] The conference of the board of managers of the Associated Hebrew Charities resolved in 1886 to "condemn the transportation of paupers into this country . . . such as are unable to maintain themselves should be forthwith returned whence they came."[32] As late as 1894, New York's *Hebrew Standard* declared:

> The thoroughly acclimated American Jew . . . stands apart from the seething mass of Jewish immigrants and looks upon them as in a stage of development pitifully low. . . . He has no religious, social, or intellectual sympathies with them. He is closer to the Christian sentiment around him than to the Judaism of these miserable darkened Hebrews.[33]

When words did not dam the human wave, German Jews moved to ease their coreligionists' pain. These were Jews in need who required the guidance and wisdom of those more knowing if they hoped to survive in their new home. Boris Bogen of the Baron de Hirsch Fund maintained, "The immigrant was a child who must be kept in his place. His benefactors knew better than he what was good for him."[34] The *Yahudim's* efforts, then, blended idealism and humanitarianism with paternalism and social control. They founded organizations and contributed money to provide food and shelter to the immigrants, place them in jobs, and Americanize them. To attack the larger problems of the community, Jewish welfare agencies such as the Hebrew Immigrant Aid Society and the Industrial Removal Office of the Baron de Hirsch Fund transported and planted immigrants in cities and towns throughout the United States. Approximately 60,000 New York City Jews were resettled with the assistance of these organizations. Also a product of Baron de Hirsch's philanthropy was the Jewish Agricultural Society. Incorporated in

1900, the society encouraged Jews to farm by offering loans, advice, and information. By 1912, it had assisted more than 2,200 Jews in acquiring farms while rejecting four to five times as many loan applications.[35]

One of the most prominent spokesmen for the Back to the Land movement was Rabbi Joseph Krauskopf of Philadelphia's Reform congregation Keneseth Israel. Born in Prussia in 1858, Krauskopf was, a quarter century later, among the first four American-trained rabbis ordained at Rabbi Isaac Wise's Hebrew Union College. Krauskopf traced his consuming interest in the Jewish agricultural revival to a meeting he had had with Count Leo Tolstoy in 1894 during a visit to Russia. Tolstoy believed that all barriers between Christian and Jew could be removed if only Jewish life was decommercialized through farming. "Make a bread producer of the Jew," he told Krauskopf, "and you will produce a change in the world's attitude toward the Jew. Let the Jew exchange the yardstick or the peddler's pack for the plow, and the world will bow to him who gives it bread to eat."[36] Profoundly impressed by the encounter and finding Tolstoy's ideas similar to his own solutions to the Jewish predicament, Krauskopf vigorously began gathering donations for a school to train Jewish boys in the agricultural sciences. In 1896, he purchased 400 acres of land outside Philadelphia and opened the National Farm School, a four-year vocational high school offering classroom instruction with in-the-field training. By 1901, the school had graduated its first class of eight students, the forward element of a rural advance that would reshape the Jewish experience. According to Krauskopf, agriculture

> will make laborers instead of paupers, bread producers instead of bread beggars. It will build up physical and mental and spiritual health instead of ghetto degeneracy and disease. It will . . . create within him anew that moral and virile fiber that in ancient times produced kings, prophets, lawgivers, bards, inspired writers to whom, to this day, the whole civilized world does homage.[37]

Jews, like Rabbi Krauskopf, had found their promised land in the American countryside.[38]

The Jewish left wing further stimulated the agrarian movement. In the wake of the 1881-82 pogroms, university students in Kiev, Odessa, and Vilna organized *Am Olam* (Eternal People) groups under the emblem of the plow and the Ten Commandments. They then migrated to America to establish model farming colonies along collectivist lines which would become the cores of a gradually evolving Jewish territorial base that would eventually be admitted to the Union as a state. While the means differed, the goal of these socialists and Marxists of normalizing Jewish life through "productive" labor converged with that of their ideological opponents. Few conservatives disagreed with I. Kasovich of the Kiev *Am Olam* who wrote, "Why should an entire people live on wind and smoke? It is a disgrace that a people should live on the labors of others. We must show the world that we can live by the work of our hands."[39] *Am Olam* groups built colonies in Louisiana, Arkansas, and South Dakota, all of which failed. The most significant in terms of size and duration was New Odessa in Oregon which contained sixty-five colonists and survived from 1882 to 1888. Like a flare, *Am Olam* blazed brilliantly and excited the imagination for a moment and then disappeared.[40]

Far more influential in radical circles and beyond was Dr. Chaim Zhitlovsky. Zhitlovsky migrated from Russia to New York City in 1908 where he published the journal *Das Naye Lebn (The New Life)*. Rejecting both assimilation and Zionism, he expounded the renewal of Jewish culture through Yiddish language and literature and the rehabilitation of Jewish life through socialism. Agriculture was central to the Jewish rebirth: "We Jews must reconstruct our lives, and function not only with our brains but as normal, wholesome, human beings in all fields of constructively productive endeavor—particularly as TILLERS OF THE SOIL."[41] For Zhitlovsky, America provided the most favorable ground for a culturally autonomous, agrarian-based, Jewish-socialist community to thrive.[42]

In the years between 1882 and 1910, the Back to the Soil call produced more than forty Jewish agricultural colonies in the United States. Despite an almost total lack of farming skills, there was no want of Russian immigrants who offered to people the colonies. The settlers, for their own individual needs as well as a sense of responsibility to the larger group, sought the land and were never pawns without will and ambition. Their interests fused with those who financed, organized, and often managed the projects, making the farm a mutually advantageous solution. Simultaneously, agricultural settlements were organized in Argentina, Canada, and Palestine in a worldwide movement to transform Jewry socially and economically. Nearly all of the American colonizing attempts were fruitless. Planning had proved hasty and inadequate and the settlements withered from a variety of diseases: inexperience, marginal land, scarce capital, and distant markets. Unforeseen but hardly uncommon catastrophes such as flood, drought, hail, prairie fire, and resulting crop failures forced the colonists to yield. Of the period's efforts, only the Jewish colonies of New Jersey survived. These did not constitute an adequate physical base or logical argument to justify further rural expansion because they were heavily subsidized and assumed the shape of model farms showcasing Jewish agriculture to visiting dignitaries.[43]

Despite the agricultural colonies' failures, the agrarian dream survived and continued nurturing the hopes of many urban Jews. For a minority the escape from tenement and sweatshop became a reality. Needing no urging from above, an estimated 5,000 Jewish families, a population of 25,000, lived on the land in 1912. Jewish farmers had settled in every state but New Mexico and Nevada, with the heaviest concentrations in New York, New Jersey, Connecticut, North Dakota, and Massachusetts. Some of the Jews who would later build Clarion predated their involvement in that colony with individual farming efforts. In 1906, David Bernstein, fired from his job as a sewing machine repairman, moved with relatives to a farm near Gurleyville, Connecticut. They stayed only a year and left "the pile of rocks" because of the death of a family member and the farm's dismal economic prospects.[44] Although the Bernsteins returned to New York City and a cold-water, walk-up flat, they would continue seeking an agricultural escape. Tsarist draft evader Samuel Chatsky boarded a train in 1907 for Ashley, North Dakota, to assess government-offered homesteading land. Discouraged by the lack of suitable sites he journeyed to Lemon, South Dakota, only to find that available land there was located ninety miles from the nearest railroad. He returned to Philadelphia and continued saving for his future farm. Both house painter Harry Yigdoll, the brother of seamstress Celia, and former Bundist Morris Bassin enrolled in the Baron de Hirsch Agricultural School seeking the skills to begin new lives. Five other members of the Clarion Colony attended Rabbi Krauskopf's National Farm School in preparation for the rural life.[45]

IV

The words of Krauskopf, Zhitlovsky, and other advocates of the Jewish agrarian movement were seeds which budded in the mind of Benjamin Brown, the organizer of the Clarion Colony. Born in 1885 as Benjamin Lipshitz, he lived as a child in the small *shtetl* of Krejopol outside of Odessa in southern Russia. In 1900, he left Russia for America, following his sister's path to Philadelphia. There Ben Lipshitz went immediately to work peddling from door to door using his only English words, "Look in the basket." At night he attended school to learn to read, write, and speak his adopted tongue. His peddling career was short-lived for it generated few spiritual and financial rewards and much rejection and humiliation. Discarding the peddler's pack Lipshitz found a job working as a farm laborer near Philadelphia. Despite little knowledge and background he quickly adapted to farm life and labor and acquired an interest in agriculture that would frame his entire career. In fact, this early experience might be likened to a spiritual conversion which profoundly shaped him. As part of his new identity Ben Lipshitz even assumed the name Brown, that of the farmer for whom he had labored. As Ben Brown, he subsequently enrolled at the National Farm School to further his education, although there is no evidence to indicate that he graduated. In 1907, he secured the assistance of Rabbi Krauskopf and the Jewish Agricultural Society in obtaining a loan to buy a farm near Covington, Kentucky, but it proved insufficient and he was unable to acquire the property. The following year he and a friend pooled their resources and bought a small farm in Bucks County, Pennsylvania, where they cultivated four acres of potatoes and twelve of corn. The *Jewish Exponent* of Philadelphia, looking for examples of successful Jewish farmers found him "happy and prosperous" after the harvest of 1909.[46] The only other source of agricultural information that Ben Brown could claim before the Clarion project was a twelve-week program offered by Pennsylvania State College during the winter of 1910-11, providing courses in vegetable farming, orchard fruits, sods, market gardening, and hay and forage crops. Despite a B average in the program and his scant farming experience, he never doubted his ability to make the colony a success.[47]

At some time between 1905 and 1909, Brown had been forced to leave farming and resume peddling. This time his selling trips brought him in contact with Scandinavian and German farm colonists in the Midwest, an experience further refining the direction his life would take. The colonists' experiment in cooperative living and working deeply impressed Brown and suggested application to his own people. Could not Jews, guided by such role models, escape the city and live, work, and prosper in the countryside? "Now I must ask again," wrote Brown, "Why not we . . . ? Why do we not use, oh Jewish workers, the opportunity to better our lot in life? Why don't we organize ourselves into groups and grasp the privileges which are open to us in this land?"[48] Brown, stirred then by the proponents of Jewish agrarianism and his own experiences, left his farm and began agitating for a Jewish colony built along cooperative lines. It would, he believed, be the first in a wave of rural settlements which would profoundly alter the Jewish experience in America.[49]

Benjamin Brown spoke of his dream to friends and relatives in Philadelphia and impressed them with his idealistic fervor, sincerity, and ability to move even the skeptical with his words. "He would," said one, "carry people away to a different world."[50] According to another, Brown was "a very eloquent, persuasive speaker . . . [who] could almost hypnotize you."[51] No wonder that Brown inspired in his followers the strong loyalty and even devotion reserved for charismatic leaders. Although driven and intense, he was also exceptionally personable, capable of charming with wit and sensitivity those who responded to his message. There was another side of Brown few perceived at this early stage. While he could inspire people and prod them to be greater than themselves, he lacked many of the leadership traits necessary to attain success. He was a poor planner, impatient and inattentive to the details of daily operation. "At times," remembered his daughter, "he lived in the air."[52] Unaware of his own limitations, he disguised his scant agricultural background behind a facade of authority and a plethora of facts. Vain and egotistical, Brown considered all criticism as personal and without merit and therefore easy to dismiss. Finally, he placed his own needs for honor and attention before the cause, thus clouding his judgement and generating dissension. "The main important fact," wrote Esther Radding, "[was that] he was too small a personality to represent a movement of that sort."[53]

In early 1909, Brown began to spend less time working his farm and concentrated more upon organizing a Back to the Land movement among Jews in Philadelphia. Meetings were conducted in Yiddish and initially held in a rented hall above a saloon on the corner of Eighth and Dickerson streets on the south side of town. Before the small groups which assembled weekly, Brown preached a multifaceted message. He beckoned Jews to the farm and its healthy outdoor life and economic security where every man could be his own boss. At the same time his words reached beyond the individual seeking to improve his life to touch upon the condition of the larger Jewish communities in the eastern cities. The labor and achievements of the Jewish farm colonies would reflect to the credit of all Jews and serve as beacons, further stimulating migration to the countryside. Brown's colony, while composed solely of Jews, would be nonreligious. That is, Judaism would be felt in terms of ethnicity, history, literature, tradition, and "folk direction" rather than ritual observance.[54] Religion would be a "private thing," with colonists providing at their own expense for rabbi and synagogue.[55] Politics, too, would be a matter of personal preference. Thus, while Brown was a theoretical socialist, he pragmatically advocated a colony resembling a modern Israeli *moshav*. The settlement would consist of privately owned farms each with its own herd of livestock yet bound cooperatively in the buying and marketing of goods. Ideology also did not keep Brown from contacting Jewish capitalists in search of financial support. The colony's leaders and managers were required to be members of the project and would be selected democratically with each settler casting one vote. Economic equality would exist initially, as well, with the quality rather than quantity of each plot being commensurate.[56]

Brown insisted that the colony be established in a western state for several reasons. The colony required a sizable piece of land and large sections were available in the West at prices far cheaper than in the East. The temptation to return to the East would be lessened and the ability to endure hardships greater the farther away the colony was located from New York City and Philadelphia. A western colony would also be less likely to become a boarder-resort as had happened with Jewish farms in upstate New York. Finally, western lands would be irrigated and thus relieve farmers of worries over nature's caprice.[57]

To stimulate recruiting efforts and expand the organization to New York City, Brown addressed a lengthy letter to Chaim Zhitlovsky's journal *Das Naye Lebn*. Brown chose this forum because of Zhitlovsky's advocacy of the Back to the Land movement and the character of the journal's subscribers. It was "read by the more advanced Yiddish speaking intellectual element of the working class. This was the class of people that we wanted to reach."[58] The letter, entitled *Far Vus Nit Mir?* (Why Not We?), was printed in the April 1909 issue and recounted the agricultural opportunities available to urban Jews and the progress made by other ethnic groups returning to the soil. The publicity gained from this piece, continued recruiting meetings, and word of mouth slowly drew more members and allowed for the organization of a New York City branch of the movement.[59]

Among the earliest recruits were Isaac Herbst and Barney Silverman, subsequently named vice-president and secretary of the organization. Herbst, a civil engineer with a degree from the University of Berlin, came to America in 1906, drawn by the reconstruction effort following the San Francisco earthquake. When a promised position failed to materialize, he remained in the East looking for work. For half of 1909, he worked as an engineer for the Otis Elevator Company; during the other twenty-six weeks of that year he was unemployed. Thirty-one years of age and married with two children, he was attracted to Brown's project for several reasons. Herbst was a socialist who supported the cooperative features of the colony as well as the effort to readjust the Jewish economy through farming. At the same time, he probably sought in the movement the personal and financial status which had eluded him so far in America. Barney Silverman, a socialist plumber who "talked like a college professor," attended a recruiting meeting in Philadelphia on the insistence of a friend.[60] Brown's speech moved him intellectually and emotionally, on an idealistic as well as a practical level. He stayed after the meeting and discussed the project with Brown for hours. Silverman vividly remembered their first encounter decades later: Brown "spoke with authority and deep perception of all topics and he seemed to have an inexhaustible fund of information."[61] Other than a few questions concerning membership qualifications and the organization's financial resources, Silverman was convinced and joined the movement. He envisioned the colony as a means to "end Jewish parasitism, make us productive, and let us live honestly."[62] Out of work for two months in 1909, he might have seen the farm as a solution to his personal and financial needs as well. Neither he nor Herbst, however, had any agricultural experience.[63]

V

By late 1909, the outlines of the future colony had grown more distinct. Brown sought up to 200 married men between the ages of twenty-five and forty years, each willing to exchange approximately $250 to $300 for shares in the colony's organization. The membership committee vaguely scrutinized character and health but paid no attention when accepting recruits to farming background or ideological and political homogeneity. The money contributed would be used to purchase land, equipment, livestock, and the materials necessary for the construction of houses and outbuildings. While a substantial outlay for the time and people involved, it was insufficient to cover costs. Brown believed that additional funds could be raised "by issuing bonds." Although the financial arrangements for the colony remained obscure, Silverman recalled, "We didn't ask many questions."[64] The colony promised to furnish every settler with forty acres of land, a house, wagon, team of horses, cows, and the necessary tools to work his farm, with repayment scheduled over a ten-year period. The Association estimated a loan breakdown for each settler as follows:

Land and Water Rights	$2,000.00
Land Clearing	40.00
House and Water Supply	500.00
Livestock	630.00
Machinery and Tools	188.00
Wagons and Harnesses	180.00
Feed and Seeds	370.00
Total	$3,908.00[65]

Friends contacted friends who spoke to brothers and cousins about joining the organization. At least fifty-eight of the men or 29 percent who participated in the project had a relative similarly involved. Members of *landmanshaften* discussed the colony in their lodges. The *Arbiter Ring* or Workmen's Circle, an important segment of the Lower East Side's Socialist coalition, contributed a minimum of sixteen of its people to the colonial undertaking. Gradually the recruiting pace accelerated. Applications were received and processed in the Philadelphia headquarters, the requisite sums deposited, and shares mailed to prospective colonists. Throughout the history of the project, however, money always trickled in slowly, many members continually in arrears. In 1910, the organization was chartered in the state of Delaware as the Jewish Agricultural and Colonial Association and empowered to buy and sell land and engage in colonization activities. Support from Rabbi Joseph Krauskopf and his assistant Rabbi Isaac Landman increased credibility and generated momentum. Similarly, newspapers such as the *Jewish Exponent* publicized the Association with favorable newscopy.[66]

The project appealed to a wide range of people. The colony's idealistic and cooperative features drew socialists such as Esther and Joseph Radding. For them this was an opportunity to "work out our special Jewish problems. To devote our entire life by becoming farmers, by working the soil. And to show those ignoramuses what we could do if we ged [sic] an equal chance to work the soil."[67] In the colony they saw a new beginning for a world "where each and everyone should have [an] equal chance to live and enjoy, and to get red [sic] forever of hatred and killing one another."[68] After discussing the project with their comrades at the Forsyth Street Free Library on the Lower East Side they applied and gained admission to the Association. Labor Zionist David Boyarsky, who had never before been on a farm, hoped to train in the colony for eventual migration to Palestine. Anarchist Isaac Isgur wanted the colony to become a working model of a society without laws, government, or violence. Socialism to former Talmudic student Louis Hamburger was Judaism's political program. After working as an organizer for the radical Industrial Workers of the World among the copper miners of Idaho and Montana, he turned toward the colony as a socialist assault upon capitalism from a different direction. In the colony he could live his philosophical principles and avoid the repressive acts of the authorities. Other union leaders such as David Cohen, Celia Yigdoll, and Alexander Geronemus may have sought similar respite from labor-management wars. With thirty-five of the colonist families which eventually farmed in Utah either socialist, Labor Zionist, formerly Bundist, or anarchist, the heterogeneous radical population comprised almost one-half of the settlement.[69]

Although the Association's leaders had planned to recruit the more "radically conscious" members of the Jewish community, the majority of members placed more practical considerations first. The colony offered families an es-

Ida and Samuel Barak in Philadelphia. Courtesy of Dr. and Mrs. Joseph Levitsky.

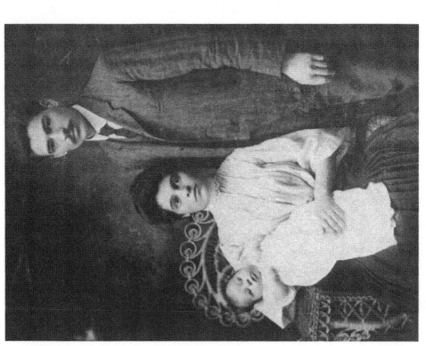

Moshe, Miriam, and daughter Sarah Malamed before Clarion. Courtesy of Mr. and Mrs. Daniel Malamed.

cape from the sweatshops and slums for a life of good health, fresh air, and economic security. Carpenter Barnet Slobodin joined because "it was hard to make a living. We were working for practically nothing."[70] The Mastrow family feared for their economic future in the city: "How could we ever acquire anything? How could we ever hope to raise our life standards? This was our chance. We had nothing to lose."[71] Sam Levitsky of Philadelphia, who had traveled as far as the gold fields of Cripple Creek, Colorado, looking for work that would adequately support his family, believed the farm offered the steady labor and income he craved. At least fourteen other recruits, whose unemployment ranged from four to fifty-two weeks in 1909, probably also hoped the colony would provide a solution to their economic misery. In addition, would-be farmers without sufficient resources saw the project as a means to land ownership. Joseph Brownstein, who had few economic worries, enlisted in the cause for his children's sake. In Abraham Wernick's words, many feared that the "children would grow up to be 'bums,' tramps in the New York whirlwind."[72]

Life-style was another consideration. Those bewildered by the pace of life in New York City and Philadelphia and who missed the sense of community they had last felt in the *shtetl* turned to the colony and its promised tranquility and harmony. With so many relatives as members, the family tie cannot be overstressed in generating recruits. Thus, Herse and Sonia Airoff applied for membership and provided financial and moral support to their relatives the Ayeroffs and Reiskys although they had no intention of actually settling in the colony. Loyalty to friends motivated others. Nathan Ayeroff sold his plumbing business and became a farmer "for the sake of the group that I was involved with. These are the people that I liked. . . . We knew them from the movement . . . [and] the various organizations. They all decided that this is the only outcome."[73] The lure of the West cannot be discounted in attracting members. Barney Silverman remembered that some longed for the life and adventures of the cowboy. "They were," he said, "actually floating in the air they wanted to get there. They were so green."[74]

While none of the above motivations was exclusive, for practicality and idealism fused in every mind, several distinct groups did emerge. Socialists, Labor Zionists, the religious orthodox, the economically insecure, and those who perceived no higher loyalty than to family or circle conceived a colony each in their own image. In such heterogeneity the weed of dissension easily rooted and was well fertilized. Distrust and discontent, however, were absent during this early period. "To most of them," wrote Silverman, "this was the greatest event that ever happened to their lives. All their thoughts, all their aspirations and hopes were concentrated upon one thing, the 'colony'!"[75]

VI

Eventually, 200 men joined the Jewish Agricultural and Colonial Association. New York, with 110 recruits, provided the majority of members while Philadelphia contributed 72 and Baltimore 11. Despite the predominance of New Yorkers, eight of the ten leaders were residents of Philadelphia reflecting Brown's initial recruiting efforts and the site of the organization's headquarters. When the Association's nine leaders who settled in Utah are excluded, the colony's male population (72) resembled the eastern residential distribution of the larger movement's membership. The Association was a project of the young (Table 2). The mean age of joiners, whether leader, colonist, or eastern supporter was twenty-seven years. Seventy percent of the members were between twenty-one and thirty with only a handful older than forty years and none more than fifty. Insufficient age data exist to allow for a comparison of Clarion members with colonists in other Jewish-American settlements.[76]

TABLE 2

Age Distribution of Clarion Members, 1910

Age Group	Colonists		Supporters		Leaders	
	N	Percent	N	Percent	N	Percent
Under 21	3	5	5	10	—	—
21–30	41	71	34	69	4	57
31–40	13	22	7	14	3	43
41–50	1	2	3	6	—	—
51–60	—	—	—	—	—	—
60+	—	—	—	—	—	—
Total	**58**		**49**		**7**	

Source: Clarion biographical data

While young in age, Clarion members were married men with family commitments. Personal histories reveal that 84 percent of the Utah colonists were married men while nearly 75 percent of those remaining in the East had a similar status. The western settlers, especially, had begun their families early with over 80 percent of the married couples having between one and six children. The leaders mirrored their followers with all but one married and all but two with children. Clarion was thus a project of the young in planning, direction, and execution. Yet, the men and women of Clarion were not immature youths without adult responsibilities. Family obligations and child-rearing demands were important factors in deciding to go back to the soil. Stable and responsible, they were at the same time willing to abandon the familiar and risk much for the sake of their families and coreligionists.[77]

Occupationally, the members of the Jewish Agricultural and Colonial Association were overwhelmingly working class (Table 3). One-half of the colonist group and over one-third of the eastern supporters held such skilled occupations as carpenter, plumber, furrier, and painter. Large numbers worked as well as semiskilled operatives in factory and garment-industry jobs. These blue-collar workers were prime recruits for Clarion because, while they suffered sweatshop and tenement abuses, they could gradually accumulate the financial resources required to participate. The movement found few joiners who could meet the monetary requirements of membership among the unskilled. Approximately one-third of the colonists and one-fourth of the supporters wore white collars in 1910. Shop owners, salesmen, and clerks probably enlisted because they were dissatisfied with the pace of their economic advance or were drawn by the more idealistic, noneconomic features of the project. The leadership circle, with one-half of its members in white-collar categories, occupied a more prominent socioeconomic position than the rank and file. Still, the voice of the movement's blue-collar majority was easily heard in decision making. When compared to the larger New York

TABLE 3

Occupational Distribution of Clarion Leaders and Members, 1910, Compared with the Occupational Distribution of Household Heads of Russian-Jewish Families in New York City, 1905

Occupational Status Group	Colonists N	Percent	Supporters N	Percent	Leaders N	Percent	New York City Russian Jews Percent
High Nonmanual	4	6	9	13	4	40	15.1
Low Nonmanual	15	23	8	12	1	10	30.8
Skilled	33	50	25	37	3	30	34.8
Semiskilled and Service	13	19	24	35	2	20	17.7
Unskilled	1	2	2	3	—	—	1.7
Total	**66**		**68**		**10**		

Source: Clarion biographical data; Thomas Kessner, *The Golden Door: Italian and Jewish Immigrant Mobility in New York City, 1880-1915,* 60.

City Russian-Jewish population, the Clarion membership was overrepre-
sented in all blue-collar categories except the unskilled and underrepresented
in the nonmanual brackets. The Back to the Soil effort did not often lure
those who were comfortable in the urban environment and were advancing up
the socioeconomic ladder. The compasses of such men pointed not to the
West but East to a better life in Brooklyn and the Bronx.[78]

Ben Brown's message had drawn young, married, family men who gambled for an opportunity to lighten the burden of the present and to improve
the chance of a future for themselves, their wives, and their children. They
sought escape from the working class and its attending tenement life-style to
become their own bosses with more control over their lives. Concomitant
with their self-interest was an idealism envisioning a sturdy and balanced socioeconomic foundation for American Jewry. This idealism and, to a lesser
degree, economic needs motivated the large white-collar minority of the
Clarion project. The movement's diversity of appeals had attracted not only a
variety of political activists but people from all economic classes. Family
ties, so crucial in recruiting, acted now to mediate group heterogeneity and
forge unity and loyalty to the whole. The leaders officially stood above, yet
were intertwined socially, politically, culturally, economically, and genera-
tionally with the rank and file. Elected annually by a group vote, they did not
dictate orders nor shirk the rigors of colonization. Rather, leaders and followers met on common ground, initially in tenement apartments and later in
the Utah desert, to discuss, plead, and convince each other of their dreams.

The cries of most men seeking change are never heard. Most dreams lie
forever stillborn. Benjamin Brown and his Back to the Soil message, however, would not suffer a truncated fate. His eloquent words had sown powerful images among a people trapped in a tenement-sweatshop existence. Their
vision of America for themselves and their religious brethren was yet unfulfilled. The practical escape from economic and social misery, fired with
the idealism of reclaiming the Jewish world spiritually and physically, drew
men and women to the cause. From the words and deeds of Rabbi Krauskopf,
Chaim Zhitlovsky, and the directors of the Jewish Agricultural Society the
movement gained momentum. These opinion makers had already prepared
the ground by advocating a return to farming as a realistic solution to individual and community needs. Young, enthusiastic, and ambitious, the people of
the Clarion project donated their money, time, labor, and hopes to the effort.
They knew they would succeed where the others had failed. The Association

gradually expanded, admitted members, erected an organizational structure, and formalized its plans. In early 1911, prodded by its impatient members, the Association began the transition from resource gatherer to farm colonizer. During the early and critical stages of this transformation much would transpire to determine the project's fate.

3

Back to the Soil

We are the vanguard of a large Jewish
movement to go back to the soil. Therefore we must succeed, we dare not fail.

Benjamin Brown, 1912

Thousands of the Jewish immigrants could
be settled on the excellent lands adjoining
those of the Jewish Colony of Utah. . . . We
shall then have dozens of Zions in our own
land, thousands of Jewish farmers helping to
make the United States to overflow with milk
and honey.

Rabbi Joseph Krauskopf, 1914

"It is no longer a dream," wrote Moshe Malamed on April 17, 1911.[1] That
morning, on a day overcast yet warm, members of the Jewish Agricultural
and Colonial Association took their first actual steps toward colonization.
Nine men gathered at the Pennsylvania Railroad Station in Philadelphia to
cheer Benjamin Brown and Isaac Herbst in their journey westward in search
of a site for the proposed colony. The two men, their expenses paid by special
assessment upon the Association membership, had planned a lengthy itiner-

ary including stops in New Mexico, Colorado, Wyoming, and Montana. Their baggage stowed, Brown and Herbst shook hands and embraced their supporters, encouraging them with reassuring words of a successful enterprise. As the train pulled out of the depot, the men on the platform waved and shouted their farewells, confident their project was in capable hands. They regrouped later at a nearby saloon to toast their future with beer and vodka.[2]

Sometime during the three-day trip to the western states Brown and Herbst probably reviewed their requirements for settlement. They sought a tract of land that was fertile, sufficiently large to settle the Association's members, with an available and adequate water supply, and linked to markets through easily accessible transportation facilities. Brown and Herbst were aware that they carried a heavy burden in the trust and hopes of their followers. They also saw themselves in a larger frame as the possible architects of a Jewish rebirth. Yet did they fully realize how unprepared they were to meet the challenges before them? Their lack of resources whether measured in monetary terms or ignorance of western agricultural conditions would have given pause to the efforts of less-assured men. Such liabilities even in the best of times would have handicapped and weakened the thrust of their movement. If conditions proved less than optimal, with natural and man-made events conspiring to make life harsh and uncompromising, such flaws could spread cancer-like to erode the colony's core and make success but a dream.

I

Brown and Herbst's search for land was neither random nor blind. The Association had sent inquiries to state land offices and placed ads in major western newspapers outlining its agricultural needs. Several states and large landowners had responded with packets of information or dispatched representatives to Philadelphia with maps and data about soil, climate, transportation, and water. The two men followed up these leads traveling first to New Mexico to inspect a promising tract of land near Deming in the southwest corner of the state. For sale was a privately owned, 30,000-acre parcel of land through which the seller agreed to construct an irrigation canal. The water for the canal was to come from wells the owner promised to dig. Herbst and Brown were impressed; the land appeared fertile and water would be made available for farming. There were drawbacks, however, for the land was located twenty miles from town and crops and supplies would have to be transported on a primitive road. Yet it was the Association's lack of financial resources which made the purchase impossible. The group's means were limited and had to be stretched to cover not only land and water rights, but seed, machinery, livestock, and the construction of houses and outbuildings. The quantity and quality of land acquired would have to correlate directly with available funds.[3]

As the disappointed men prepared to leave New Mexico they received a telegram from Rabbi Joseph Krauskopf of Philadelphia. Krauskopf suggested that Brown and Herbst add Utah to their itinerary and investigate agricultural opportunities there. The Association had discounted Utah early as a possible site because of reports that the climate was inhospitable to farming and that available land was unsuitable, located in either desert or mountain regions. Rather than displease their most prominent supporter, the two men bought tickets for Salt Lake City. Krauskopf had several reasons for proposing Utah. While the Association was making inquiries about western lands, Rabbi Krauskopf had acted independently to gather information concerning the conditions of settlement. To survive the initial, difficult years, Krauskopf believed the colonists would require assistance from a financially secure and politically well-connected, local Jewish community. Prominent Jews could intercede with government officials and area businessmen to insure favorable treatment and advantageous terms in the myriad of dealings their coreligionists would undertake. The colonists never doubted that this assistance would, if necessary, be more substantial. "They would not let us down," said Barney Silverman. "Should it come to a financial squeeze, they would see us through."[4] A group of such men, long known to Krauskopf either as personal friends or financial supporters of the National Farm School, lived in Salt Lake City. Their ties to Krauskopf had been further cemented through the Rabbi's son, Harold, who had resided in the city during 1910. Among those whom Krauskopf contacted were attorney Daniel Alexander (who had attended Congregation Keneseth Israel while studying at the University of Pennsylvania and now sat on the board of directors of the National Farm School), political and business leader Simon Bamberger, and mining entrepreneur and land developer Samuel Newhouse. These men then approached members of the Jewish community, civic organizations such as the Commercial Club of Salt Lake City and the Utah Development League, and Governor William Spry and enlisted their support. Krauskopf also recommended Utah because of its large Mormon population. People who had experienced the difficulties of settlement and had suffered religious persecution, he felt, would be more receptive to a Jewish colony than more typical Americans. A Jewish settlement could not survive in a socially hostile environment, for it required a good working relationship with the Christian majority as a necessary foundation for successful colonization. A subsequent telegram

UTAH'S PRINCIPAL CITIES,
MOUNTAIN RANGES, & RIVERS

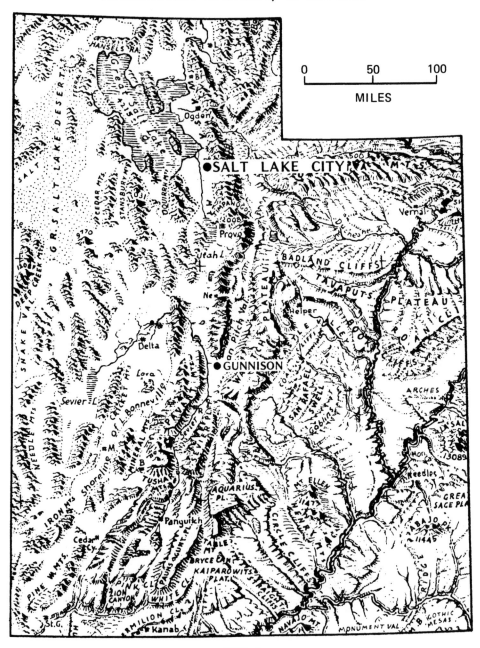

MAP 4

from Samuel Newhouse welcoming Brown and Herbst to Utah reinforced Krauskopf's advice.[5]

The needs of the Jewish colonists merged with the efforts of state officials who were actively promoting a sell Utah campaign. To lure settlers, the Utah government in conjunction with business and civic groups were disseminating facts and figures throughout the nation boosting the state's people, economy, and climate. The state spent $30,000 to erect displays and exhibits promoting Utah at the Lewis and Clark Centennial Exhibition in 1905 and $85,000 for similar activities in San Francisco and San Diego in 1915. In 1911, the Utah State Board of Statistics was reorganized as the Bureau of Immigration, Labor, and Statistics with a prime function the attraction of new settlers to the state. The bureau advertised Utah agricultural opportunities by providing potential settlers with information about farm acquisition, acreage availability, land values and prices, costs of production, and crop yields per acre. The Utah State Agricultural College in Logan, meanwhile, issued bulletins for farmers, with and without experience, concerning dry farming and irrigation. State leaders felt a special urgency in 1911 to draw farmers. Utah was in the process of constructing the sixty-mile-long Piute Canal which would water an estimated 35,000 acres and thus open desert land to cultivation. No wonder, then, that Salt Lake City Jews questioning government officials about land for a proposed colony found them quite responsive.[6]

A representative of the Utah State Board of Land Commissioners, which was charged with the sale of state-owned land, met Brown and Herbst after their arrival in Salt Lake City and personally escorted them to several available sites. The two men were particularly interested in a state-offered section of land in south-central Utah below the Piute Canal. The more than 8,000 acres were in a tract eleven miles long and from one to two miles wide. Three miles to the west was Gunnison, a small town serving as a station on the Denver and Rio Grande Railroad line. This railroad provided a direct transportation link with the Salt Lake City market, 150 miles to the north. The land, situated in the foothills of the Valley Mountains, overlooked farms colored in season with ripening alfalfa, oats, and wheat.[7]

The tract itself was virgin soil covered with sagebrush and wild grasses. After walking over some sections of the tract and holding the soil in his hand, Brown was convinced it was "of good quality."[8] Governor William Spry would later agree with Brown's assessment, declaring the parcel "among the very choicest agricultural lands in the state."[9] Satisfied as to the land's fertility, the Jews were similarly assured about water availability. When finished, state

THE CLARION TRACT

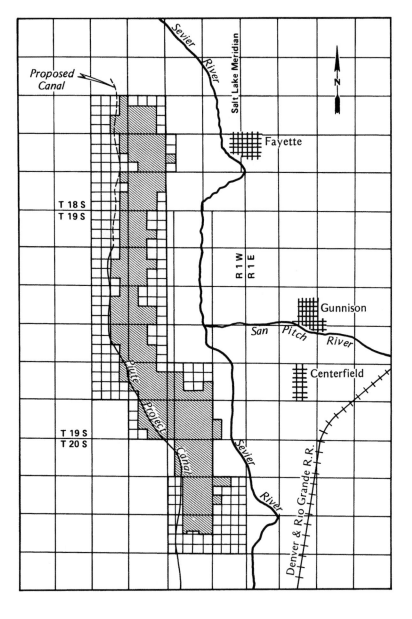

0   2
MILES

N

Sevier River

Salt Lake Meridian

Proposed Canal

T 18 S
T 19 S

R 1 W
R 1 E

Fayette

Gunnison

San Pitch River

Piute Project Canal

Centerfield

T 19 S
T 20 S

Sevier River

Denver & Rio Grande R.R.

MAP 5

officials boasted, the Piute Canal would provide abundant water and end the farmer's dependence upon the weather. This expert advice added to state construction and ownership of the canal probably assumed for the would-be colonists the form of an official guarantee of its viability and assurance against all mishap. This naivete is suggested in a recollection by Barney Silverman: "What impressed people in the east . . . [was] the magic word known as irrigation. . . . All you got to do was like stepping over to a sink."[10] The party then traveled to Gunnison for meetings with the mayor and local businessmen. The Jews were touched by the townspeople's friendliness and expressions of moral support and financial goodwill. Not only were land, water, and community variables measuring positively for the tract, but the state's selling price was within the Jewish Agricultural and Colonial Association's reach. The Association's leaders agreed to purchase at the public-land auction on August 7, 1911, 6,085 acres for $46.50 for land and water rights per acre. Ten percent of the purchase price of the land, or $6,815.50, was due immediately and the rest with interest of 5 percent per annum payable in equal installments over ten years. Payments for water rights ($35.00 per acre) were postponed until after the state canal was functional. For the convenience of the colonists, all installments would fall due after harvesttime. The state of Utah retained title to all land and water rights until colonists had paid principal and interest in full. To satisfy Brown's requirement that the colony be ethnically and geographically homogeneous, the state informally agreed to discourage non-Jewish farmers from bidding on the designated lands. Actually, there was very little possibility that local farmers would compete for the land. Several later told colonist Sam Chatsky, "We would never let our children go on land like that."[11]

Ben Brown and Isaac Herbst returned to Philadelphia and reported favorably to their supporters on a Utah location for their colony. The members accepted their recommendation and voted unanimously to settle on the proposed site. Association member Abraham Wernick remembered the atmosphere at the New York City branch gathering held to consider the question:

> The meeting took place in a small, basement room in Harlem. It was crowded to suffocation. I stood there and thought: Here we are pressed together in a tiny room. How accurately it symbolizes the situation of the lives from which we are trying to escape! With our votes at this moment we may decide the fate of the colony—if we choose the right place we will succeed; if not, we'll fail.[12]

The decision made, the leaders beat the drum for funds, asking current members to meet their financial obligations or seeking new recruits with the nec-

essary monetary resources. In the summer of 1911, an Association delegation consisting of Brown, Herbst, and Louis Flax resumed and finalized
negotiations with Utah government officials in Salt Lake City. The August
land auction in Sanpete County held no surprises. Under the slogan, "the
State of Utah has a farm for you," land board representatives sold the desired
acreage to the Jewish contingent.[13] Because the federal government had given
the land to Utah with the promise it be sold only to individual settlers, the
men bought the parcel in forty- and eighty-acre plots in the names of Association members. Later, according to their plan, each family would reassign its
land to the Association. The reassignment occurred, but it would be accompanied by considerable discontent and dissension which, said Brown, "never
healed."[14] Ironically, the Association's initial check to cover the down payment on the land did not clear because of insufficient funds, a clear portent
for those who chose to see it. Instead, the air in New York City, Philadelphia,
and Sanpete County was filled with optimistic predictions of coming prosperity. The editor of the *Manti Messenger* was typical of the forecasters, noting
that the colony would be

> composed entirely of men who are farmers by choice and who have
> been sufficiently successful to lay up some money and the associa-
> tion will come into this county with a bank account of between
> $40,000 and $50,000. They have with them professors of agricul-
> ture, artisans in all branches, and propose to do thoroughly modern
> and up-to-date farming. It is a very desirable addition to our popula-
> tion.[15]

II

Brown planned settlement in stages. Twelve men would be chosen to go to
the colony immediately to prepare the land for planting and irrigation. Working the land as a team they would receive wages for their efforts. The second
stage would commence in the spring of 1912 with the arrival of carpenters
and plumbers who would construct homes and help clear and plow the land.
Later that year, the tract would be divided into forty-acre homesteads and
fifty men and their families planted in the colony. With homes already built
and fields ready for planting, organizers hoped that the colonists' difficult
transition to an agricultural life would be facilitated. The psychological and
physical burden of starting with and from nothing would be eliminated by
those who came before, thus shepherding the fragile store of emotional and
mental energies necessary for colonization. Each year thereafter, the colony
would grow by increments of fifty families until all Association members had

removed from the East. A lottery system would determine in an equitable manner the sequence of arrival. The colony's leaders, always vague about the financial underpinnings of their project, did realize early on that members' contributions were insufficient to fund the costs of settlement. Internal sources of funds combined with bountiful harvests, they assumed, would carry the colony through the initial stages provided no serious financial setbacks occurred. Once the colony had stabilized, funds from Jewish philanthropists would be forthcoming and see the project through to completion. Convinced that their plan would succeed, concern over financial stumbling blocks did little to break the colonists' stride.[16]

The Piute Canal held the key to the colony's future and its ability eventually to attract financial supporters. Begun in 1908, the canal was fed from a reservoir near the town of Joseph in Sevier County and ran south to north past Richfield and then to Sanpete County and a planned terminus west of Fayette. By 1911, the canal had reached the southern one-third of the eleven-mile-long tract of Jewish colony land. Although predicted that all Jewish land would be under the canal by 1913 and thus open to irrigation, construction had only approached the middle one-third by 1914 and was not completed until 1918, more than two years after the colony's demise. The Jews, however, had more to contend with than just construction delays. The newly built canal had sides of dirt and lacked the necessary gates and weirs designed to regulate the water each farmer received. Farmers on the southern end of the canal, then, had the first opportunity to secure water. Nothing prevented them from diverting more than their fair share except their consciences. Moreover, because there were no past data concerning canal capacity and the amount of water which would be lost through seepage and evaporation, state officials could only estimate the eventual quantity available for delivery. As late as October 1911, the State Board of Land Commissioners was unable to advise farmers about water availability since the state engineer's report on the subject, "has not been made to date."[17] A local farmer also criticized the board for contracting to sell water rights at two acre feet per share for land requiring double that amount. The Jewish settlers on the northern end of the canal were thus at the mercy of their southern neighbors' sense of morality and gambled upon the reliability of state officials' impressions about the quantity of canal-carried water necessary for farming. Prospects for an adequate water supply for the colony were cloudy at best and in drought years when water was far from plentiful, quite dismal. Colonist Barnet Slobodin's lament was heard all too frequently during the life of the settlement: "We were on the end of the canal and by the time water reached us it disappeared in the ground.

We couldn't get enough water to raise a crop."[18] Problems with the Piute Canal would plague the colony throughout its existence and area farmers to the present day.[19]

III

On Labor Day 1911, amid applause, tears, and farewells, the first eleven colonists departed Philadelphia by train for Utah. During a stopover in Buffalo, New York, they recorded their historic moment in a photographic studio before a backdrop of Niagara Falls. The picture captured the images of eleven unsmiling, would-be farmers in business suits and ties, earnest and sober on the eve of a task with possibly momentous results. Perhaps they were aware of recent events which would have steeled their resolve to bring renewal to Jewish life. On September 8, news dispatches from Russia reported yet another Jewish expulsion, this time from the city of Nikolaev. From Palestine on the same day came indications that the future of Jewish agricultural colonies in the Galilee was in jeopardy. Chosen for their honesty, mechanical skills, strength, experience with horses, and "seriousness," the group included two carpenters, a plumber, a peddler, and a furrier. All but four of the men were from Philadelphia, for Ben Brown wanted the first colonists to be men he knew personally and whom he could trust. In addition to Brown who awaited them in Utah, only one, a graduate of the National Farm School, had any agricultural background. The group traveled for six days by train, finally reaching Gunnison on September 10. On arrival, the men gathered their gear together and clambered onto the platform where Brown greeted them in Yiddish. The colonists then boarded an open wagon for the trip to their land. Gunnison residents stopped and stared at the newcomers who sang Ukrainian folk songs as they drove through town.[20]

While the sight and sound of the colonists startled Gunnison residents, the Jews surely felt disoriented in what was to them an alien environment. Just a few days before, the men were enmeshed in a Jewish world organized in Yiddish with tenement and sweatshop borders. Their community was an enclave where Christians were external, confronted only occasionally and in a manner denying friendship or closeness. The ghetto provided a sense of physical and emotional security while nearby Christian neighborhoods, generating fear, loathing, and conceit, were avoided. Christian intrusion into the Jewish world in the guise of politician, police officer, shopowner, or missionary was tolerated but hardly welcomed. Never really having been exposed to Christian America, the Jews were now thrust to its heartland.

The first colonists bound for Utah: front row, left to right, Barney Silverman, Berel Horowitz, Isaac Herbst holding his daughter Theresa, Samuel Levitsky; second row, Samuel Sack, Harry and Rebecca Martin and child, Eli Sendrow; third row, Isaac Friedlander, Aaron Binder, Joseph Furman, Joseph Miller. Courtesy of Sarah Sack Bober.

The Jewish experience in New York City and Philadelphia, grounded in *landmanshaften,* synagogues, or radical political organizations, had little relevance in rural and Mormon Sanpete County, Utah. The county claimed no village containing more than 2,500 people. Gunnison, the community closest to the Jewish colony, had a population of 905 in 1910, an increase of just 121 residents during the previous decade. The county's foreign born numbered 2,440 people, with nearly three-quarters having migrated from Denmark, England, and Norway. Ethnically and culturally similar to the native population, these immigrants intensified the homogeneity of the county. Before the arrival of the colonists, Sanpete County counted only two Jewish merchants among its 16,704 people. Jews were so unusual a sight that the appearance of a Jewish peddler in 1910 occasioned a news item in the *Gunnison Gazette.* Thus, Gunnison citizens were informed when an advance party of the Jewish Agricultural and Colonial Association was in their town with a news note headlined, "JEWS HERE."[21] In fact, the Jewish population for the entire state of Utah was only 670 persons in 1916, equivalent to a few blocks on the Lower East Side. The only element of religious heterogeneity in the Gunnison area other than the Jewish colony was a small congregation of the Presbyterian Church. Gunnison, like nearly all of Sanpete County, spent its Sundays attending religious services in the ward houses of the Church of Jesus Christ of Latter-day Saints.[22]

The Jews' new home seemed alien for other reasons. Just two months before the colonists' arrival, the county voted for Prohibition and closed all of its saloons. Most of Gunnison still relied on kerosene to fuel its lights, with electrical power introduced only in January 1911. "Greater Gunnison" boasted one doctor, one lawyer, one bank, and one pool hall. "However," editorialized the town's only newspaper, "do not for a moment think this is a 'one horse' town."[23] The small-town atmosphere was reflected in the *Gunnison Gazette* which filled its weekly six pages with notices of local social events, family reunions, and sicknesses, columns titled "Giggles, Gossip, and Gabble," and brief reviews of state, national, and foreign news. Government business was conducted on an annual budget of $2,900 and was absorbed with brush clearing, garbage collection, and street widening. Crime in Gunnison and the rest of Sanpete County was negligible. In 1912, the county recorded no murders, robberies, assaults, or rapes. Incorrigibility was the most frequently cited offense with four young people confined during the year. Local politics was a quiet affair between Republicans and Democrats, with the proper religious credentials a prerequisite for office holding. The Socialist

Original settlement in the southern section of the colony, 1911-12. Courtesy of Sarah Sack Bober.

Party in the 1910 election counted just two votes in the entire county for its candidates for the U.S. Congress and the Utah Supreme Court.[24]

As Ben Brown steered the wagon westward out of town, the colonists strained to see their land. Visible to all were the four large white tents which would serve that winter as communal living and dining shelters. As they drew nearer to the encampment, the climb uphill became more obvious, the horses reducing their speed to "almost a crawl" as they pulled hard against their harnesses.[25] Although lacking in farm experience, Barney Silverman became concerned. The land sloped steeply, resembling the sides of "a large saucer."[26] The "raw earth," as Isaac Friedlander described it, was bare of trees and covered with sagebrush, shadscale, and tall, thin grasses. Large patches of ground were devoid of any vegetation. Dry washes and gullies pierced the terrain, cutting the land into irregular strips. Small stones and large rocks littered the tract conjuring up frightening images of what lay below the surface. Closer inspection of the soil revealed a sandy, gravelly loam approximately a foot in depth underlaid by a hardpan subsoil. A present-day farmer likened the land to "gravel beds."[27] When divided into forty-acre farmsteads this marginal land would prove inadequate to support a family. The site of the base camp was a particularly dubious place to begin cultivation. Yet, this determination was out of the Jews' control. The stage of canal construction had dictated the initial area of farming in the southern part of the colony on some of the worst land in the tract. Silverman also noticed that no well had been dug for water. Ben Brown reassured the anxious men. Balanced on his haunches he bent down and scooped up a handful of the light-brown dirt. He tightened his fist about the earth and then loosened his grip, revealing a compressed clod which subsequently split into small pieces. This test, he told the colonists, demonstrated the "tremendous richness of the soil. This earth contains all vital elements of highly fertile soil and with the application of the right amount of water, this land is capable of producing the highest yield per acre anywhere in the country."[28] The men relaxed, the expert has assuaged their anxiety. "Coming from his mouth," said Silverman, "nobody doubted it."[29]

Although they were unaware at the time, the poor quality of the soil was only one of the difficulties they would face. The area had a short growing season with frosts coming late in the spring and early in the fall. Sanpete County's season averaged 124 days, yet experienced farmers knew that their margin of growing safety was only 95 days.[30] Their growing time was thus a full month shorter on the average than that experienced farther north in Utah and Salt Lake counties. Precipitation for local crops was minimal. Mountains bordering the valley acted as barriers to moisture from Pacific storms moving eastward. Despite an elevation of more than 5,000 feet, the area was semi-arid, measuring slightly more than twelve inches of precipitation per year. Further, three-quarters of this amount was practically useless to local farmers as it fell as snow during the winter months. Water delivered through the irrigation canal arteries was, then, the lifeblood of Sanpete County farming. Seasonal extremes would pose another obstacle to the colonization effort. Initially, Utah's climate enchanted the Jews with the temperate, "almost perpetual summer" season. "But," declared Isaac Friedlander, "the reality was the opposite, we found: the summers were short and terribly hot; the winters long and severe."[31] Temperatures reached the high nineties in the summer and could fall as far as seventeen degrees below zero in the winter, with a mean of forty-six degrees. While unusual, snow could accumulate to over seventy inches as it did during the winter of 1913-14.[32]

The day after their arrival, the colonists outfitted in Russian workers' caps and peasant blouses rose early and reported for work. Ben Brown divided them into committees with tasks of land clearance, clerical work and purchasing, horse care and water supply, and surveying. The six men assigned to clear the land pursued their task in steps. To create farmland, they hitched two teams of horses to an iron rail which was then dragged along the ground to uproot the sagebrush. The detached brush was raked into large piles and burned. Next, the men unearthed and stacked the larger surface rocks. With shovels, picks, and hoes the colonists did their best to fill in holes and low spots in the emerging fields. The land was now ready for the gas tractor which scraped, leveled, plowed, and harrowed the soil. The tractor, the first used in the county, quickly proved ineffective as it was susceptible to frequent mechanical breakdowns. It would remain both a financial and physical burden for the colony because none of the men knew how to repair the machine or maintain it in operation. As a result, plowing was accomplished primarily through horse and man power. Despite this setback, the men prepared 1,500 acres during the fall of 1911 for the coming spring's planting. Irrigation ditches leading from the canal to the fields were also laid out and dug. But the lack of farming experience was soon apparent. Brown and Joseph Miller's education at the National Farm School had been geared to Pennsylvania conditions. They could rely for instruction only upon a course titled "Soil improvement by means of drainage, irrigation, cultivation, manuring, (and) rotation," which met for two recitations per week and treated its topics solely upon a theoretical level.[33] Thus, they eagerly accepted the advice of local Mormon farmers and followed the directions of a professor sent at the governor's insistence from the Utah State Agricultural College. In addition, two men were charged with the care of the horses and the ferrying of water by wagon from Gunnison. Meanwhile Isaac Herbst and a survey team laid out roads and plotted lines dividing the tract into individual farms.[34]

Regardless of his task, each man in return for his labor collected $15 per week in wages. The amount earned, however, was of little importance. The men knew that their Association operated on a pittance. They knew, as well, they had been chosen to initiate the ground-breaking stage of an experiment with implications not only for themselves and their families but the Jews of the American ghettos. Their toil now would be decisive. The financial health of the colony required bountiful harvests or the promise of a Jewish agricultural showcase which would attract the support of wealthy philanthropists. It is hardly surprising that, as Ben Brown proudly recalled, "they worked twenty-five hours a day."[35]

Even in this initial phase of colonization expenses were beyond the Association's means. Although bought with credit, tents, tools, wagons, and horses had drawn heavily upon the organization's budget. The tractor alone had cost $4,000 with one-fourth of the purchase price paid down immediately. Wages added $180 to the weekly drain. To support the men, Association members in the East redoubled their efforts to raise the required funds. Leaders convinced families to loan money to the Association above their membership requirements. Members voted to assess themselves additional fees to maintain the project. Settlement in Utah was prohibited until all of a member's financial obligations had been met. In addition, names of reserve members were added to the rolls and their money collected in case earlier participants were forced to withdraw from the Association. Recruiters became excessive in the pursuit of their cause. Thus, Rabbi Isaac Landman declared in an interview with the *Jewish Exponent:* "The fact is that if a colonist is so lazy that he will do nothing else except cut his alfalfa crop three times a year he will be able to make a living and to meet his obligations to the State."[36] The rabbi later assured the reporter that only the industrious and energetic would find places in the colony.

Fund raising occupied only a portion of eastern supporters' time. Prospective colonists were also preparing to enroll in a crash program of study "that will practically amount to a short course at the [National] Farm School or in one of the State agricultural colleges."[37] After a few months of classroom instruction in animal care, the cultivation of wheat and alfalfa, and the handling of tools and machinery, the colonists believed that they would be ready for farm life.[38]

The colony suffered two defections during the first winter. One colonist, pessimistic about farming prospects, returned to the East. Another attempted physically to bully fellow colonists and was banished from the colony for three months "for behavior unbecoming a pioneer."[39] Rather than accept his dismissal he voluntarily resigned from the Association and left Utah. Graduates of the National Farm School with "no experience in irrigation farming, but . . . [whose] general knowledge in agriculture was very extensive" replaced the men early in 1912.[40] Political differences among the colonists aroused little concern during this time. A sense of common purpose, a spirit of camaraderie under adverse conditions, and the preoccupation with daily chores smothered ideological disagreements. The drinking water situation continued to cause difficulties. With well drilling postponed until the spring, water was hauled in a large tank from Gunnison twice a week with the six-mile round trip consuming most of a day. The water problem would grow in intensity as the colony's population increased.[41]

Despite the defections and the water shortage, morale remained high. The men perceived themselves as the vanguard of a movement that would change the course of lives of tens of thousands of people. "Let us make a good go of it here," said colonist Joseph Furman, "and you'll see the whole people returning to the land."[42] Their progress, too, was obvious and generated much pride. Hard work and sweat had reclaimed desert and prepared it

for new life. Satisfied and confident, the men snapped photographs of themselves and their accomplishments and mailed them home as postcards to family and friends. Encouraging letters returned, firing the men in their work.
For those repelled by the squalid tenements, the Utah environment proved
intoxicating. Barney Silverman wrote that

> the evenings and nights were exceptionally cold during the winter,
> but that did not hold back the pioneers from venturing out from their
> tents. They were well repaid for their courage in more than one way.
> The sky they beheld was not like anything they ever saw back East.
> The sky was always clear blue, with never a speck of cloud and
> studded with myriads of stars and they looked so near and so
> bright.[43]

Similarly, Isaac Friedlander recalled a trip by the colonists into the mountains
to gather firewood and to explore which "evoked in us . . . a religious exalta-
tion":

> We are amazed by the concurrence here of summer and winter. Be-
> low, Indian summer warmth prevails, attended with flies and mos-
> quitoes, while the wooded ridges and high crevasses are mantled
> with snow. But the ultimate thrill of religious ecstasy seized us when
> a sudden clap of thunder was heard to arise somewhere in the depths
> of the mountains, and then it faded away. We sang and danced for
> joy, B[enjamin] B[rown] was possessed of even more delight and en-
> thusiasm than the rest of us. He mounted a massive stump, spread
> his arms heavenward and spoke to God like a prophet. These shout-
> ers and jumpers could have been mistaken for a sect which comes
> into the wooded mountains to adore their God. . . . Although we
> felt like insects in comparison, we felt greater than our ordinary
> selves, because we had had this transcendental experience.
>
> Very little wood was gathered that day; our wagons returned half
> empty. But our hearts brimmed over with happiness and song—the
> happiness of freedom from care and from anxiety for the morrow.[44]

IV

Rabbi Joseph Krauskopf's impression that the Mormon world would be hos-
pitable to Jewish aspirations was soon confirmed. The Mormons, rather than
perceiving the colony as an alien outpost in their midst, received the Jews as
lost kin. Like many Christians, the Mormons considered themselves chosen
in a spiritual sense, having, through faith, covenanted with God to follow His
commandments. Yet, the Mormon conception of selection went beyond that
of other Christians for it was rooted in a claim to literal descent from the

Benjamin Brown and Isaac Herbst (on the right, respectively) reviewing the colony's books. Courtesy of Sarah Sack Bober.

Communal mealtime for the original colonists. Courtesy of Sarah Sack Bober.

ancient tribes of Israel. "We are," said George Reynolds in 1916, "of the house of Israel, of the Royal seed, of the royal blood."[45] Acceptance of Mormonism transformed the convert into a latter-day Israelite with a line of descent extending to the patriarchs of Judaism. Thus, church leader Brigham Young declared in regard to Mormon proselytizing: "We are now gathering the children of Abraham who have come through the loins of Joseph and his sons, more especially Ephraim."[46] Although accepting Jesus Christ as the Messiah, Mormons resuscitated various Old Testament customs and Hebraic practices. For example, Mormon leaders restored their conception of ancient Hebrew priesthood orders, reintroduced polygamy, and preached the "Word of Wisdom," a code of dietary laws designed to maintain physical health as well as serve as a symbol of unique status.[47]

The events and sites of nineteenth-century Mormon history bolstered this theological identification with Jews as Biblical brethren. In the 1830s and 1840s, the Mormons suffered pogrom-like violence as they fled before mobs which murdered and assaulted them in Ohio, Missouri, and Illinois. After the killing of their "Moses," Joseph Smith, Brigham Young as a latter-day Joshua led the Saints in an exodus across the Mississippi River and into the American wilderness. The self-proclaimed "Camp of Israel" found its promised land in Utah. It was hardly coincidental, they believed, that the climate and geography of their refuge resembled the land of Israel. Like the Holy Land, Utah possessed its own Dead Sea tied by a river they appropriately named the Jordan to a body of fresh water. When labeling terrain and communities, Mormon settlers occasionally turned to the Bible for inspiration, creating Utah counterparts of Goshen, Jericho, Mount Nebo, and Moab. At the center of the Mormon Zion, in its capital city, was erected the main temple just as Jerusalem had sheltered a similar holy edifice during the reign of King Solomon. In both the religious and secular worlds, then, Utah Mormons affirmed their identity and destiny as a chosen people in accordance with a Jewish model.[48]

Latter-day Saints were, as well, fervent Zionists, predicting in accordance with ancient covenant and prophecies the eventual gathering of the Jews to Israel. According to the *Book of Mormon,* Jesus Christ on a visit to the New World Israelites reiterated God's promise to His people: "I have covenanted with them that I would gather them together in mine own due time, that I would give unto them again the land of their fathers for their inheritance, which is the land of Jerusalem, which is the promised land unto them forever."[49] Similarly, in 1893, church President Wilford Woodruff pleaded at the dedication of the Mormon Temple in Salt Lake City: "O God of Israel, turn thy face we pray thee, in loving kindness toward thy stricken people of the House of Judah. . . . May the days of their tribulations soon cease, and they be planted by thee in the valleys and plains of their ancient home."[50] The recreation of a Jewish nation, Mormons believed, was a necessary precondition heralding the return of Christ to earth and the beginning of the Millennium. To further God's plan, Mormon apostles were first sent to Palestine in 1872 to rededicate the land for the return of the Jews. This ceremony was subsequently reenacted four times. With the Jew's fate so intricately intertwined with their own future, Mormons were vitally interested in Jewish society and happenings. "Organizational activities in Jewish life," wrote scholar Rudolf Glanz, "and general Jewish news are more frequently reported in the Mormon press than in other general American newspapers and magazines."[51] Thus, theologically inclined Mormons made special note of the emergence of Theodore Herzl and the organization of the World Zionist Congress, considering such as the working of God's hand in human events. Because conversion of the Jews was expected to occur only after their return, Mormon proselytizing efforts were inconsequential throughout the nineteenth and early twentieth centuries.[52]

When Jews actually met Mormons in Utah, relations were quite cordial. In 1866, Brigham Young donated a parcel of land to the small Jewish community of Salt Lake City to serve as a cemetery. The following year, Young offered a Mormon church building to local Jews for Rosh Hashanah services. Half a century later at the colony, Mormons welcomed Jews as neighbors, tending advice, food, friendship, tools, labor (hired and voluntary), and moral support. "They acted to us," recalled Nathan Ayeroff, "not as strangers but as brothers."[53] While most would stay within their own groups, some Jews and Mormons established close personal relationships visiting and dining at one another's homes. Their children in school and at play would expand these contacts even further. In several instances these ties long outlasted the colony's life. Early in the colony's existence, Gunnison residents held a banquet which drew nearly 400 people to honor the Jewish settlers. Although the Jews "felt out of place" at the affair, Mormons lauded the "pioneers" with speeches and entertained them with song.[54] Judge A. N. Cherry welcomed the colonists on behalf of his community:

> We feel that we need you and are truly glad that you came. We hope to help you and know that you will be of great advantage to us. We stand ready to join hands with you; let us work in harmony, dwell together as brethren in unity and strive together to build up the brightest, wealthiest and healthiest spot in the great state of Utah.[55]

Historical celebrations would later attract visitors from the colony and even Jewish floats in the local parades. President Joseph F. Smith, citing Mormon-Jewish relations in the Gunnison area as of a "most cordial and neighborly character," contributed $500 in support of the colony on behalf of the LDS Church.[56] Still, he was apologetic because the church's need to assist Mormon settlers uprooted by the Mexican Revolution had precluded a larger donation. Certainly, the economic stimulus the Jews infused into the county facilitated their reception. By purchasing food, clothing, livestock, and equipment, Isaac Friedlander bluntly asserted, "We brought prosperity to Gunnison."[57] The editor of the *Gunnison Gazette* agreed as to the Jewish economic impact: "As the colony builds up [it] will add considerably to the tax valuation."[58] Yet, it was most importantly the sense of common identity—past and present, religious and pioneering—which united the two peoples and laid a sturdy foundation for effective working and congenial personal relationships.[59]

In a column in the New York City Yiddish newspaper, *Tageblatt*, colonist Moshe Malamed wrote, "There is not a sign of the anti-Semitism which is often found in the East."[60] Malamed exaggerated, for interactions were not always so positive. Several colonists remembered Mormon neighbors and merchants who cheated, harassed, and ridiculed them. Surely local usage of the noun "Jew" as an adjective—as in "Jew house" and "Jew farm"—grated upon colonists' ears as it does to present-day Jewish visitors. Children could be especially cruel to those who are different and their slurs are most frequently reiterated. "Where are your horns?" high-school student Herman Lieberman was asked.[61] Al Pally recalled frequent fights with those who chose to taunt him because of his religion. Bigotry as an answer, however, provides little explanatory power. Difficulties arose more from ignorance, economic competition, and personality than ideology. In so homogeneous an environment, then, religion became in some minds a stigma for the lack of any other symbol of nonconformity.[62]

V

With the coming of the winter of 1911–12, the ground froze, land clearing halted, and outside work dwindled then ceased. Snow blocked the road to town and isolated the colony. Mail went undelivered and the men felt, in Isaac Friedlander's words, "confined to a ship in the middle of the ocean, worlds away."[63] The "jarring yelping" of the coyotes only intensified the colonists' feelings of sadness and loneliness.[64] Keeping warm, mending harnesses, fixing machinery, and endless discussions occupied tent time. Does God exist? Will capitalism crumble under its own weight? What name shall the colony bear? The men also hammered out the objectives and purposes of the colony in this time of enforced inactivity. Their colony was to be the first of a multitude of Jewish settlements planted throughout the United States. Initially, the colony would engage solely in the cultivation and marketing of a variety of crops. Later, the settlers would diversify and establish a canning factory to process their produce. From these beginnings a town would grow where every branch of agriculture, commerce, manufacturing, and mining would thrive. A new society rooted in all of these economic endeavors would revitalize the Jew in his as well as others' eyes. In a promotional pamphlet the colonists optimistically declared:

> We are confident that the next ten years will witness a great exodus from the congested cities toward the country. . . . It will greatly contribute towards the reduction of misery and poverty of our over-populated cities; new and fresh blood will begin to circulate through our enfeebled Jewish veins, it will lay the foundation of permanency, and, moreover, will serve as a powerful proof to the world, that wherever the Jew has an equal opportunity and receives human treatment, he throws off his peddling pack and yard stick and is off to the infinite bountiful prairies of the West and under God's blue skies our best children of old Israel will establish their abiding peace.[65]

As the harbingers of the Jewish economic and social future in America, the colonists had issued a call. It was appropriate that they named their experiment Clarion.[66]

The colony's economic problems continued to fester. Money flowed from Clarion's coffers without compensating dollars added to the organization's ledger. Operating expenses rapidly absorbed hard-to-replace funds. The state of Utah expected the colony's 1912 installment for land by the first of the year. To stress the urgency of the colony's plight, Ben Brown left Utah and returned to the East to solicit money. Six months on the soil had worked a transformation intensifying Brown's determination and heightening his self-confidence. "This was no longer the Brown of old who used to come to meetings loaded with suggestions. He did not suggest anymore—he demanded, and he was right."[67] Brown's power, in words and presence, firmed the members' resolve and they squeezed themselves further for Clarion. Members made good their initial pledges and also assessed themselves another $50 fee in the colony's support. Between $4,000 and $5,000 was collected. In light of Utah's decision to postpone collection of the land payment for one year, the amount was sufficient to restore the colony's financial health briefly.[68]

Work began again in earnest at the end of February 1912, with the plowing and planting of wheat, oats, corn, and alfalfa. By late March, 1,500 acres had been prepared and awaited water from the Piute Canal. Under the direction of Utah State Agricultural College experts and local farmers, the colonists also finalized the digging of the irrigation ditches. To combat the steep slope of the land, the channels were cut in a zigzag pattern forcing the water to run more slowly, allowing its deeper penetration, and lessening soil erosion. The arrival of four more settlers, three of whom had recently graduated from the National Farm School, augmented the work force and expanded the colony's knowledge base. Additional contingents of six settlers in June and five in September freed some of the men from field work to construct a common storehouse for the harvest and individual homes for colonist families. Meanwhile, several Association members eager to begin new lives had come from the East to Utah and rented or bought land near the colony tract. By the fall 1912, fifteen wives and twenty-six children had settled in Clarion bringing the population to sixty-eight. While farm work remained communal and the coming harvest the property of all, living arrangements centered around the nuclear family. "Our colony," wrote new settler Abraham Wernick, "began to take on the look of a small *shtetl.*"[69]

Toward the end of April, green sprouts had broken through the soil in the fields. The happiness this caused, however, was short-lived. The reality of farming as opposed to the dream soon became apparent when strong winds, dust storms, heat, flies, and mosquitoes began plaguing the colonists. The colony's tractor remained difficult to maintain, and hired mechanics could coax it to run only intermittently. Water still had to be carried in barrels from Gunnison, the trips now more frequent and thus more burdensome. The colonists dug wells to alleviate the shortage, but they all were dry. Partially to combat the problem, civil engineer Isaac Herbst planned and supervised the construction of a concrete cistern to store canal water which, after filtration, would be suitable for the animals and clothes washing. The colonists devoted several days to the project, cutting a ditch from the canal to the reservoir, hollowing out a hill to provide support for the structure on three sides, building forms, and pouring concrete. The night the reservoir had filled with water, "a loud and splitting boom" shook the colony.[70] Men and women rushed from their beds to the site to find the unsupported wall, built without reinforcing rods and with poor quality cement, lying on the ground shattered into large pieces. The project was abandoned, the wall never rebuilt.[71]

Samuel Sack in his Russian worker's cap and peasant blouse preparing the land. Courtesy of Sarah Sack Bober.

The colony's "prized" tractor. Courtesy of Beckie Mastrow Pullman.

Farming inexperience aggravated these difficult conditions of life and work. The transition from city to farm proved more difficult than most had imagined. The little "tricks" learned through experience, generation to generation, were not so easily transferred. Words of advice were hard to implement when all one knew was the urban world. Nathan Ayeroff, one of the recently arrived settlers, remembered that these eastern tailors and peddlers "didn't know to go to a cow, to sit down and milk a cow, they were afraid to touch it."[72] Harnesses, hitches, and tools were similar mysteries. Even the graduates of the Farm School had difficulties as their training in the East had not prepared them for irrigation farming on marginal soil in the arid West. While the men and women of Clarion would harden and adapt to their environment, their awkwardness in this early period left the colony with a foundation as unsteady as their ill-fated cistern.[73]

Worse were the problems infecting the colony's lifeline – the Piute Canal. State engineers had been unduly optimistic about the construction schedule, the quantity of water that could be delivered, and even the quality of the canal itself. The state had promised to begin delivery of the water for the entire Jewish tract in mid-April, sufficient time before the irrigation season to allow the soaking and testing of the laterals extending from the canal to the fields. Water did not arrive until May 3, when the canal covered only the southern one-third of the land. To the colonists' chagrin, the water which had appeared that morning disappeared by afternoon. For two days thereafter the canal was dry. A small stream reappeared May 6 and flowed until May 12, only to vanish for three days. The water supply, to the anguish of the settlers, continued to run in this intermittent manner throughout the summer months. Twelve feet wide by four feet deep, the canal had not settled and was unreliable, its banks lacking stabilizing and anchoring grasses and willows. Muskrats and gophers easily burrowed through the dirt sides of the channel causing six breaks and leaving the colony without water for thirty-five days. State officials, desperate to aid the stricken farmers, augmented the rodents' work by ordering that additional quantities of water be sent down the canal. This further weakened the structure, warned E. A. Crowley, the secretary of the Sevier Valley Canal Company, because it "has insufficient capacity to carry the volume of water you are attempting to carry, and that there is danger of the canal breaking if such amount is continued in said canal."[74] Meanwhile Ben Brown frantically telegraphed the Board of Land Commissioners on May 20, "SEND WATER TO OUR LAND AS SOON AS POSSIBLE. . . . OUR EARLY WHEAT IS ABSOLUTELY BURNING. WE MUST GO AT IT IMMEDIATELY OR WE LOOSE [sic] MOST OF OUR CROPS."[75] Again, on June 13, he wrote that the canal was dry and "We are ruined if that will keep up."[76] When the canal was in repair less than one-fifth of Clarion's water needs could be met. For only two days during that summer was the water flow adequate to irrigate all of the colony's 1,500 acres. According to assistant Piute Canal watermaster, Anton Jensen:

> There was hardly a day that the water would remain stable in the canal and as a result the stream kept on fluctuating. . . . On a couple occasions they had sufficient water . . . but that kept up for a few hours only, and after each such increase in the stream, it generally diminished to either a very small stream . . . or it disappeared."[77]

The green of spring became "scrawny and sparse vegetation. The soil looked very dry and thirsty as if it would need a river of water to slacken its thirst."[78]

Having had water in the canal would not have relieved all of the colony's troubles. The area initially cultivated consisted of marginal land used even today only for grazing. "When the water hit it," explained a Mormon farmer, "why, it was just like sugar. It just melted. There was no sod so the water just ran off the ground and took the ground with it."[79] Unskilled in irrigation techniques and farming on steeply sloping virgin land, the men and women of Clarion found their fate as uncontrollable as the water and their circumstances eroding as fast as the soil.[80]

Salt Lake City Jews reached out to the colony in that summer of despair. From the colony's beginnings, Jews such as Samuel Newhouse, David Alexander, George Auerbach, and Simon Bamberger had acted as intermediaries with machine and tool suppliers to insure that the settlers received the most favorable terms and the fastest delivery of goods. Bamberger, who in 1916 would become Utah's governor, bought lumber for the construction of Clarion's homes and outbuildings. Often, these Jews would personally call upon Governor Spry asking him to intervene with the State Board of Land Commissioners or to obtain agricultural advisers on behalf of colonists. Salt Lake City's rabbis, one representing the Reform congregation and the other the Orthodox synagogue, visited Clarion often, the former writing articles publicizing the colony.[81] Realizing that the colony's internal monetary reserves had been exhausted and the prospects of a good harvest now remote, Salt Lake City Jews moved to help Clarion farmers over their financial hurdle. In June 1912, the above men plus six prominent local Jews organized the Utah Colonization Fund to facilitate Clarion money raising. Under its auspices Ben Brown assumed the role of bond salesman and began to tap external financial sources for support. He offered investors 4 percent bonds, secured by the colony's land and water shares and other assets, with payment in full promised by 1924. Those who were receptive to Brown's appeal obviously had other motives than a quick and profitable return on their investment. The ten Salt Lake City Jewish directors of the corporation inaugurated the drive with subscriptions of $100 each to the cause. The Mormon Church bought an additional $500 in bonds. With the state of Utah retaining title to the colony's tract of land and water rights until its indebtedness had been cleared, this financial plan was dubious legally.[82]

Many colonists believed that the *Yahudim* (American Jews of German extraction) could and should have made greater efforts on behalf of the project. They attributed the lack of stronger local support to several factors. Salt Lake City Jews did not view the colony as either an idealistic experiment or a practical solution to eastern congestion. They were simply not interested in the Back to the Soil movement, nor did they believe that farming was the necessary alternative to commerce and manufacturing. Local Jews, in fact, had succeeded in boosting themselves through peddling and the factory to prominence in the urban environment. Rather, these Jews perceived assistance for the colony as charity. Jews in need must be helped because they are Jews. "They never expected," Abraham Wernick believed, "to see their money again, even if the colony turned out to be a great success. Understandably, in a situation like that, you don't hand out thousands. . . . As soon as our emissary left, they forgot all about us."[83] Moreover, it seemed that appearances before the gentiles had to be upheld. "They kept a watchful eye on the colony," maintained Isaac Friedlander, "to make sure nothing was done that would reflect disgrace on themselves but [sic] everything was being done properly."[84] The colonists soon resented the paternalistic "inspectors" who graded houses, fields, gardens, and work and awarded prizes as incentives to raise standards. Distance was also a product of the distinct political, economic, and social worlds the two groups inhabited. Mutual suspicion clouded the interaction between Jewish radicals and the Jewish bourgeoisie, the economically marginal and the comfortable, the newly arrived and the established. Distrust, while pervasive, remained for a long time concealed. The Clarion colonists, aware of their precarious position, muted their differences to avoid antagonizing their benefactors.

To help promote the colony, to show their appreciation for local support, and to gain a brief respite from their burdens, the Clarion settlers invited state officials, Salt Lake City Jews, and neighboring Mormons to a preharvest festival on August 18, 1912. More than one thousand people attended the gathering including the governor, the board of directors of the Utah Colonization Fund, Philadelphia Rabbi Isaac Landman, and the local leadership

of the Mormon Church. Following serenades by the Gunnison and Centerfield city bands, the large crowd welcomed to the podium a series of
speakers who extolled the Clarion promise and praised the warm relationship
that had developed between Jew and Mormon. In Governor Spry's words: "It
certainly seems . . . that Judah and Ephraim have joined hands and united in
the desert. We now see a garden of grain and will soon see a garden of flow-
ers in the place of a desert and a beautiful cluster of homes."[85] Almost as a
benediction, Gunnison's Mormon Bishop James Rasmussen declared, "Let
Jews, Gentiles, and Mormons be one."[86]

Also, to advertise the colony and assist in the accumulation of financial
capital, Clarion's leaders issued a pamphlet entitled, *The First Successful
Jewish Colony in the United States.* Claiming assets of $406,950 which in-
cluded land and water rights, equipment, and livestock, against liabilities of
$289,550, the colony asked not for charity, but investment in a viable enter-
prise with meaning far beyond Utah. Help us "to issue a clarion call from the
mountains and broad valleys of the Far West to the suffocated brethren and
sisters of the Ghetto."[87] Just $150,000 raised through a bond issue would
guarantee the settlement of all Association members and establish the necessary financial foundation for successful farming. Pictures of sturdy homes,
fertile fields, and happy children decorated the promotional literature and
created the image of a stable and secure colony. Included, in addition, were
endorsements from Governor Spry and the Mormon Church hierarchy proph-
esying a prosperous future for the colony. The pamphlet concluded with a
list of traits that assured Clarion's promise: business-like operations, a firm
financial base, fertile soil, favorable climate, and a reliable water supply.[88]

Despite their toil and courage, the Clarion colonists reaped a disastrous
first harvest. The combination of poor soil, inexperience, and especially the
lack of water had doomed their efforts. An early frost in September added to
their misery. Optimistic predictions of thirty bushels per acre in the wheat
fields and forty bushels per acre of oats were unfulfilled. Only 250 acres produced a satisfactory yield while another 600 acres gave just half of the
amount expected. The remaining 700 acres were totally lost. Ben Brown,
shaken by the news, informed Association members in the East: "The income
of the land which did receive enough water wasn't enough to pay for the
seeds."[89] The loss in costs and labor was estimated at $14,250. The colonists,
however, found some solace in their time of misfortune. A delegation of
Clarion settlers presented a claim to the Board of Land Commissioners requesting reimbursement for losses because of the state's failure to provide water. They readily expected the Utah legislature to grant them redress during

its 1913 session. They also felt that hard times were behind them, an un-avoidable part of the ground-breaking stage of colonization. The future could only be better. "Nothing more terrible," wrote Isaac Landman to Rabbi Krauskopf "can ever happen than occurred this year. . . . I believe that we will succeed in the long run."[90]

The results after the first year on the land were decidedly mixed. The transition from city to farm had been difficult and shattered any illusions about an idyllic pastoral existence. The soil remained marginal, water to drink scarce, and water for irrigation uncertain. Financial shortages pressed the colony and continued unresolved. This would be a struggle without res-pite, a battle against long odds with a determined foe. Yet, the people of Clarion were far from surrender, refusing to resign themselves to ultimate defeat. The colonists were still confident and sure of their decision while their eastern supporters clamored to begin the settlement process. The elu-sive good life could be achieved on the farm and their beacon to the cities would soon shine. Much had been done. Raw earth had been broken and cul-tivated, houses erected, precious skills and experiences gained. Women and children had arrived, transforming Clarion from a tent camp of men to a fam-ily community. The state of Utah promised to widen the canal, strengthen its banks, and improve water delivery. Good relations had been established with Salt Lake City Jews and the local Mormon population. Ben Brown made ready to approach investors with a farming reality rather than an unrealized blueprint. Much still remained to do. Just after the harvest, in the fall of 1912, the colony began the second stage of settlement, moving from commu-nal labor to the cultivation of individual forty-acre plots. The colonists wel-comed the long-planned shift to private land ownership believing that self-interest would intensify the colonial effort. With various collectivist fea-tures retained and the sense of common purpose still strong, few perceived the move as a retreat from the ideal. In this new time, however, old problems still festered and unforeseen difficulties would emerge. When the promise could not be kept, the colony would turn inward against itself, becoming a hot house for conflict and despair.

4

Struggle on the Land

Let us make a happy life even if we
must sacrifice our personal matters.
We must become martyrs in order to
see a happy world.

Esther Radding
Clarion colonist

A piece of string became a treasure.

Beckie Mastrow Pullman
Clarion colonist

The Clarion colonists eagerly awaited the privatization of work and land
holdings at the beginning of their second year on the soil. Like a *moshav* in
modern-day Israel, the colony's land would be divided into individual farmsteads with settlers buying and selling cooperatively and sharing large equipment. The Association attempted to ease the transition by providing each
family with a weekly stipend until it became self-supporting. Social and
ethnic ties, Association membership, and mission would combine with this
continuing economic relationship to cement the community. While the coop-

erative effort continued, a change in emphasis had occurred. Each farmer would now be his own boss, responsible to and for himself and his family. The engine of self-interest would be securely harnessed to Clarion's cause not only for personal gain but to energize the Back to the Soil movement and its supporters in the eastern ghettos. The shift in work and organizational patterns, however, would bear no connection to the roots of the colony's problems. None had complained in the first year of coworker laziness or lack of initiative. Instead, farming and colonization had been attempted in a harsh environment hardly amenable to success. Human error had compounded these natural defects to besiege the colony and make life difficult.

The human factor, appearing in another guise, would also act to frustrate the project's future. This was a movement of strong-willed men and women divided according to ideological, religious, and personal interests. None of the settlers was a communist and there was no objection to the division of land. The colonists believed in private property for personal and family use and found no reason to fashion Clarion as a collective farm. Nor were the colonists social radicals who believed in free love or the elimination of the institution of marriage. Disagreements, instead, concerned the Jews' purposes in creating the Clarion colony. Former Bundists saw Clarion from a Jewish-nationalist perspective. The colony would be an integral part of the Yiddish-speaking Jewish community of the Diaspora. It would be a model society with a balanced economic structure which other Jewish groups could emulate. In America, Russia, and elsewhere, colonies such as Clarion would effect the self-transformation of the Jews. For Labor Zionists, Clarion was only a partial fulfillment of their dreams. Their ultimate goal was the creation of a Jewish-socialist state in Palestine. Acquiring agricultural skills, teaching children the Hebrew language, and building group cohesiveness were steps forward to eventual settlement in *Eretz Israel*. Clarion's handful of anarchists and those socialists who rejected an ethnic-religious frame of reference added their voices to the discord. Still, all of these groups combined were a minority when compared to the apolitical majority. Clarion's majority placed personal and family concerns above ideology. In Clarion, they found their answer to the sweatshop and the tenement. Within the majority, and requiring delineation, were the religious Orthodox. They expected the colony not only to fulfill their economic needs but to meet their religious requirements as well. Despite this heterogeneity, conflict and discord in Clarion were usually dormant. The day-to-day rhythm of farm life and work, the solidarity engendered by hard times, and a sense of purpose had reduced the salience of ideology. Yet, in the face of continuing setbacks, the potential for internal dissension could become explosive. Factionalism would thus pose almost as dangerous a threat to the colony's existence as soil quality or the quantity of water.

I

On the morning of September 19, 1912, the colonists awoke early and gathered before the tent housing the Association's office. Nervous with anticipation, yet buoyed by expectations, each awaited his turn to draw a number from a hat which would designate the location of a tract of land that would become a farm. The land raffled that day was confined to previously cultivated parcels already irrigated by the Piute Canal. Association members still waiting in the East, on the other hand, drew lots for land in the northern sections of the tract fixing their holdings for future settlement. Because the land was of uneven quality, the plots were not equal in size. Land the leadership judged fertile and relatively easy to farm was apportioned in forty-acre parcels. Even these "better" plots proved economically unviable, far too small to support a family. Those who selected more marginal land were compensated with additional acreage either attached to their plot or in strips located elsewhere in the colony. Extra land rarely made a difference. Sam Chatsky's land "was just like a cemetery, full of rocks. We couldn't do nothing there, so many rocks. If you go over it with a wagon, the two wheels go in one ditch, the other two wheels in another ditch."[1] Although Chatsky decided to stay and work the land, his brother accepted his advice and remained in Philadelphia. The leadership excluded the poorest land from the drawing and called for volunteers to undertake its cultivation. Among those, noted Abraham Wernick, who sacrificed "their own personal interests for the general good of the colony" was Benjamin Brown.[2]

The distribution of land, based upon Isaac Herbst's survey, occurred despite the Association's initial purchase of land in forty- and eighty-acre plots in the names of individual members. The colony's leaders argued, and their followers agreed, that Herbst's dividing lines better reflected the disparity of soil quality on the tract and was more conducive to fostering economic equality among the settlers. Herbst's survey had also arranged the colony more conveniently by having as many farms as possible front the settlement's main road. Although the new survey and subsequent land division had won the approval of the Jews and the Board of Land Commissioners, it was not in accord with the legal documents held by the state of Utah recording Clarion

Isaac Herbst and his surveying team fixing farm boundaries and marking the colony's main road. Courtesy of Sarah Sack Bober.

land ownership. This discrepancy and its meaning would not remain unnoticed very long.[3]

The conversion from communal to private operations involved more than the redistribution of the land. Livestock, equipment, and buildings also had to be reassigned to those on the land while the similar needs of those yet to arrive would have to be met. To execute these functions and, as previously indicated, to aid Ben Brown in the solicitation of funds, the colonists on September 17 had transferred their land and water rights to the Jewish Agricultural and Colonial Association. Under a Deed of Trust, the Association acted on behalf of the colonists as an intermediary with the state in making payments for land and water. According to the same legal instrument, the organization promised to assist each colonist in clearing land, building a home, finding water, and buying the tools and machinery necessary for farming. The Association also offered loans to colonists for the purchase of food and supplies, expecting repayment of debts with a share of their crops. Aaron Binder's account was typical: On December 24, 1912, the Association supplied feed, a cow, a horse, and provisions totaling $263.38. Binder offered a note to cover this sum due at harvesttime, 1913. A month earlier he had signed a promissory note payable in thirteen years for $2,305.34 plus interest in consideration of advances by the Association for land, water, and settlement expenses. Thus, a member's initial contribution and subsequent donations and assessments to the organization had allowed him and his family to participate in the project and entitled him to future assistance, financial and otherwise. His small stake had provided an opportunity which alone he could not have pursued. While neighbors would assist one another during harvesttime, in cutting wood because mountain trails made the task dangerous, in cooperative buying and selling, and in certain community-wide endeavors, the colony's communal stage was completed. It now appeared that "each man was on his own."[4]

The sense of optimism felt in Clarion that fall did not emanate solely from the independence and self-reliance which the Jews experienced in the wake of the shift to individual farms. Tangible evidence of increased permanence and progress continued to accumulate. In early September, the colony's first child was born amid much rejoicing. Although plans to bring an additional fifty families to Utah were postponed because of a lack of resources, the colony grew when wives and children were reunited with husbands already on the land. More and more houses were built to replace the temporary tent shelters. Further, Clarion's population had stabilized and no new defections had occurred. Impatient eastern supporters still pressed to begin farming, cheering colonists with their enthusiasm. Clarion's children resumed their education with ten attending elementary school in Centerfield while others entered high school in Gunnison. In October, Ben Brown, fortified by letters of introduction from Jewish and Christian businessmen in Salt Lake City, wrote from St. Louis that he had already raised $1,500 in bonds. Before he left that city, the first stop on his bond-selling tour, he collected $6,300 for the colony.[5]

Beneath this optimism and close to the surface was an anxiousness fed by fear and distrust. The farming difficulties experienced the first year and the disappointing harvest had stunned the colonists and shaken their faith in Brown's judgment and qualifications. Brown, questioned about his choice of site and agricultural expertise, grew defensive and less compromising and seemingly more arbitrary in his decision making. "The whole undertaking," wrote Abe Wernick, "was in the hands of a man who seemed to know little about what he was doing, but who thought he already knew everything—he consulted with no one and did what he pleased."[6] Brown became even more vulnerable when, although married, he romantically pursued the sister of one of the colonists. She later left the colony to give birth to his child. The affair quickly became public knowledge in a community where "everyone knows everyone else and what's cooking in their neighbor's pot. (Sometimes even in their neighbor's bedroom.)"[7] Brown and his wife Clara separated and she and their two children returned to the East. Most were morally outraged. Some, as self-declared "radicals," refused to judge Brown in such a way, instead becoming alarmed about the effect of their leader's affair upon the cause. Was Brown sufficiently responsible to lead the movement? How would the *Yahudim* react to their project if they became aware of the incident? Further compromising Brown's position were problems involving those with whom he had entrusted responsibility and leadership. Inaccurate bookkeeping by the Association's secretary generated charges of chicanery and led to his demotion. His replacement was similarly accused and replaced. Personality clashes, exacerbated by rivalry among the wives, led to bickering between Brown's lieutenants and organizational paralysis. "A 'you said, he said' politics developed," recalled Brown, "that reached way to our members in the East."[8] Brown and anti-Brown camps, inchoate and ill-defined, had begun to emerge in the colony. Ben Brown's reaction to these challenges alternated between intransigence and complete surrender, with neither option implying a willingness to relinquish control. Thus, when confronted, Brown "would always take an unyielding position. . . . To oppose him on anything meant an open fight and not everyone was strong enough for that, so they let it pass."[9]

A reflective moment for Benjamin Brown. Courtesy of Sarah Sack Bober.

At other times, he threatened to resign leadership and withdraw from the project. Playing upon his central role in the movement and the loyalty of the majority, he could bully his detractors into submission. Such tactics, however, would gradually lose their effectiveness. As the colonists became more sure of themselves and life in the settlement deteriorated, Brown would find his base of support eroding beneath him.[10]

There were other sources of conflict which heightened discontent and inflamed relations between the colonists. In the aftermath of the land distribution colonists grumbled about the quality of their land as opposed to that of others. Some accused Brown of rigging the lottery in favor of his supporters. The inequality of colonist family possessions elicited envy and bitterness. Other complained about the substandard norms of local schools and the lack of a "Jewish" education for their children. The formation of a literary and cultural discussion group also provoked antagonism because membership was limited to those with proper ideological credentials. The colonists chafed, as well, under the restrictions the Association imposed. Gunnison's bank dealt directly with the organization and would not make loans to individual colonists. A colonist was prohibited from selling his land or water rights without permission. The larger pieces of equipment remained in the organization's hands to be shared by the colonists. Brown and the Association continued to make decisions concerning land and amount of tool and machinery purchases. Scarce resources meant minimal outlays for supplies and livestock. National Farm School graduate David Friedman criticized the Association for allowing only $35 for the purchase of a cow: "You can just imagine what kind of cow . . . [you] can get for this."[11]

In Clarion's air and soil the only crop to be had in abundance was dissension. Disagreements easily degenerated into quarrels and arguments into combat. In fact, there were five fistsfights in the colony during its short life. The closeness of living and the bareness of existence are necessary but not sufficient to explain the extent and intensity of the discord. Clarion warred with itself because it lacked shared moorings and bonds. Personal self-improvement and vague aspirations to turn the Jewish people toward the land proved weak shields when confronted with adversity. The privatization of land accelerated the trend toward disunity as it did much to dissolve the sense of common interest and purpose that framed the first year. External enemies were also absent thus eliminating possible rallying points. The ideological heterogeneity of the movement further militated against unity. Anarchists, international socialists, Jewish socialists, nonaligned radicals, and Labor Zionists grew suspicious and more intolerant of one another as the energy that fostered the united left-wing effort diminished. Especially indicative of the seriousness of this problem was the one issue upon which cross-cutting loyalties were built and thrived. Only in their opposition to Brown could the diverse factions find a common ground and goal.[12]

The religious Orthodox, as well, became embroiled in the turmoil. Approximately fifteen colonist families observed the Jewish High Holy Days, Hanukah, and Passover. A lay rabbi and cantor conducted Saturday morning services with the site alternating among the observants' homes. When the members of the group petitioned the Association to assist them in observing their beliefs by providing funds for a *Sefer Torah** and a ritual slaughterer to furnish kosher meat, they were rebuffed. Nathan Ayeroff, a nonreligious colonist, asked Brown and the Association's directors to reconsider: "They are plain simple people. They have nothing in their heads about socialism or whatever ism it is. They believe and you have to satisfy their feelings." Obstinence on this matter, Ayeroff argued, would cause desertions: "What the hell were they going to stay here for?"[13] Insisting that religion was a private matter in the Jewish colony, the Association refused all entreaties. Eventually, the Salt Lake City Jewish community donated a *Sefer Torah* to the colony. Kosher meat was beyond the colonist's means and the religious either abstained while at Clarion or compromised their beliefs. The Association's neglect of the religious kindled an anger and resentment which still flares in the sons and daughters of Clarion's Orthodox Jews.[14]

II

The colonists spent the fall of 1912 working their farms preparing for the coming growing season. They removed rocks, built fences, repaired irrigation channels, dug root cellars, erected barns, and sealed their homes against the cold weather with tarpaper and plaster. The men traveled in caravans to collect firewood in the Valley Mountains because the steep, poorly marked roads made accidents real possibilities. The Association's credit standing with local merchants remained good and food and supplies were available for the settlers. The winter that year was especially harsh. Babies' hands were wrapped in cloth to prevent frostbite. Men driving wagons could not hold onto the reins for the bitter cold and let the horses find their own way home.

---

*Jewish scrolls of the law containing the Five Books of Moses handwritten on parchment.

Water still ferried from Gunnison froze on the trip. The colony's first accident also occurred when the water wagon struck a hole, throwing Joseph Furman beneath the wheels and breaking his leg.[15]

More serious for the future of the colony was the loss of two of Clarion's most influential supporters. Rabbi Joseph Krauskopf suffered the first of a series of strokes in October forcing him to suspend his activities at Congregation Keneseth Israel and the National Farm School and on behalf of the Clarion Colony. In late 1913, still unable to resume his duties, his congregation sent him on a trip around the world to aid in his recovery. Not until September 1914 did Krauskopf regain his strength and return to his work. His assistant, Rabbi Isaac Landman, pushed forward on all of Krauskopf's fronts. He was particularly enthusiastic about the Utah project, telling the *Jewish Exponent,* "Our soil in Clarion will grow anything and grow it well."[16] Landman, while energetic and persistent, lacked the presence and prestige of Krauskopf, one of the most powerful voices in American Jewry. His absence would be measured not only in its effect upon Clarion morale, but the extent of financial support the colonists could hope to attract. The other casualty among Clarion's friends was Colonel Samuel Newhouse of Salt Lake City. Prominent in colonists' eyes for his financial generosity and sway in Utah government circles, Newhouse had become by the late summer of 1912, "a leading member of the down and out club."[17] Investments in mining and real estate had proven ill-advised and had eliminated his impact upon Clarion's course.[18]

A money shortage, a continuing theme in Clarion's history, became acute once again. The colony required immediate funds to maintain those already on the land during the nonproductive months until harvesttime. Additional resources were needed to carry forth plans to settle new families, for eager Association members in the East demanded an acceleration of the colonization schedule. Moreover, if Clarion was to become the herald of Jewish rebirth, it had to pull itself from the financial wall to which it was pinned. A secure financial base for Clarion would not only guarantee the colonists' futures but offer Jews everywhere hope and a model for personal and group fulfillment. With settlement costs conservatively estimated at $1,900 per family for the purchase of a house, wagon, tools, livestock, seed, and supplies, a large financial transfusion was critical.[19]

Again, Clarion turned to the Salt Lake Jewish community for funds. This time, local Jews raised $10,000 to aid the colony. Jewish Agricultural and Colonial Association members in the East were called upon once more to give whatever they could. "The response," wrote Barney Silverman, "was phenomenal; they pawned whatever they had of value, they borrowed from friends and relatives. No sacrifice seemed too great for them in this hour of need for the colony."[20] This money, in addition to the collection of the balances owed upon unpaid membership dues netted $4,000.[21]

After a successful selling campaign in St. Louis where he raised over six thousand dollars, Ben Brown traveled to Chicago in search of Clarion bond subscribers. There, with the aid of an introductory letter from Rabbi Krauskopf he arranged a meeting with Julius Rosenwald, chairman of the board of Sears, Roebuck, and Company. Rosenwald was impressed with Brown's presentation and made a startling proposition. He would buy $65,000 in Clarion bonds if Brown could convince the Jewish Agricultural Society, the established authority and lending agency in all farming matters, to match his offer with a loan of its own. However, if the Society did not deem the project worthwhile, he would withdraw all support. Brown also contacted financier Jacob H. Schiff regarding the colony. Schiff subsequently wrote to the Society informing it of Brown's proposal and inquiring as to its position on the project.[22]

The Jewish Agricultural Society, while monitoring the Clarion project from its beginning, had remained aloof. In 1911, colony organizers had approached the Society seeking direction and support only to be referred to Rabbi Krauskopf and the National Farm School. When Brown and Herbst went west to inspect land for settlement they asked the Society to send an adviser, but it declined. These rebuffs combined with Brown's self-confidence and fear of dictation to curtail further interaction. The Society's directors were wary of the Clarion effort. While they worked for Jewish land ownership—and the colony was the most significant farming experiment at the time—they frowned upon large-scale agricultural settlement. In light of the failure of Jewish colonies to root permanently in the nineteenth century, they believed that their resources could be more efficiently and effectively allocated to individual farmers. Pressure, however, from Clarion supporters Rabbi Krauskopf and later Rabbi Landman and now the Rosenwald offer and Schiff note forced the Society to abandon its studied indifference. The directors dispatched an investigator to Clarion to report upon the capabilities and characters of the colonists and the agricultural potential of the settlement. The Society's representative interviewed the colonists and surveyed the area forwarding a very favorable assessment to his superiors. The colonists, he wrote, were "young men of intelligence, good appearance, who showed en-

terprise and energy, and who should, upon the whole, make successful settlers." He concluded that the colonists "would prosper if they could raise the
necessary funds to get started properly."[23]

On December 3, 1912, the Society invited Brown and Rabbi Landman to
its offices in New York City to discuss their Clarion proposals. The meeting,
which Brown compared to an "inquisition," lasted five hours.[24] The directors
praised "the earnestness of the leaders of the Colony and . . . the progress
thus far attained by it." Yet, the men refused to support the project: "While in
full sympathy with their aims, try as hard as we might, we could not discovered a basis on which we could co-operate with them and help them.
Their financial structure crumbled as soon as it was put under scrutiny."[25] The
directors attacked Brown's estimates of future expenditures, charging that the
$130,000 sought was merely one-fourth of the capital necessary to cover the
costs of colonization. They argued further that the colony could face a deficit
of $100,000 within just three years even without calculating the possibilities
of defections, members' delinquent payments, and additional agricultural setbacks into the financial equation. Moreover, the directors criticized the idea
of agricultural colonies, believing that private farming was the most practical
path back to the soil. As a parting blow the men confronted Brown with evidence of colonists' dissatisfaction with their leaders and internal feuding.
Clarion, they concluded, was an impossible dream. Following the meeting
the Society sent letters to Rosenwald and Schiff advising against support, for
Clarion was a "scheme doomed to failure on its face."[26] Rosenwald and Schiff
still sent donations of $2,500 and $5,000 to Clarion as signs of respect for
Rabbi Krauskopf. Appended to the contributions, however, were explicit in-
structions that Brown not bother them again about the project.[27]

The Jewish Agricultural Society did not terminate its relationship with
the Clarion project at this juncture. The organization maintained a detailed
record of Clarion news and its dealings with colony members and supporters.
It interviewed disaffected colonists and logged reports of discontent. After
one such account, Eugene S. Benjamin was quoted in the Society's official
chronicle: "We are absolved from all responsibility."[28] The Society, however,
did a great deal more than merely gather information. It initiated and vigorously pursued a campaign to cut Clarion from outside funding and support.
The directors circulated their negative findings about the colony to philanthropists, advising that they too should reject Clarion entreaties. The Society
even went so far as to prompt editors of Jewish newspapers with facts,
figures, and interpretations to refute articles favorable to Clarion. Thus the
editor of the *American Hebrew*, contemplating support for the colony, shifted

his stance upon receiving society officer Leonard Robinson's letter of rebuttal. He printed the message as an editorial, verbatim and without attribution. Robinson's note barely muffled with halfhearted praise the death knell the society sounded for Clarion: "I can therefore see no reason why anyone who feels so inclined should not subscribe to the debentures of the Colony provided he understands that he is assisting a worthy though doubtful experiment and does not look upon them as an investment."[29] As the news spread, Brown had more difficulty selling bonds and the number of those reneging upon bond purchases climbed sharply.[30]

The Jewish Agricultural Society adopted its position on the colony for several reasons. Clarion's collective features and the left-wing complexion of its settlers were the antithesis of the society's stress upon individualism and capitalism for successful Jewish farming. Past colonizing efforts had failed, and the society considered itself a protector not only of investors but potential colonists who would gamble everything in such risky ventures. Yet the ferocity of the attack and unyielding position the society assumed suggest that the anti-Clarion effort may have been grounded in less-noble motives. Perhaps, although initially ignoring the Clarion movement, the directors felt usurped, having lost control of the Jewish agrarian effort. Clarion was the major topic in Back to the Soil circles and the society had fumbled its opportunity to play a central role in its organization, selection of members and site, and method of operation. Having excluded itself from the experiment and later pressured to some involvement by Clarion proponents, the society may have sought self-justification in its failure. Perhaps, on some level the guilt of nonsupport should be figured into its resistance. Such feelings would only be assuaged when prophesies of Clarion's defeat were fulfilled. Not to be dismissed was the immigrant and Russian-Jewish complexion of the Utah colony. The *Yahudim* of the Jewish Agricultural Society may have felt the darker side of paternalism, an arrogance and anger that the less knowledgeable and less experienced had had the audacity to reject their guidance. Only in Clarion's defeat would the society achieve the vindication of its opposition, influence, and power.

The money Ben Brown collected in the winter of 1912 was sufficient to move Clarion into the next year. The nearly $30,000 raised, supplemented by a loan of $10,000 from the Gunnison bank, amounted to three-quarters of the $50,000 that colony leaders had estimated as the minimum necessary to meet the settlement's needs. The state of Utah aided colonists again by postponing payments for land and water rights to compensate partially for the failure of the canal the previous summer. The deferment of debts another year, as had

the governor's visit, reflected the state's sense of responsibility and commitment to the colony. Utah wanted Clarion to succeed and actively worked to
that end. While deeply disappointed about the drive's failure to generate more
capital, the colonists looked to the future and steeled themselves against continuing shortages and difficult times. Success would surely come in 1913
proving their detractors wrong and loosening philanthropists' purse strings.[31]

III

The farming cycle began anew in spring 1913. While each farmer was responsible for his individual plot, cooperative effort was needed to ready the
land for planting. The distribution of the Association's limited supply of tools
and livestock into many hands had stretched resources and required continued sharing. Inexperienced farmers also sought out those who had previously
worked the land. The colony's housing arrangement further promoted this
mutual assistance and collective action. Strong social ties nurtured in the
farm groupings devised by Clarion planners facilitated the sharing of horses
and equipment already predicated upon harsh economic realities.[32]

The settlers again sowed wheat and alfalfa while simultaneously repair-
ing irrigation channels in anticipation of the filling of the Piute Canal. Unlike
the previous summer, the water arrived in the canal on time and in sufficient
quantity. Yet even an adequate water supply caused problems. To quiet complaints that some colonists had appropriated more than their fair share of water, Clarion leaders petitioned the State Board of Land Commissioners to
install weirs and thus insure a more equitable distribution. The colony also
appointed one of its members to oversee allocation of the water. While the
Jewish water regulator was soon in place, the board found no money in its
budget to fund the weirs. The planting of trees that spring along the colony's
main road enhanced the settlers' pride in their progress and strengthened the
sense of community. The colonists, in addition, felt a growing stability with
the appointment of a committee to negotiate with local utility companies for
the extension of electric power and telephone lines. The Clarion Colony
seemed to have emerged from the rawness of the frontier and had begun to
accumulate the trappings of permanence. Looking ahead to a glowing future
the colonists quickly forgot their latest agricultural failure. A winter potato
crop, harvested in the spring, had yielded poorly because the farmers had not
covered the ground properly, the vegetables freezing then rotting with the
thaw.[33]

As farm work proceeded, the colony moved as a body toward the completion of several long-delayed tasks. To survive, the settlers had to locate a

water source in their tract and end the chore of hauling it in wagons from Gunnison. The drinking, cooking, and cleaning needs of an expanding population had transformed an inconvenience into a hardship. In May, the Association purchased a well-drilling rig for $1,500 and began searching for water. After several failures, water was found 200 feet below the surface near the Lieberman farm. The water was welcome even though it was always covered by an oily blue film. The well would also prove undependable, the pump in continuous disrepair and the dropping water table requiring repeated drilling. Despite later attempts, this would unfortunately be the colony's only successful well. While it relieved some of the burden associated with the trips to town and was seen at the time as a beginning, it was a slender reed and boded ill for long-term success.[34]

Also related to Clarion's future was the group's second task—the construction of a school. The local school board, in light of the colony's growing population, created a Clarion district and agreed to appoint a teacher provided that the settlers erect a building. The Mormon board allowed the colonists the option of hiring, at their own expense, a second teacher to offer religious instruction for the children. In a common effort and with great hope, a two-room school, housing grades one through five, was built to accommodate the colony's twenty-eight children. To offer their children the greatest educational advantages, the colonists even assessed themselves additional fees to keep their school in session a month longer than required.[35]

What was begun in harmony and fueled by a cooperative spirit soon degenerated into bitter feuding when the program of Jewish education was considered. The clash over the school curriculum is understandable only when placed within the context of ideological diversity which predated the colony and had begun to fester within it. Jewish nationalists and former Bundists wanted to hire a teacher who would nurture identity through Yiddish language, literature, and folklore. Yiddish culture, they argued, would transcend national borders to unify Jews everywhere intellectually and socially. Labor Zionists also sought a teacher versed in Yiddish language and culture. A Jewish secular education would make the children aware of their ties and responsibilities to coreligionists who remained in the Diaspora. International socialists felt that an emphasis upon "Jewish" subjects would distract students from the worldwide struggle for socialism. The religious minority requested instruction in the Hebrew liturgy. Finally, some were content to employ only the Mormon teacher the school board selected. Jewish education, whether secular or religious, had no place in a public school. The education controversy tore at the fabric of Clarion society by reopening old wounds and firing simmering resentment. At stake was more than a grade-school curriculum. Under debate was the meaning of Clarion to its members and the wider world. Never before, in so open a forum, had the colonists confronted this issue. Discussion went on late into the night on several occasions, "evoking outbursts of temper, hysterics, and what was worse, it posed a threat to our very existence."[36] A serious rift had occurred, and some threatened to leave over the question. The colonists eventually compromised by calling for a teacher who would instruct students in Yiddish language and literature while interpreting Jewish history from an international-socialist perspective. Hardly anyone was satisfied. Colonist Moshe Malamed wrote: "Long after these meetings there was tension in the air, and the opposing factions did not look at each other when they met."[37] After just eighteen months on the land, the ideological cracks had grown wider and more exposed, seriously weakening Clarion's base.[38]

Although tensions remained just under the surface, tempers subsided and the education controversy lost its salience. The schoolhouse along with the well were additional symbols of settledness. Other signs demonstrated the colonists had a future in Utah. The Jewish farmers built a cooperative store near the school and a common granary. By the summer, the number of houses constructed on the Clarion tract had increased to fifty-two sheltering a population of 156 persons. Almost 2,400 acres were under cultivation and fed by a now reliable irrigation system. Between October 1912 and June 1913, only five families had left the colony. Their departure did not demoralize those who remained but was welcomed as it lessened discord and ill will. The National Farm School graduates had also returned to the East to pursue careers in farm management and teaching. Their withdrawal provoked concern among the colonists that Rabbis Krauskopf and Landman's enthusiasm for the project might diminish. Such fears, however, proved groundless. Association members in the East who had sufficient funds to establish themselves without aid were allowed to settle in the colony and quickly replaced those who had left. There was no scarcity of willing easterners ready to begin farming, and a lottery remained in effect to determine the order of arrival.[39]

Salt Lake City Jews who visited the colony that summer were quite impressed with the progress of a year. "ALL IS WELL WITH THE JEWISH COLONY," summarized the *Manti Messenger* after interviewing the members of one inspection party.[40] The *Gunnison Gazette* quoted Max Weil of the same group as saying: "They have made a success of it. Last year where there were sage brush wastes there are four and a half miles of alfalfa, wheat, oats, and barley, all in a promising condition. All the colonists are well satisfied."[41]

(Apparently the colonists had not been particularly candid with their coreligionists.) The visitors unanimously concluded that the Clarion farmers were hardworking, able, and deserving of support. Ben Brown, constantly in search of funds to maintain the settlement, embellished such recommendations in a colorfully embroidered article titled "A Message from the Jewish Colony in the Far West." The piece is as interesting for what it actually said about the colony as for what it failed to reveal:

> The hills west of the colony are thickly covered with pine and cedar trees, affording ample free fuel and material for fences and outbuildings. During certain seasons of the year the nearby rivers simply teem with fish. . . . The sun shines in the valley for at least 325 days a year, the climate invigorating, and few days in the year prevent outdoor work. The blue skies overhead by day and the teeming, starry night and moonlight fill men's hearts both with joy and faith. It seems that no sin can thrive here for it is so open and free that God's eye is not obscured anywhere.[42]

Despite such heavenly images, life in the colony was hard. Each colonist family lived in a one-room shack, twenty-five feet square, set upon a concrete foundation covered by boards. The house had a kitchen, two bedrooms, and a living room distributed by corners with no wall partitions. Cooking was performed on a wood-fueled stove, coal being too expensive. The stove was also the family's sole source of heat. Kerosene lamps provided the only light at night. The houses, of course, lacked running water which was carried in pails from the colony's single well. Clarion's builders had left the walls unfinished with upright two-by-fours exposed. Heat and cold cracked and shrunk the lumber, allowing the wind to whistle through chinks in the walls. Many of the children remember the high-pitched sounds of the wind and even blankets covered with snow falling through the warped wallboards. Some of the colonists had combated the elements with plaster while others hung tarpaper as a crude wall covering. To lessen the sense of isolation and loneliness, the colonists built their houses within easy walking distance of their neighbors. Some constructed their homes in groups fifty to seventy-five yards apart (see Map 6). As previously noted, colonists took advantage of this proximity to farm more efficiently. Close personal ties were forged in these clusters which extend to the children living far from Utah today. At the same time, others found proximity to their neighbors simply another burden in an already difficult situation.[43]

With Clarion so much a struggle, life in the eastern slums probably appeared inviting. This was especially true for the women. They hauled water,

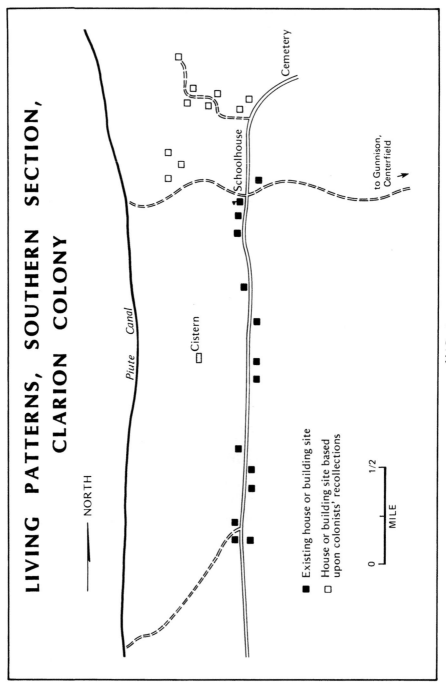

LIVING PATTERNS, SOUTHERN SECTION, CLARION COLONY

NORTH

Piute Canal

Cistern

Cemetery

Schoolhouse

to Gunnison, Centerfield

■ Existing house or building site

□ House or building site based upon colonists' recollections

0   MILE   1/2

MAP 6

The Mastrow family's Clarion home. Courtesy of Beckie Mastrow Pullman.

baked bread, made butter and cheese, dressed meat, and cooked on a primitive stove. They also tended the vegetable gardens, their labor necessary to supplement family diet and income. The care and feeding of the chickens, cows, and turkeys were counted as well among the women's chores. Clothes constantly needed washing and mending. Keeping a clean house was difficult in the normally crude conditions of Clarion and impossible when cold weather required that the animals be sheltered in the house. The demands of babies and young children further drained mothers of their time and energy. Added to the daily stresses of a life without respite or convenience was the round-trip distance to Gunnison and its doctor and midwife. If help was called for in the fields the women responded by praying for stronger backs and more hours in the day. When husbands left the colony to seek extra income in Gunnison or far-off Salt Lake City, farm operations and family responsibilities fell completely on them. Clarion offered no escape from the physical or mental pressures. Even privacy was denied the women in the one-room shacks. The colony took a heavy toll. The Bernstein children remember their mother "exhausted and irritable much of the time" from her daily labor. "Her memories of the farm . . . were to her like a bad dream."[44] Alice Furman Woll recalls in her mother "the feeling of being imprisoned in a valley surrounded by mountains . . . the resentment of having to leave the city."[45] Pauline Brownstein, said her children, simply "cried and cried."[46]

Money was scarce in the colony and eggs, milk, vegetables, and cheese were bartered in town for needed commodities. Luxuries and even many necessary items were denied, for in Clarion, said one of the children, "a piece of string became a treasure."[47] The county tax assessment records reflect the hand-to-mouth existence that was Clarion. In 1913, Joseph Furman was assessed a tax of $6.24 on personal property, livestock, tools, and improved acreage valued at only $195. Aaron Binder's assessed tax was $6.88 for total property worth $215. Harry Modell, with a $200 value placed upon his improved land and ownership of three horses and a cow, was the colony's leading taxpayer with an assessment due of $14.88. To make matters worse, during the summer the Association cut one dollar off the weekly allotment it gave to each family. In the fall, the stipend was eliminated entirely.[48]

IV

Life on the economic edge combined with the colony's existing personality conflicts and ideological heterogeneity to create an instability that counterbalanced the optimism born of struggle in difficult circumstances. Disagreements, real or imagined, were magnified in this atmosphere with people intolerant of compromise. Fear and anger riddled trust and respect as sides formed and made ready to fortify their positions with what resources were at hand. Inflexible and bellicose words pitted conversation when opponents colored each other in the darkest shades, interpreting every action according to a preconceived pattern of malevolence. In such a situation combatants would not yield, forcing triumph or defeat with no one truly able to claim victory. The rising pressure erupted in June and July 1913 in a controversy which integrated fears for economic security with questions of Ben Brown's judgement and leadership abilities. The issue was colony land tenure and it ignited the tinder of slowly accumulated resentment and distrust. This division proved far more dangerous than the quarrel over the program of Jewish education. It drew destructive power from its potential economic consequences and the centrality of Ben Brown.

Isaac Herbst's resurvey of the parcel had adjusted the original property lines to compensate for the varied quality of the land and to lay out the settlement so that as many farms as possible abutted the colony's main road. Colonists who were already on the soil were then apportioned land under the canal. No attention was paid at the time or upon the arrival of new colonists to the variance between the official documents of title registered by the state and actual occupancy of colony land. With suspicion and tension choking the air, the problem soon came to a head. Some colonists feared that their efforts were in vain because they were working land which legally belonged to others. The land ownership question also appeared to undermine individual responsibility and the private control of property. How could one sell his land if it was created from parcel sections owned by different colonists? What would be the result if the legal owner of all or part of your farm defaulted upon his financial obligations? Would not the inefficient drag the more capable down? Abe Wernick, for example, worried about "those who let the hired hands do all the work while they themselves 'rested.' "[49] Barnet Slobodin rebuked one farmer who failed to feed his horses and another unable to find time to milk his cow regularly. Did not the employment of the Association as a vehicle for dealing with the state protect the lazy and work to the detriment of the industrious? "In reality," wrote Isaac Friedlander, "the good would suffer for the not so good. If some colonists were not able to or willing to pay their debts or taxes, then the Association as a whole would be responsible."[50] During seemingly endless sessions, anxious farmers conceived every possible legal complication, losing themselves in a maze of fear and confusion. Those who were unable to follow the debate could still wade into the fray by deriding Ben Brown for his incompetent handling of the situation. In fact, discussions often digressed from the real legal issues to a question of confidence in the president of the Association.[51]

Led by Barney Silverman and Isaac Herbst, who disagreed with Brown about policy and chaffed under his authority, a dozen dissatisfied colonists petitioned the State Board of Land Commissioners to resurvey the tract, recognize the validity of the present configuration, and issue deeds to individual settlers. The "disrupters," as they were labeled by the colonists, also sought the support of the Salt Lake City Jews while informing the Jewish Agricultural Society in New York City that conditions within Clarion had deteriorated. The Society added this news to its file bolstering its conviction that the colony would never succeed. Thirty-eight colonists, while concerned about the issues raised, sided with Ben Brown and reaffirmed their faith in his leadership. However, in response to their wishes, Brown did appear before the land board requesting official recognition of the colony's survey and the granting of individual titles. Government officials rejected both petitions convinced that the requests would prove too consuming of money and effort. Some members, questioning the colony's permanence, thought a resurvey to be simply a waste of time. The dissidents and their families left the colony after their defeat and were quickly replaced by Association members from the East.[52]

The land dispute had sapped the colonists of time and energy and demolished the personal aspirations and ideological missions of a significant minority. Even more devastating to the colony's future was a series of weather calamities which damaged the crops and denied the labor of a year. On August 9, a "heroic storm," in Isaac Friedlander's words, struck the colony. "The sky was aglow with hot coals."[53] Barney Silverman, who was packing to leave the colony, recalled

> the first sounds of the howling winds which grew louder by the minute. Then came the rains not in heavy drops, but in literally heavy columns of water. The mixture of the howling winds and the tremendous deafening roar of the flood, sounded like the very mountains are crumbling and are rolling over the colony down into the valley below. The loud claps coupled with the noise of the wind and falling water were so terrifying that it could best be described by the words—inferno or cataclysm.[54]

Heavy runoff from the Valley Mountains to the west combined with the rains over Clarion to fill the dry washes leading to the canal. The water flowed in such volume and velocity that the conduits under the canal were inadequate to handle the discharge and became clogged with debris. The water rose over the canal, breeching its banks, and then flooded the ripening hay, alfalfa, and wheat fields. Gravel, tree limbs, stones, and sand covered the land, burying the crops. It appeared "as if it had hailed rocks all night. . . . The place looked like the aftermath of an earthquake."[55] The water had moved with immense force deepening existing gullies and creating new ones which "cut some farms in two."[56] Another storm struck the area on August 27, and "many of the farmers have suffered loss that will prove quite a hardship to them."[57] Maturing crops and the irrigation canals had again sustained heavy damage. A storm in the fall and an early frost later thinned the fields even more.[58]

The colony's most profound tragedy also occurred in August 1913. Twenty-nine-year-old Aaron Binder, one of the twelve original settlers, decided to perform a local feat of bravery to prove that a Jew was the equal of any Christian. Isaac Friedlander described Binder as "a physical Jew." "He was not interested in our ideological motivation in returning to the land; he was simply called by the land. . . . He was our blue ribbon, model farmer, with whom we showed off before the Mormon farmers who came to look."[59] Although woodcutting was a communal effort because it was considered dangerous, Binder drove a wagon alone 7,000 feet up into the Wasatch Mountains to saw timber for a shed for his horses and cow. On his return down the steep trail, his load overturned, crushing his chest and killing him instantly. The colonists buried Binder on a barren hill overlooking the valley. His gravestone inscribed in Hebrew read:

> Here lies
> a man young in days
> [who] met death in the Wasatch Mountains
> Aaron son of Abraham
> Set free [from this life] on the eleventh
> day of Elul 5673
> May he be accounted among the
> righteous in the life to come[60]

As a eulogy Isaac Friedlander wrote that Binder was "a son of our people, a humble, hardworking Jew, with a great Jewish soul. He died a martyr, in the cause of raising our level and not permitting shame on the Jewish name."[61]

Binder left a widow and five children. His fellow colonists vowed to remember their friend and work the family's farm as long as Rose Binder remained and until the children had grown. "After a while," recalled Wernick, "as usually happens, we stopped thinking about the man who had been killed."[62] The Binder family's Clarion tragedy was completed when a baby died of meningitis and was buried near his father. Soon after, the family returned to Baltimore where Rose Binder, unable to feed or clothe her children, temporarily placed them in an orphanage.[63]

The poor harvest was anticlimactic, the storms and marginal land producing a crop smaller than the most pessimistic predictions. A mechanical breakdown of the threshing engine further exposed the mature crop to the vicissitudes of the weather, thus lessening the marketable output. The colonists gathered approximately thirty bushels of oats and wheat per acre which brought $12.00 to $14.00 in income. With half of the crop owed to the Association and, after deductions were made for expenses and various payments, most of the farmers could expect to clear only $150 to $200 for all of their efforts. Even the trees planted the previous spring along the colony's main road were casualties. The weather, a lack of care, and grazing cows and horses had taken a heavy toll.[64]

Clarion was demoralized. "It was very hard to go on," remarked Nathan Ayeroff.[65] "Soul searching" meetings both planned and spontaneous occurred. Can we be successful? Is Clarion worth more work and hardship? Should we give in? "How much more," asked Isaac Friedlander, "can we take?"[66] With only a few dissenters the group decided to continue on the land and not return in defeat to the city. Some worried about the reaction of friends and relatives who had counseled against the project. Others felt too much had been invested to surrender. Clarion's call to the Jews of the ghettos had not yet been heard. What would the Mormons say of the Jews who yielded so quickly? But it was farming and its accompanying life-style which held the Clarion settlers to the soil. Isaac Friedlander believed "they had integrated themselves into the land."[67] Nathan Ayeroff concurred: "To be on [the] land, to be free, to work for yourself, not to have a boss or a foreman; to breathe fresh air all the time. . . . How could you leave a place like this and go back to New York, to the factory?"[68] Despite all that had occurred, all of the frustrations and defeats, Clarion, said Abe Wernick, "nevertheless felt like a *Jewish* home."[69]

The Jews picked up the rocks and again cleared the fields. Irrigation ditches were repaired, sheds rebuilt, and fences mended. It was not an optimistic sense of the future that drove them, but rather a fatalistic determination. To survive that winter, the colonists marketed all of their grain, leaving nothing for seed in the spring. When the harvest money was gone, furniture, dishes, and anything of value were sold to buy food and clothing and to pay

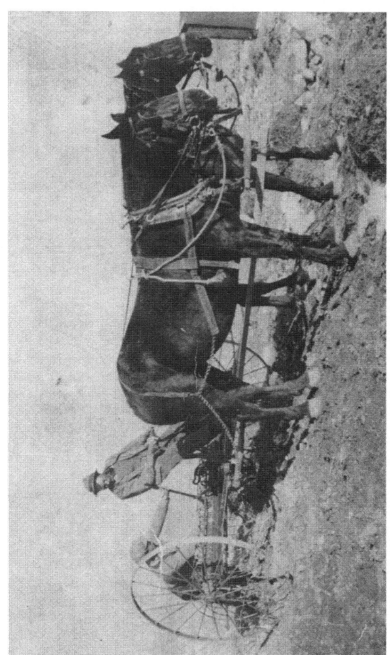

Aaron Binder and an unidentified Jewish farmer preparing to work their fields. Courtesy of Sarah Binder Steinberg.

debts. Joseph Brownstein obtained funds to support his family by selling all of his remaining property in Philadelphia. Men took odd jobs in and around Gunnison and Salt Lake City collecting scrap iron and hides and tailoring. Money from eastern relatives tided others over the difficult months. The *Yahudim* in Salt Lake City made an emergency collection of funds to aid in the relief of the colony. Diets changed, with barley, beans, and potatoes the daily staples. The Ayeroff family remembers eating cats to stave off hunger. The Furmans ate pigeons. That winter the colonists also had to dig a third grave in Clarion's cemetery when Isaac Lieberman died before his first birthday.[70]

In this desperate situation, the colonists again placed their faith in a financial miracle upon Ben Brown and his persuasive abilities. Brown left Utah and traveled east seeking subscriptions for the bond issue. This time, Utah Governor William Spry, Attorney General A. R. Barnes, and President William D. Candland of the State Board of Land Commissioners joined him in his quest for funds. In Philadelphia, Governor Spry lauded the "rapid progress the Jewish colonists had made in adapting themselves to Western customs and adopting modern farming methods. . . . The colony has been remarkably successful. We regard the colonists as extremely desirable citizens."[71] In fact, Spry issued his own call for a return to the soil: "To the man in the East who is dissatisfied with his work or living conditions, Utah offers a chance to lead an independent life under favorable conditions far from the congested tenement districts of the large cities."[72] Rabbi Isaac Landman who met him in Philadelphia quickly promised the governor that 100 more families would depart for Clarion within the next few months. The newspapers also interviewed President Candland, who described the Clarion tract as "one of the most fertile to be found in the West."[73] None of the men elaborated upon their remarks.

The Utah delegation with Brown and Rabbi Landman traveled to New York City for a meeting with the directors of the Jewish Agricultural Society in a final attempt to procure funding for the colony. The Utahns came away from the conference believing that the Society would assist the colony if the state resurveyed the land and registered each parcel in the name of its actual owner. The funds, however, were never forthcoming. Inexplicably, the Society later reneged and refused all support. The selling campaign did succeed in raising $6,000, the money more a charitable bequest than an investment. This amount was sufficient to purchase seed, forestall the repossession of wagons, harnesses, and tools, and buy time. Yet, everyone knew with colonist Moshe Malamed that, "the knife was at our throats."[74]

1913 was to have been the colony's year of renewal and progress. The traumatic first harvest would lie forgotten as individual initiative and self-interest combined to produce a bountiful crop. Dependency and financial insecurity would fade in this thrust toward self-sufficiency and stability. Instead, 1913 brought frustration, conflict, and a harvest of failure. Human will could not overcome poor soil, scarce capital, and capricious weather. Economic and environmental realities, in turn, conspired with human nature to inflame the ideological and political discord which ruptured the community. The colonists' optimism and missionary fervor had seriously eroded by the winter of 1913-14. There was little to cheer the colonists forward as they began the farming cycle again. The sources of financial assistance had vanished. Clarion had not demonstrated to the outside world its viability as a model for the Jewish agrarian future in America. In fact, those who challenged Clarion for ideological and personal reasons had moved beyond passive opposition. The Jewish Agricultural Society was engaged in active sabotage of the project. The situation was financially futile, the colony had been torn internally, geographic and agricultural circumstances had not improved, and the Jews of New York City and Philadelphia ignored and even scoffed at Clarion's call. Yet, the colonists held on in stubbornness and in hope that the coming year would allow them the life they craved. Their vision was now fixed less upon Jewish regeneration and personal success and more and more upon survival.

5

Land of Stone, Country of Promise

A chain has many links. When one
weakens and falls out, others follow.

Moshe Malamed
Clarion colonist

. . . the courage to go on was gone.

Isaac Friedlander
Clarion colonist

Internal inadequacies and pressures had so far defeated the Clarion project. Inexperience, undercapitalization, unsuitable farming conditions, and factionalism had drained the colony of energy, resilience, and resources, leaving it vulnerable to mortal blows. The colonists, however, retained their courage and determination, refusing to await such a fate passively. They prepared the land, attempted to diversify their operations, and continued the search for financial aid. Yet, in 1914 and 1915, new difficulties, now from the outside, enveloped the crippled colony. The combination of internal weaknesses and external shocks destroyed Clarion and what it represented—the dream of personal fulfillment and the hope of Jewish rebirth. Individual achievement and

Jewish advance would not come on the farm but in the business and professional worlds of America's cities.

I

With the money raised during the winter through bond subscriptions, the
Jewish farmers of Clarion again plowed and planted their fields in wheat,
oats, hay, and alfalfa. The water appeared on schedule that spring, delivered
in a canal that state construction teams had strengthened and improved. The
northward progress of the Piute Canal was sufficient to allow the Jews to oc-
cupy more farms and to increase their area under cultivation to 2,800 acres.
Although hard pressed, the colonists refused to concede. Only a few had surrendered and the settlement's population stood at over 200 people. "The miracle," wrote Ben Brown, "is that . . . [they] remained. It became a kind of
sacredness. I am forced to confess that the dedication of the forty-nine families that remained had influenced me to find new means of carrying on the
work."[1] Once more he packed his suitcase and went east to seek funds, this
time to untapped sources in Cleveland and Cincinnati.[2]

In an attempt to revive Clarion, the colonists planned a major diversification of their efforts. With a crucial financial transfusion from Simon Bamberger and other Salt Lake City Jews, they purchased baby chicks and the
lumber and netting needed to house them. The money came in the form of a
loan, but neither lender nor borrower expected it to be repaid. Fortified by a
lecture about poultry raising from a professor at Utah State Agricultural College, the colonists purchased the fowls and began construction of coops and
runs. The Jewish farmers decided to buy chicks instead of hens. Abraham
Wernick explained their reasoning: "If we bought full grown hens, the possibility of an immediate regular income from the eggs would be more actual,
but we were concerned about the future. We therefore made the decision to
suffer a little now for the sake of the long-range benefit."[3] Buying chicks and
waiting four to five months for them to mature was a common farming practice and also less costly in terms of an initial outlay. Still, with the colony
financially strapped, postponing additional income raises doubt. The colonists had chosen to gamble upon a present which they barely grasped for a
future that was fast disappearing. Several colonists, again following a college
professor's lecture, chose to supplement their income by raising pigs. They
quickly calculated their profits based upon the expected size of a sow's litter
and found the path out of their financial morass. For most, in light of Jewish
dietary habits, "the idea was a little bit disgusting. . . . The women particularly were opposed to it. One woman warned her husband that if he ever

Miriam Malamed feeding the chickens on the family farm in Clarion, 1915. Courtesy of Mr. and Mrs. Daniel Malamed.

Moshe Malamed returning home after a day on the land. Courtesy of Mr. and Mrs. Daniel Malamed.

brought a pig to their farm she would leave the colony."[4] Unfortunately, both experiments in diversification ended in failure. Many of the chicks died en route or during their first few days in the colony. "What the reason was for this calamity we did not know."[5] Each family's small flock of chickens was all that remained of Clarion's experiment in large-scale poultry production. A cholera epidemic later decimated the colony's pig population. With cattle and other livestock too expensive, Clarion's diversification plans were halted and the farmers concentrated upon their grain fields and irrigation ditches.[6]

These setbacks accelerated the project's descent into economic quicksand. "That summer," wrote Wernick, "hunger came knocking at our door. None of us had any income."[7] The colonists bartered milk, cheese, and eggs for necessary supplies. Borrowing was common until Gunnison merchants imposed ceilings upon unpaid balances. Rumors spread that the county sheriff would soon appear to enforce claimants' demands for repossession of Association-acquired wagons, harnesses, tools, and livestock. Assessment rolls in 1914 once more testified to the continuing bareness of life in Clarion. That year, only five of the colony's thirty-five farmers had property valued at more $200. More typical of the standard of living was Nathan Ayeroff who paid a tax of $3.56 on property worth $95. Sam Lieberman was assessed $4.50 for his land, horses, and tools valued at only $120. Joseph Brownstein's horse, cow, equipment, and land were appraised at just $140, and he paid $5.25 in taxes. Considering the time, effort, and funds each colonist had already expended in pursuit of his dream, these figures proved cold reminders of a reality beyond control.[8]

To make matters worse, the flow of water in the Piute Canal had become insufficient and irregular by mid-May. The soil cracked under the sun and the crops withered. "We didn't know what to do first—water the land that wasn't watered yet, or let that part burn up and water the same area again. This situation gave us no peace."[9] The problem this time was unrelated to construction. Rather, the Jews experienced an inconsistent flow because of their neighbor's greed. In the hot and dry weather, farmers below the colony took advantage of the cover of night and the absence of locks on the canal gates and used more than their allotted share. The Jews complained to the Board of Land Commissioners which, in turn, called upon the watermaster to insure an adequate stream for the colony. He, however, was tied to the water thieves by blood and religion and intervened only in a perfunctory way. In fact, he attributed the entire controversy to the inexperience of the Jewish farmers which led to their improper utilization of available water. While the more recent arrivals from the East were unfamiliar with irrigation techniques, the trouble stemmed far more from the indeterminable and large fluctuations in the supply which on occasion caused overflow and waste. The board granted the colony's request to supplement the watermaster's efforts with its own canal rider, yet his labors proved insufficient to solve the impasse. After repeated letters, telegrams, and delegations to the board had brought no redress, the frustrated and angry Jews acted. On July 4, 1914, Brown and thirty of the colonists marched along the canal, seized control of the water gates, and forcibly closed those belonging to the Mormon farmers. Order was eventually restored, but no one had benefited. Meanwhile, the loss of colonist David Bernstein, who had developed gangrene and died despite the amputation of his leg, only added to the settlers' misery. Bernstein left his wife and seven children in the colony's care. The group assessed itself a special tax to meet this new emergency.[10]

It was clear long before threshing time that the harvest would not boost the colony into the next year. The colonists had compounded their water problems with incompetence. They had planted wheat developed for dry farming, which requires a winter dormant period, rather than the seed which grew best when sowed in their irrigated fields in the spring. "At the time we did not yet know the difference."[11] The wheat crop was thus a total loss. The marginal soil had, as well, taken its toll on crop production. While the colony harvested its alfalfa and oat fields, the yields were inferior to those on neighboring farms. "Altogether," recalled Abe Wernick, "it meant that the general income from the crop was smaller than the previous year and that the outlook for most of the colonists was quite bleak. In short, it meant that they would go hungry that winter. . . . Each one of us had privately gotten so deep in debt that there would be nothing to live on."[12] Nor did Ben Brown return with good news from the East. The outbreak of World War I had diverted philanthropists' attention toward Europe, to which they now funneled aid to support displaced Jews. No one would listen to his pleas for a financially distressed colony in Utah. If these events weren't sufficient to test colonists' wills, the only well in Clarion again became undependable and water once more had to be ferried from Gunnison. "Our spirits were low and the weather was turning cold. Quarrels broke out among our people."[13] Three families left that fall. Only news from the East that jobs were difficult to find deterred others from abandoning the project.[14]

If Clarion was to survive, the colonists had to raise $10,000 to meet outstanding debts and to sustain them into the next year. The dwindling number of Association members in the East had long since exhausted their support capabilities. Some of the colonists made a desperate appeal to the antagonis-

The Bernstein family in Clarion. Courtesy of Michael Bernstein.

tic Jewish Agricultural Society but were rebuffed. With all other support channels blocked, the Jewish farmers turned to the *Yahudim* of Salt Lake City. The board of directors of the Utah Colonization Fund, aware of the difficulties, was prepared for the colonists' urgent request for assistance. The directors were receptive but, before help would be forthcoming, required consent to certain preconditions. The *Yahudim* demanded a formal dissolution of the Jewish Agricultural and Colonial Association and an end to all of Clarion's collective features. That is, each farmer would resign from the group, sever his cooperative buying and selling ties, and abrogate his share-cropping contract. The Association would no longer handle machinery and livestock purchases and the sale of the colony's crops. With debts to the Association paid, farmers would keep all of the profits gained in the marketplace. Loans would then be made on an individual basis to the productive while the lazy and inefficient would be pruned from the enterprise. Although taking charge, the Jews of Salt Lake City did not expect to carry the entire financial burden by themselves. They believed that the Jewish Agricultural Society would look favorably upon their actions and the new "capitalistic" orientation of Clarion and extend aid. There was, however, no evidence that the Society had any intention of changing its stance on the matter. To bolster the new arrangement, the colonists and *Yahudim* would also press the Board of Land Commissioners to recognize the Clarion land survey and deed the plots to their owners. Finally, the Salt Lake City Jews deemed it advisable to appoint a farm manager who would oversee affairs in a business-like fashion until the former colonists had become self-sustaining. "In other words," contended Moshe Malamed, "we would lose our independence. This was the opposite of the goal for which we were striving, which we were trying to avoid."[15] With their backs to the wall, the colonists could do little else but agree to all stipulations.[16]

To discuss individual farmer's conditions, and to appraise clearly circumstances within the colony, a delegation traveled from Salt Lake City to Clarion. Neither side welcomed the encounter: "From the moment they arrived there was great tension; they were critical of our venture."[17] For the *Yahudim*, the colony was an unwanted financial and moral burden from which they sought relief. To the colonists, the meeting was necessary but humiliating. They saw themselves degraded, their hands outstretched for alms while they tried to justify their needs. The confrontation came at a public gathering the first night. The *Yahudim*, led by Simon Bamberger, called upon each farmer to state his requirements to remain on the land. Several arose and indicated that only a few hundred dollars were sufficient to make them indepen-

dent. Moshe Malamed resented the attitude of the delegation, believing that
they sat in judgement of him and his comrades: "They cross-examined several
of us harshly, to determine just how good or bad our situation was."[18] One of
the Jewish farmers, speaking what others thought, berated the Salt Lake City
Jews for neglecting the colony and reneging upon earlier promises of substantial financial assistance. Bamberger exploded, remembered Wernick,
who quoted him as shouting: "Who the devil brought you out here? I'm fed
up with the lot of you! I'll have nothing more to do with any of you!"[19] He
then stormed out of the meeting. The *Yahudim* at that point ceased their
efforts to effect a full-scale reorganization of the colony and to reclaim it
along more individualistic lines. Still, they would not allow their coreligionists to perish economically. When creditors threatened repossession of tools,
equipment, and livestock, Salt Lake City Jews interceded to forestall economic collapse. They arranged a compromise in which the colony returned to
the claimants the trouble-plagued tractor and raised $2,500 as a temporary
settlement for other business debts. The colonists had thus gained just a little
more time in which to turn Clarion's fortunes.[20]

The colonists' breathing space proved limited. The Board of Land Commissioners, prompted by complaints of colonists' water misuse and a reckon-
ing that Clarion's demise was close at hand, attempted to recover what funds
it could from the Association. It refused the Jewish farmers any further extension on the money due in principal and interest for the land and water
rights. In addition, the board demanded immediate payment on present and
deferred obligations by January 1, 1915, or the forfeiture of the Clarion tract.
Except for its initial down payment, the Association had given the state no
money on its purchase. In 1912, because of the failure of the canal, the board
had granted the colony a twelve-month extension on the payment of principal
and waived the first year of interest as compensation for crop loss. At the end
of 1913, the Association had informed the board that it would be unable to
meet the payment schedule. While the board did not officially approve another extension, "we did not pay them any money."[21] Now, in the winter of
1914, with current and past debts totaling $57,400, the board would wait no
longer. Again, Salt Lake City Jews came to the defense of the colony and
hammered out a compromise. They persuaded the state to delay collection for
a few months while the colonists agreed to make payments on the interest
owed and return their 3,000 uncultivated acres for resale. This arrangement
would cut the colony's obligation by one-half. In addition, the *Yahudim* promised to intensify their efforts among eastern financiers to raise money for the
colony. Although the agreement ended their opportunity for a new life on the

farm, eastern members of the Association unanimously concurred in the decision. The colony would thus continue in a truncated form, but its future had become more and more apparent.[22]

II

Only fragments of information are available about life in the colony during its last year. Fifty-two families remained on the land, with Association members arriving from the East as late as January 1915 to replace those who had departed. Conditions continued to deteriorate. "Things were so bad," reported Abe Wernick, "that many of us no longer had any flour to bake bread."[23] As the circumstances of living became more unbearable, morale and personal relationships decayed. "We had come to the realization that we ourselves would no longer be able to continue to live amicably together. The demoralization among us was so bad that no one trusted anyone else."[24] This depression was deepened when Clarion endured another casualty. Sarah Mastrow, the wife of Isador and mother of two, suffered a stroke and lost the use of the left side of her body. Her family and the rest of the colony blamed the tragedy on a life that transformed the healthy and ambitious into the maimed of body and mind. In the spring, Ben Brown resigned as Association president in reaction to popular dissatisfaction and his own sense of personal failure. He could no longer command the loyalty of a majority of his fellow colonists or the confidence of Mormon businessmen in Gunnison or Jews in Salt Lake City. His replacement was anarchist Abe Wernick who assumed control only to preside over the liquidation of the colony. Agricultural disaster continued to afflict colonists when a hay crop planted in March was thin when cut in June owing to a late frost. Creditors demanded their money and more repossessions of equipment and livestock occurred, rapidly eroding Clarion's supply of resources. As life became more difficult during the summer, a notice was published in the Gunnison newspaper informing all potential buyers that the Association held a chattel mortgage on the tools, horses, and cows which colonists were seeking to sell to survive. A depressing harvest in the fall was the final shock for many.[25]

The cumulative blows—agricultural calamity, a life without economic, social, religious, and cultural necessities, the death of two colonists and two infants, and the departures of others—had robbed the Jews of the will to continue. Approximately thirty of the families reluctantly agreed to accept the money raised by the *Yahudim* and buy railroad tickets to Los Angeles, Chicago, Philadelphia, and New York City. They surrendered quietly: "It seemed they opened the doors of their homes, walked out, and disappeared."[26] The shacks did not remain in Clarion either. Creditors sold the houses to local farmers who pulled them to new sites where they served as toolsheds and animal shelters. The concrete foundations that remained, remarked Barney Silverman on a return to the site years later, stood like "tombstone[s] where many hopes, many beautiful dreams lie buried."[27] A public auction disposed of the rest of Clarion's meager possessions. Four hundred dollars was all that remained after the liquidation of the Association's resources. Wernick donated the money to the People's Relief Fund, a charity in New York. In the wake of the project's failure, the anti-Clarion *American Israelite* editorialized: "It is to be hoped that when the next colony is being planned that the people will be wise enough to refuse to give it financial support."[28] Other Jewish newspapers either did not note the colony's demise or relegated obituaries to the back pages of their editions.[29]

While most of these settlers returned to the city, some could not immediately escape the farm's attraction. Barney Silverman wandered the western states for two years working as an orange picker, sugar beet harvester, and sheepherder before resuming the plumbing trade in Philadelphia. David Cohen farmed with his brothers in upstate New York until 1917. Moshe Malamed operated a farm in Bucks County, Pennsylvania, near the National Farm School. The Yigdoll, Modell, Hamburger, and Barak families went west and homesteaded in California.[30]

III

Seventeen families refused to submit to the inevitable and clung to the land. The end, however, could not be long delayed. On November 5, 1915, the Board of Land Commissioners carried out its threat and declared the Jewish parcels foreclosed and cancelled for nonpayment of nearly $70,000 for land and water rights. The board authorized a public sale of the land to be held on January 18, 1916. Handbills advertising the auction described the tract as situated in "one of the most fertile valleys in the State" with a climate both "mild and healthful."[31] According to William D. Candland, president of the board, "This land seems to be wanted by a lot of citizens."[32] Ben Brown, chosen to represent Clarion's remnant, appeared before the board and cajoled its members into a last concession. Those who sought to remain would be allowed to retain title if they made a down payment immediately and met the prescribed financial schedule in the future. "We feel," pleaded Brown, "that we are entitled to that much consideration for all the hardships we went through, and for the loss of money we sustained during the first four years in the Clarion project."[33] The land auction thus excluded from sale those plots the Jews had claimed. The auction proved a disappointment for its sponsors. A heavy snowstorm plus a scarcity of eager buyers resulted in the distribution of less than 800 of Clarion's 6,000 acres.[34]

Most of those who remained lived in the area for only three or four years. Hyman Basow held on to his parcel paying taxes and land fees but moved to Gunnison, supporting his family with a plumbing and general repair business. The Liebermans stayed until 1919 and then returned to Philadelphia. Sam Kristol also sold his property in 1919, using his earnings to buy another farm in Bucks County, Pennsylvania, which he worked through the 1920s. The Plonskys went east after World War I and bought a farm in northern Indiana where they remained until 1924. Barnet Pally and cousin Barnet Slobodin found that their farm incomes were insufficient to meet costs and support their families. Rather than relinquish the land, they traveled during the winter collecting cattle and sheep hides from area farmers. When this did not bring financial comfort, Pally opened a tailor shop in Gunnison. Finally in 1924, the Pally and Slobodin families left Sanpete County and, after temporarily residing in Salt Lake City, departed for Los Angeles and New York City, respectively. The year before, the Mastrows succumbed to the hardness of a life without respite and abandoned the farm for the city.[35]

Only the Joseph Brownstein and Nathan Brown families overcame the economic hurdles of local farming. Brownstein bought a succession of farms which were situated under the more dependable Westview Canal. The stimulus of World War I and the opening of a plant to process sugar beets in nearby Centerfield brought a measure of financial security. Nathan Brown, the brother of Benjamin, carefully budgeted his money and diversified his grain production with cattle and poultry raising. When the Brownsteins sold their farm in 1925 followed by the Browns the year after, it was not financial adversity which drove them from the land. As the number of Jewish families had declined, the proselytizing efforts of the Mormons had intensified. During the colony's early years, the majority of Jews had looked to their coreligionists for fulfillment of personal and cultural needs. The colonists projected an image of unity and formidability, dissuading most Mormons from approaching on other than an economic level. Physical distance from non-Jews further expanded the social space insulating the two groups. The Jews were thus geographically and economically within the community, yet not participants in political, legal, social, or religious institutions. The colony had remained an island distinct from the Mormon sea surrounding it. Now, missionaries approached adults on the farm and children in the schools pressing them to read the *Book of Mormon* and to grasp a new faith. "We were always on our guard," remembers Lena Brown Marinoff.[36] Resistance to conversion became more difficult as the Jewish presence had thinned: "It was kind of a hard situation when there was only one or two of us."[37] Even harder to combat was the subtle pressure toward assimilation which occurred as children of the different religions interacted socially. Jewish boys and girls visited Mormon friends in their homes, attended ward house meetings, and dated their neighbors. The fear of assimilation and the inability to nurture their children in a "proper" ethnic, Jewish environment forced the final Jews to leave. "If I was going to stay there," declared Joseph Brownstein, "I gonna lose all my children."[38]

Benjamin Brown had also continued to live in Clarion, sharing a farm with his brother. In labor he sought escape from the idealism which had brought forth the ill-fated project. "I have to confess," he wrote,

> that I had lost interest at first in all problems relating to Jews. And, I had revulsion for all pretensions of any sort of radicalism among Jews. I threw myself wholeheartedly in my farm work and found tranquility and happiness in the beautiful landscape of my field. The smooth skin of my animals calmed my enraged spirit. My fine horses took the place of human friendship. My sugar beets, potatoes, wheat and hay always won prizes in the farm exhibits.[39]

In 1923, spurred by the financial opportunity presented by a large surplus in Sanpete County's egg production, Brown left the farm and organized a marketing agency for area farmers. With the help of Mormons Clyde Edmonds and Bert Willardson, the operation added grading and packaging to its functions and expanded first to Sevier and Juab counties and later the entire state. The Utah Poultry Association, subsequently renamed the Intermountain Farmers' Association, enabled producers to buy and sell cooperatively, thus attaining more control over prices and costs. The organization proved so successful that two years after its creation, Brown left Utah to open a New York City office to facilitate marketing in the eastern states. Brown, however, assumed the position for more than organizational and financial reasons. "I had the feeling that I was dying a sweet death; as you would douse one in a barrel of sweet water. I felt that I must tear myself away from my non-Jewish atmosphere and return to my people."[40]

Brown's involvement in two unrelated Jewish colonization efforts marked the end of his self-imposed exile. In 1927, the Soviet Union designated the Biro-Bidzhan region in Far Eastern Siberia as a National Jewish District. This vast underdeveloped region, the size of the states of Massachusetts and Connecticut combined, was 5,000 air miles from Moscow with a population of only 34,000 people. The government planned to transform Soviet Jews into "competent and exemplary builders of the new socialist life."[41] Jews would be dispersed from the provinces of the former Pale, returned to the soil, and productivized. Upon this territorial base Jewish identity and nationality would be preserved and life normalized. The creation of a Jewish center in Siberia, it was also assumed, would deflect Zionist aspirations and zeal. Far more important, Soviet leaders hoped the project would accelerate Jewish assimilation through diffusion, begin the economic transformation of Siberia, and create a defensive barrier to Japanese expansionism. To finance this operation the government expected large infusions of Jewish funds from abroad. Ben Brown visited the district as a member of a fact-finding delegation at the behest of its opponent Chaim Weizmann, the future first president of Israel. Ironically, civil engineer Isaac Herbst, one of the Clarion's Colony's former leaders, was in Biro-Bidzhan at the same time. Convinced of the futility of a Jewish Palestine, he had left the United States in 1930 to build a Soviet-Jewish homeland. He later returned to America broken in body and spirit. The Biro-Bidzhan project never elicited significant Jewish support, popular or financial. Long winters, short summers, cultural isolation, inadequate capital, and government capriciousness discouraged large-scale settlement. Between 1928 and 1933, 19,600 Jews traveled east to the region but of these 11,450 departed, most after only a year of colonizing. Purges in 1937 decimated the Jewish cadre in party and government positions further weakening the effort. By 1959, 14,629 Jews lived in Biro-Bidzhan constituting only 8.8 percent of its population. The only evidence of a Jewish influence in the region at that time was a two-sheet Yiddish newspaper (Jewish in language only) and street signs printed in both Yiddish and Russian.[42]

Ben Brown participated more directly in a second proposal, the New Deal-sponsored Jersey Homesteads, later renamed Roosevelt. Twenty years after Clarion, Brown wrote, "I still regret my inexperience then of undertaking a colonization project due to ideals. . . . We dare not forget that such an ideal demands in the practical realization, not only knowledge, experience, a definite market, etc., but also a positive source for financing, otherwise the ideal flies out of the chimney."[43] Brown had never relinquished his dream to lead Jews back to the soil and create colonies founded upon cooperation. The New Deal provided him the opportunity to garner sufficient capital to effect his goals. In 1933, the Division of Subsistence Homesteads of the Department of Agriculture's Resettlement Administration was created to foster industrial decentralization and establish farm cooperatives. Brown approached government administrators with a proposal. He planned to settle 200 families on a 1,200-acre tract of land fifty miles southwest of Manhattan. Each family would subscribe $500 to the project which entitled it to ownership of a single-story house on an acre lot and membership in a food cooperative. Residents would work together in the spring and summer on the community's farms and in a cloak factory during the fall and winter months. Extensive capital resources plus supplemental employment income, Brown believed, would assure the success of the settlement just as their absence had helped determine Clarion's fate. Brown was convincing and the Division of Subsistence Homesteads approved a loan for $500,000 to buy the land and build the roads, factory, and houses for this experiment in agricultural-industrial cooperation.[44]

The first families moved to the Jersey Homesteads in July 1936. Government bureaucracy, labor union opposition, competition from established firms, and general hard times plagued development. The cloak factory failed to make a profit during the decade and closed during the 1940s. Successive businesses since that time have arrived and departed. Agricultural inexperience also handicapped residents. The cooperative farms have been sold and are now in private hands. Today, Roosevelt is a town of nearly 900 inhabitants, half of whom are Jewish. Most breadwinners commute to work in New York City or Philadelphia. Ben Brown never saw the outcome of his efforts for he died in 1939, at the age of fifty-three years.[45]

IV

Except for the few who continued farming, Clarion's colonists returned to the city and resumed their occupations, attempting with fellow Jews to scramble up the ladder of socioeconomic mobility. While all of the former colonists "were partially – and many completely ruined financially," Clarion's members were successful in achieving status and economic security in their trades and businesses.[46] Many advanced out of blue-collar ranks by opening stores or by obtaining nonmanual positions. The children of Clarion often surpassed their fathers, securing middle- and upper-middle-class positions in law, journalism, medicine, and education. Seventeen-year-old Maurice Warshaw would travel only to Salt Lake City but progressed from pushcart to department chain store owner. A colonist's son would rise to become the president of the Morrell Meat Company. Another would become a Republican national committeeman.[47]

Political assimilation followed closely upon social and economic mobility. Most of the colonists and their children saw their radical beliefs dissolve into the main currents of American liberalism. The Democratic Party and the welfare state replaced Socialism and government ownership of the means of production as the heralds of the nation's future. Some of the colonists, however, would maintain their left-wing ties through both of America's Red Scares and until their deaths. A few went beyond verbal and voting commitments. Joseph Radding, leaving his wife Esther to care for their daughter, returned to the Soviet Union to participate in the creation of "a better life [,] a better system. . . . A government by the people and for the people."[48] David Reisky also booked passage for the Soviet Union to help build a revolutionary society. But the violence and brutality inflicted in the name of the people would profoundly disillusion the men and force their withdrawal. Reisky's son Albert later adopted the name of the radical author John Reed and fought and died with the Abraham Lincoln Brigade in Spain during the Civil War. Manya Ayeroff, whose wounds suffered at the hands of the tsarist secret police had helped turn brother Nathan toward the Bund, left America for the Soviet Union and joined the Comintern. She eventually became a director of the official news agency of the People's Republic of China. The drive to return to the soil, as with the majority of American Jews, was experienced vicariously. Clarion's Jews pledged funds or joined organizations in support of Zionist activities in Palestine and later, Israel. Only Sivan Hamburger, who was born in the colony, made an *aliya* (ascent), attending agricultural school in Palestine from 1929 to 1933.[49]

V

With the dispersal of the Jews, Mormon families settled the lands in and near the former colony. By 1925, the population had climbed to 166 people, sufficient to designate Clarion as a ward in the LDS Church. A few years before, seven Japanese families had settled under the reliable Westview Canal where they truck-farmed cabbage, cauliflower, and lettuce. Growth continued until 1926, when drought enveloped the region. The Mormons called for days of fasting and prayer but there was no relief. Finally in 1932, so many families had departed that the ward became unviable and was disbanded. Twelve families now live under the Piute Canal and are farming sections of the Clarion tract. Even with modern farming techniques, the use of chemical fertilizers, and far more water than the Jews had, just half of the land is cultivated. The rest remains barren and unproductive. Local farmers continue to expect less yield from their Clarion fields than other acres harvested.[50]

Most of the land, today, is as colonists found it in 1911. Sagebrush and tall weeds cover Clarion. Bare ground, cracked by the lack of water and covered with rocks, surround the sparse vegetation. The desert has reclaimed all of the colony's wheat, hay, and alfalfa fields. Only the foundations of the houses, the faint lines of the irrigation ditches, and the gravestones remain.

The Clarion project failed both as a means to restructure Jewish-American society and as an attempt to effect long-term changes in the lifestyles of 200 families. The Clarion call was barely heard and certainly not heeded in the ghettos of New York City and Philadelphia. For the colonists, the farm became a memory, a life out of step in their urban world. Many shared responsibility for the colony's fate. Clarion's leaders, mesmerized by the word irrigation, erred initially in their choice of a site with marginal soil and an undependable supply of water. It was, as well, located in a region where their little agriculture experience was almost inapplicable. Too cavalier about the financing of their project, they found themselves powerless when undercapitalization straitjacketed their plans. Ben Brown and his lieutenants, in addition, quarreled, postured, and placed their needs before the interests of the group. In these ways they effectively and efficiently expunged the moral and personal power which energized their claim to leadership. Without these resources, their command existed in title only. The Jewish Agricultural Society stunted the colony's growth by shutting off the financial tap at its source. It denied Clarion crucially needed funds for reasons ranging from a sense of obligation to the Jewish farm movement and its financial supporters to the personal antagonism and jealousy felt by the directors. The state of Utah boosted its canal and property beyond reason. In the crucial year of 1912, the canal's collapse pushed the colony to the wall, a position from which it would never extract itself financially. The colonists, themselves, frittered away goodwill, energy, time, and supplies with inexperience, ideological divisiveness, and personal animosities. They lacked the cement of their neighbors in Utah and coreligionists in Israel who sensed hostile enemies, were bound by common ideologies, and conceived themselves as builders of Zions. The group will necessary to sustain the colony in adversity, whether man-made or natural, never really materialized. Everyone looked to his own with the common good frequently sacrificed. Alternatives, moreover, were readily available and detracted sharply from commitment. The relative comfort of New York City, Los Angeles, and Philadelphia made burdens more difficult to bear and easier to discard. The hard times inevitable in colonization generated in many minds thoughts of escape rather than kindling renewed efforts of conquest. A few would succeed but their achievements proved hollow. The threat of assimilation gutted their progress, for Jewish farmers could exist as such only in the presence of other Jewish farmers.

There is, however, another Clarion, a paean to hope and determination. The Clarion colonists felt no shame in defeat. Their children, today, collect all available information about the colony, gather to discuss the experience, attempt to contact the sons and daughters of other settlers, and make repeated pilgrimages to the colony's site. They perceive the time in Clarion as a high point in their families' lives, a time of sacrifice and dedication. For Clarion was a dream, a battle for the future which sought for the individual and his family the full potential of American life. Economic security and personal tranquility for themselves and their children were worth years of sweat and toil and pain. Yet, the colonists did not stand in isolation. Their efforts were enmeshed in the love of and identification with the larger group. They were the vanguard of a movement to end prejudice and discrimination and insure the economic and social equality of Jews. They fought against impossible odds and were overcome on all fronts. It is a wonder that they held onto the soil as long as they did. That they failed in Clarion is their history. That they dreamed and struggled and were greater than themselves is their legacy.

6

Clarion and the Jewish Agrarian Experience

We sought for a vision.

Avraham Ben-Shalom
Kibbutz Ain Hachoresh

There is no greater patriotism than that
of no alternative.

Unknown

Clarion was an instant in Jewish time. It appeared as a brief, compressed interval of drama, intensity, courage, and pathos – and vanished, a fragment of the past whose image was nearly effaced. The colony deserves reconstruction and recall merely for itself. It is proper to recount the lives, hopes, and struggles of the men and women who dared to scratch the resisting Utah soil. Without regard to success or defeat, Clarion's history reveals a partially lost experiment which enriches the inheritance left by the Jewish immigrant generation to its descendants. The Clarion colonists' path from Russia to America and then to the soil was a departure from the mainstream, yet added another dimension to the Jewish presence in the twentieth-century golden land. With Clarion, agrarian threads must be sown into the urban fabric of American Jewry. The search for Jewish farmers need not begin and end 6,000 miles from America's shores.

Viewed thusly, Clarion provides much of value. An approach, however, which considers the colony in isolation and as a foil has serious drawbacks. Clarion becomes an eccentric episode deviant and alien from prevailing patterns. Its defects and failure become magnified and consume attention: Why did the colonists with so little experience attempt to farm? How could they have succeeded in the face of marginal soil, scarce water, and harvest calamities? In light of the worldwide movement to large-land holdings and technological farming, was not the project doomed from its inception? (Curiously, Israeli *kibbutzniks* operating under comparable conditions escape such questions.) It is necessary, therefore, to consider Clarion from another perspective. While every second and moment in time exists apart and distinct, each draws meaning as a piece of a larger whole. Similarly, to avoid distortion, Clarion must be conceptualized according to a wider framework. Clarion was one of over forty Jewish agricultural colonies in the United States as well as ideologically and temporally a part of the international drive to return to the land. Clarion may serve, then, as a heuristic tool to probe this larger effort and to offer insights into its present configuration. What variables were critical in affecting Clarion's fate? What kinds of relationships existed among the variables? Did their interactions vary over time? Why? The history of Jewish farming activities in the United States and Israel can then be considered in light of the variables drawn from Clarion's experience. Why did these colonies succeed or fail? Why has the Palestine and later Israeli environment alone been able to nurture a Jewish agrarianism which is both economically viable and ethnically secure? Perhaps from so unlikely a place as the Utah desert can be gleaned the factors which helped fix the course of modern Jewish farming and may shed light upon its future direction.

I

Five interrelated variables, their influence changing with time, were crucial in determining Clarion's fate: farming experience, environmental conditions, capital availability, colonists' morale, and the existence of alternatives. Except for a small minority of Clarion's settlers, the farm represented the unknown. They were city people with urban occupations—shopowner, clerk, peddler, tailor, and factory worker. Even the few with farming experience were handicapped since their knowledge was limited to eastern agriculture and left them unprepared for the semiarid conditions of Utah. Inexperience added to the ordinary toil attendant upon colony ground breaking. Plowing, planting, irrigation, building, and livestock and poultry tending consumed excessive amounts of time, energy, and finances. Their poor choice of a site further compounded difficulties brought about by inexperience. Water scarcity, an undependable irrigation canal, marginal soil, and capricious weather hastened the drain on the colony's enthusiasm and meager supply of monetary resources. Yet, neither lack of experience nor the environment were insurmountable. Each day on the land increased the colonists' agricultural dexterity and knowledge. Hard work, trial and error, and Mormon farmers' aid and advice bolstered the Jews' confidence and enhanced their ability to remain on the soil. The sequential arrival of Jewish settlers from the East also facilitated the sharing of painfully acquired skills and enabled newcomers to avoid earlier mistakes. The success of the Jews who remained on the land in Utah after the colony's demise or who farmed elsewhere testifies to the Clarion colonists' will to adapt to agriculture. The experiences of those who stayed reflect, as well, the change in environmental conditions. The environment, while still a dangerous foe, had begun to shed its harshness and become more predictable. The most difficult tasks had been accomplished. The land had been cleared and fields created. Fences and outbuildings had been constructed. Homes had been built more carefully and were more comfortable. The canal had become increasingly dependable. Farmers diversified their crops and livestock and were financially more steady. While water and weather would always be a source of concern, economic security would no longer hinge upon a single harvest or storm. After the initial stages of colonization, then, the variables of experience and environment no longer claimed their previous centrality.

Clarion's life could have been extended if it had had the means to sustain it through the difficult years—available capital and high morale. Without either, the impact of alternatives became pronounced. Adequate financial resources were needed to enable the Clarion colonists to survive the early colonization period, gain experience, and control their environment. Subsidies would have bought the colony time to attain stability and become economically self-supporting, although on a scale smaller than envisioned by its planners. The specific amount essential for successful colonization is difficult to estimate as it varies with time of settlement, place, technology employed, and means of organization. For Clarion, that figure, like the total actually contributed to the cause is uncertain. Still, if the patronage of an outside agency with abundant funds would have softened the hard times, it would not alone have been sufficient to insure the colony's future. To hold the colonists to a resistant land also required an intense and cohesive morale. The hardship, denial, and self-doubt which accompany any colonization project can be held at bay, if not dispelled, when men and women are bound mentally and emotionally to a common goal. Clarion could draw only briefly on such reserves. The colony's avowed purpose was to rebuild the Jewish people through agriculture. The pioneering work of the first year, done on a collective basis, fired the settlers in pursuit of their goal. In the second year, with the privatization of land and labor, Jewish redemption became a slogan and faded in the daily life and routine. The apparent unity unraveled and the diverse factions focused their energies against one another dissipating strength in an endless series of internal explosions. Personal animosities and political and cultural disagreements rotted the core of goodwill and sacrifice so essential to success. Further eroding morale was the silence of the outside world. The Mormons did not threaten the colony and offered no common ground for the quarreling groups. When Clarion's call was ignored and financial contributions failed to materialize, their greatest fears were reified; their mission had no meaning. Nor did Clarion possess a man commanding in authority, respect, or intellect who could impose order and rally the faithful. Rather than offering unity and healing, the colony's leadership exacerbated divisions. For the Clarion majority, idealism had always pulled less upon thought and action than had self-interest. Recruited primarily to raise capital for the cause, these men and women looked first to their own needs for direction. When conditions deteriorated they could find few things to justify continued allegiance.

Directly related, yet separate, was the existence of alternatives. New York City, Philadelphia, Salt Lake City, and Los Angeles called to the Jews as it did to Christians, offering rescue and release from farm life. The familiar urban world, even with its drawbacks, promised solution to economic uncertainty, deteriorating relations with fellow colonists, and idealism gone sour. Encouragement from relatives left behind, agricultural setbacks, and philanthropists who rejected the colony as unworthy of support made the decision to return easier.

The Clarion case delineates the critical interplay between the five variables. Inexperience and harsh environment shackled the experiment from the beginning but were not sufficient to explain its defeat. Adequate capital and a continuing sense of mission were not available to buffer the colonists during the trying period of foundation building. Neither the pride of achievement nor the idealism of a cause could silence the siren of alternatives. Clarion's

obstacles to economic self-reliance and ethnic viability proved too formidable
to conquer.

II

The Clarion experience was typical of the great majority of Jewish colonies
founded in the United States, for the same variables interacted to influence
their evolution and outcome. The first attempts, isolated and disconnected, to
colonize Jewish groups in farm settlements occurred in the early decades of
the nineteenth century. In the 1820s colonization was undertaken in Florida
but unfavorable environmental conditions and malaria forced withdrawal. Attorney and diplomat Mordecai M. Noah purchased in 1825 over 2,000 acres
on Grand Island on the Niagara River near Buffalo, New York, for an agricultural refuge for Jews. A lack of interest aborted Noah's plan. A decade
later, thirteen Jewish families created the Sholem Colony, but marginal soil
and poor harvests led to their early departure.[1]

Large-scale colonization began only in the 1880s. Jewish immigration to
America in the wake of the Russian pogroms touched off efforts to turn the
refugees to the soil. Farming could provide a livelihood for the immigrants,
avoid urban congestion, and dispel commercial stereotypes. Aid societies in
New York City and Philadelphia prepared to direct and fund the colonization
movement: the Hebrew Emigrant Aid Society, Russian Emigrant Relief Committee, Hebrew Colonization Society, and the Montefiore Agricultural Aid
Society. The Alliance Israelite Universelle and the Baron de Hirsch Fund
also provided support. In addition, philanthropic agencies appeared in Cincinnati, Boston, New Orleans, St. Paul, and St. Louis. The work of these
groups combined with the desires of individual immigrants and the more organized *Am Olam* societies to activate the Back to the Soil movement in
America. Approximately forty colonies were founded between 1881 and
1910 in such states as Louisiana, North and South Dakota, Kansas, Colorado, Michigan, Wisconsin, and New Jersey.[2]

The first colony of Russian Jews were planted on Sicily Island, Louisiana, in 1881. With aid from the Alliance Israelite Universelle and the New
Orleans Agricultural Society, sixty families (many members of *Am Olam*)
were established on 2,800 acres of land. Despite adequate supplies, the colony could not survive its infancy. Inexperience in a hostile environment of
swamps, oppressive heat, floods, snakes, and malaria-carrying mosquitoes
devastated the settlement. Most of the colonists returned to the city. Others
journeyed to South Dakota to participate in the formation of Cremieux in

1882. This colony grew to include 200 people and encompass 5,000 acres. Yet within three years of its creation it had disappeared, succumbing to drought, prairie fire, hailstorm, and insufficient reserves. Also in 1885, the nearby *Am Olam* settlement of Bethlehem Yehudah perished after an eighteen-month existence, the victim of crop failure and factionalism.[3]

Of the six North Dakota colonies, Painted Woods, established in 1882, was the most substantial. Initially, the colony consisted of twenty-two families each homesteading 160-acre tracts. At its height, 232 colonists plowed and planted wheat, their operations subsidized by the Baron de Hirsch Fund and the Montefiore Agricultural Aid Society. This support, however, proved insufficient as fire, drought, crop failure, and severe winters ravaged the colony. After four years nearly all of the colonists had surrendered to the elements.[4]

Kansas, with seven settlements, was the most active western site of Jewish colonization after the Dakotas. In 1882, the Hebrew Union Agricultural Society placed sixty Russian Jews on 160-acre farms in the Beersheba Colony. The society maintained strict supervision of the project by appointing a manager and placing the settlers on a weekly ration. "The Superintendent of the colony at Beersheba," boasted the *American Israelite*, "has the people completely under control, and they obey the word of command as soldiers; they were at first unruly and self-willed, but by a systematic course they now are tractable and docile."[5] To the chagrin of its patron, Beersheba ceased to exist by 1886. Poor location, marginal soil, parsimonious support, and friction between the colonists and their overseer all contributed to its decline. Even less was accomplished in the Hebron, Montefiore, and Lasker colonies. All organized and funded by the Montefiore Agricultural Aid Society, they suffered from undercapitalization because of their sponsor's overextension. None of these efforts lasted more than four years. Touro, another colony, died within a year of its birth. Little information has survived concerning Kansas's two other Jewish colonies.[6]

The Cotopaxi Colony of Colorado shared a similar abbreviated life. With support from the Hebrew Emigrant Aid Society, thirteen immigrant families (only one with prior farming experience) were settled on government land in the central section of the state. "It was," said an observer, "the poorest place in the world for farming, poor land, lots of rocks and no water."[7] The colony vanished in a year, its members returning to the East or relocating in Denver.[8]

A decade after the colonization surge of the early 1880s, settlement was attempted in Michigan. A group of peddlers, without any agricultural background, sought financial security in farming. They purchased sixteen farms on marginal land that lumber companies had cut and burned over. Begun in 1891, the Palestine Colony experienced difficult times, suffering crop failures in 1893, 1894, and 1897. Yet, the Jews refused to submit, supplementing their meager incomes with peddling and emergency grants from the Baron de Hirsch Fund and the Detroit Jewish community. Only in 1899 did they cease their struggle, unable to support themselves and their families on the soil.[9]

The Arpin Colony in Wisconsin was also situated unwisely upon cutover land, with blackened tree stumps offering an additional obstacle to successful farming. In 1904, the Milwaukee Jewish Agricultural Society obtained 720 acres and installed eight families on farms. By 1906, three more families had joined the project, all receiving five dollars per week from the society. Little favorable news, however, was received from the colony where inexperience, loneliness, and low morale sapped the energy from the effort: "The Russian and Roumanian immigrants who settled in the colony did not care about farming at all and accepted the chance to get on farms only because there was nothing else for them to do."[10] Just three families continued to till the soil at Arpin in 1909.[11]

This brief overview of the Jewish-American colonization effort offers a litany of idiosyncratic causes for failure. Despite much sacrifice and hardship, marginal soil, malaria, hailstorms, floods, prairie fires, inadequate water and fuel supplies, factionalism, high interest rates, inexperience, and low capital reserves prevented the colonies from rooting in American soil. Agricultural societies acted too hastily and with too little foresight when choosing site and settler and estimating project costs. Even the timing of the effort was wrong. In the last quarter of the nineteenth century, the American agrarian sector was in decline, with overproduction, excessive interest and transportation rates, high costs, and low prices forcing foreclosures and an exodus from the countryside to the city. The Back to the Soil movement in America had become an exercise in futility and its goal of social, economic, and geographic diversification of the Jewish population terminated before germination.

Concentration upon the particular or specific, however, disguises as much as it reveals. Patterns highlighting the common features of events can easily be obscured. Moreover, it brings no closer an understanding of why Christian settlements in the United States or Jewish colonies elsewhere operating under similar conditions were able to survive. The short histories presented indicate that colonization failure was not monocausal but the result of an equation comprising five components. Farming experience, environment, capital availability, the existence of options, and morale all played a role in the destinies of the colonies, their values shifting with each case. Thus, Sicily Island's failure, while certainly tied to environment must also be understood in terms of decaying morale and the existence of urban or other colonial options. Capital was available to the Sicily Island Colony and, while important, was less critical in determining its fate than that of less favorably endowed settlements. The negative interaction of all of the variables is apparent in the Beersheba Colony, although internal friction and factionalism clearly give significant weight to the morale factor. Arpin's history, too, should emphasize a lack of will without overlooking the other problems that the colonists confronted. Simple answers to failure such as an absence of water or prairie fire will not suffice. The colonies were complex creations involving the mobilization of diverse people and resources. They require an interpretation both multifaceted and analytical.

The relative success of the Jewish colonization effort in New Jersey was, similarly, a function of the variable interplay. Twenty Jewish colonies dotted the New Jersey landscape with one-half surmounting the obstacles of the initial settlement stages. Among the largest and most significant of these colonies were Alliance, Woodbine, Carmel, and Rosenhayn. Like Jewish colonists in other parts of the United States, these farmers were immigrants coming to the soil with little or no agricultural expertise. Often their small farms were located upon marginal soil which other farmers had avoided as unsuitable for cultivation. Many New Jersey colonists, however, overcame the limitations of inexperience and environment. Economic success was achieved because they received large infusions of financial aid enabling them to build the capital and knowledge base to handle crises and gain stability. Philanthropic societies approached their New Jersey colonization projects as "privately subsidized social experiment[s]."[12] Their "model" farms required patient cultivation, careful weeding, and continuous care: "Those who wished to do things differently lacked the power; a few were expelled as troublemakers. Policy decisions usually came from above."[13] Later, when philanthropic aid and direction decreased, farmers and their families supplemented their income with local factory employment. Success, however, cannot be measured solely with a ledger book. The New Jersey colonies did not remain Jewish endeavors. Within two generations, the colonies had begun to lose their distinctive religious identities. New Jersey's Jewish farmers could not look beyond their own families and farms for a rationale to remain on the land. The close markets of Philadelphia and New York, previously an advantage, now became economic and social magnets attracting Jewish farmers and their children back to the urban world. Self-interest and private need had dictated departure and thus the loss of the colonies' ethnic viability.[14]

The Alliance settlement was representative of these trends in New Jersey Jewish colonization. In 1882, the Hebrew Emigrant Aid Society, with the support of the Alliance Israelite Universelle, purchased 1,200 acres near Philadelphia and placed twenty-five families on fifteen-acre plots. The area was linked to a large urban market by railroad and was spared both flood and drought dangers. To ease the immigrants' transition to agriculture, the society hired a farming instructor, gave each family a monthly stipend, dug wells, built homes, and financed the acquisition of tools and equipment. The following year, cigar and shirt factories were opened to provide additional employment opportunities and income. By 1887, the colony began recording good harvests and a yearly profit. The population had also risen to 529 people. In the 1890s, the Alliance Colony suffered through agricultural depression with the rest of the nation's farmers. Farm prices and profits dropped and foreclosure threatened. In this crisis, the Baron de Hirsch Fund financially salvaged the colony by refinancing mortgage debt, offering farmers longer payment schedules at lower interest. The opening of another local factory further bolstered the colony. By 1905, Alliance was again growing, counting 891 inhabitants. Three years later, it disposed of its colonial and cooperative features and assumed the shape of a community of factories and shops surrounded by private farmers.[15]

Financial security did not ensure ethnic stability. As early as 1919, non-Jewish families comprised one-third of the Alliance population. This demographic shift was also apparent in Rosenhayn where eighty-seven Jewish and seventy-eight Christian families lived and Carmel with sixty-nine Jewish and twenty Christian families. The original Jewish settlers had departed, with Italians and Poles buying land and cultivating farms in the formerly homogeneous colony areas. Between 1901 and 1919, the Jewish population in the colonies had become relatively static. In 1919, only 219 persons of the region's total Jewish population of 2,739 had lived on the land more than fifteen years. The tide, with nothing able to slow it, had turned and America's Jewish farmers left for the city.[16]

III

Those who disparage the Back to the Soil movement in the United States as anachronistic in the modern period or unrealistic because of settler inexperience and inappropriate site selection fail to appreciate that the same factors affected the colonization effort in Palestine. The participants of the First (1882-1903) and Second (1904-1914) *Aliyot* settled in Palestine simultaneously with the Jewish colonization movement in America. The creation of Degania, the first *kibbutz,* preceded Clarion by only two years. Palestine's colonists were Eastern European, born and raised in the *shtetl,* and were as prepared for the fields as their American coreligionists. The environment they encountered was equally hostile—poor soil, a shortage of water, swamps, and insufficient rainfall. An observer described the land as the colonists had encountered it:

> On the slopes the ancient terrace walls were for the most part broken down and destroyed, and the soils have been completely washed away leaving only narrow strips of fertile land lodged in the valleys or low spots. . . . The former forests, dating from biblical times, have disappeared. Now the herds of goats of the Bedouin and the Fellaheen roam over the barren land searching for a leaf or a blade of grass during the long dry summer. Windswept sand dunes along the coast have been blown inland and are filling stream channels. Stream and flood waters were impounded behind the moving dams of sand, which . . . formed vast swamps between the hills and the sea, making the area uninhabitable by the curse of deadly malaria. The centuries of neglect and primitive methods of farming during which erosion had done its destructive work . . . has reduced the production of the land to a minimum.[17]

Despite these restraints, one-quarter million Jews inhabit the land and hundreds of *moshavot* (settlements), *kibbutzim* (collectives), and *moshavim-ovdim* (workers' cooperatives) dot the Israeli landscape. Today, Jews all over the world herald the accomplishments of these farmers and bask in the labor that has brought life to the desert. A Jew in the fields is now taken for granted when but a brief time ago the image was considered unnatural and forced. Few, however, reflect upon an obvious disparity. Why did the Jews succeed in Israel yet fail in America? To interpret this success it is necessary to trace briefly the course of Jewish colonization in Palestine since the late nineteenth century. Again, the centrality of the five variables in directing the course of settlement is readily apparent.

As the massive human flood pushed west from Russia in the 1880s, a small stream trickled south toward Palestine. Approximately 20,000 to 30,000 Jews formed this First *Aliya* fleeing from the pogrom-ravaged Pale.

Like *Am Olam,* the BILU Movement* inspired many of these *chalutzim* (pioneers) with a vision to rebuild Jewish life through agriculture. They would create a Jewish peasantry from which a revitalized nation would arise. By 1898, these men and women had launched twenty-five colonies including Rishon le Zion, Zikhron Ya'akov, Rosh Pinna, and Petach Tikvah, collectively sheltering 5,000 Jewish farmers. The colonies had not rooted easily. Inexperience, a lack of funds, malaria, and Arab harassment had combined in the first years to choke growth. The timely intervention of Paris banker and philanthropist Baron Edmund de Rothschild averted the colonies' collapse. Between 1884 and 1900, he poured £1.5 million into the settlements, purchasing land, livestock, and equipment while providing each family with a weekly wage. Rothschild believed that the colonies would become self-supporting if they directed all activities toward grape growing and wine production, and he dispatched agricultural managers to effect his plan. He not only financed these operations, but bought and marketed the total output. This capital transfusion, while stabilizing the colonies financially, brought dangers of another kind. The colonists became "wards of the Baron," hired hands without power to chart their settlements' futures.[18] The idealism which had stimulated the colonies' creations was now blanketed in apathy and resentment as profit became the only goal. With the loss of the sense of mission, self-reliance and initiative ebbed and gave way to paid Arab labor. The arrogant and contemptuous manner of the colonies' managers made matters even worse. Their postures reflected the baron's claim: "These are my colonies and I shall do what I like with them."[19]

By the end of the nineteenth century, Rothschild had lost patience with the colonies' slow progress toward economic independence. In 1899, the Baron de Hirsch-organized Jewish Colonization Association (ICA) assumed responsibility for the settlements and prodded a shift from viticulture to citrus, grain, and cattle. It also underwrote new settlements based upon the cultivation of field crops. This diversification reduced the colonists' dependence upon a single crop and did much to firm their financial situations. Morale, however, continued to suffer as colonists and managers clashed over procedures and policies.[20]

After twenty-five years of gradual weaning, the colonies had planted themselves permanently. Baron de Rothschild and later the ICA had provided

---

*BILU is the acronym for *Bet Ya'akov Lekhu Venelkha* (O House of Israel, come ye and let us go. Isaiah II:5).

the capital investment to allow the settlers to pass through the traumas of early colonization. By 1910, the colonists had attained a settledness, with fields and groves expertly tended and producing for market. While the colonists were pleased with their material status, they had lost sight of broader national goals. Jewish farmers spiritually bound by the fences enclosing their property indicated the hollowness of purpose pervading the colonies. This privatization of aims had eroded any self-image the colonists may have had that they were in the vanguard of Jewish renewal. It did not, however, lessen the individual's commitment to his colony group nor extinguish the settlement's ethnic identity. In Palestine, unlike the American sites of colonization, Jewish farmers clung together in defense. The hostile population surrounding them tightened their sense of commonality while they bonded culturally and socially. There were, moreover, few alternatives to break the colony circle. The urban centers of Palestine were undeveloped, offering few economic, educational, and emotional inducements to leave the soil. A refashioned morale based upon group loyalty, then, unified and sustained them during which time the city left them unmoved. In a sense, these men and women were trapped in their Jewish enclaves and would maintain their ethnicity and agrarian lifestyle regardless of their intentions.

The *moshavot* had initiated modern Jewish agriculture in Palestine. They would not, however, serve as ideological or practical precursors for the major thrust of Jewish agrarianism. Zionist leaders disparaged these villages as "at a blind alley" because they did not offer a sufficient foundation to erect a national homeland for Jews.[21] After three decades, the twenty-five *moshavot* had lost their idealistic drive, becoming divorced from national goals. Their individualistic message could not kindle the interest or enthusiasm which would attract financial contributors or recruits to the cause. The *moshavot,* while expanding, had been unable to absorb the number of immigrants needed to strengthen the Jewish community in Palestine. In fact, farmers in these settlements, by hiring more tractable Arab laborers and denying Jews jobs and experience, voided Zionist efforts to balance the Jewish social and economic structure through agriculture. Nor had these settlements' growth been adequate to suggest that they were the most effective vehicles to secure a sizable land base to justify a Jewish claim to the country. Thus, to carry forth efforts to accelerate immigration, expand territorial possessions, and reform Jewish society, another solution had to be discovered. Profit, it should be noted, was a minor consideration to Zionist planners in their search for an answer. Financial gain, argued Zionist Arthur Ruppin, had to be subordinated to the higher demands of our national movement. To me the training of workers or . . . the revitalization of a colony . . . are assets of the highest value. . . . I am at a loss to understand how . . . the occupational restratification of the Jews and their transformation from city dwellers into land workers can be decided by consideration of dividends. We might just as sensibly demand that our schools be run at a profit.[22]

Although unplanned, the pragmatic needs of Zionist organizers fused with the ideological dreams and demands of the members of the Second *Aliya*. Beginning in 1904 and ending in 1914, this wave of immigration brought 35,000 to 40,000 Jewish settlers to Palestine. Many were Labor Zionists who sought to build a new Jewish nation in Palestine upon socialist principles. The time for debate and construction of theoretical models had passed. They hoped now to create settlements which drew strength from the ideal: to each according to ability and sharing according to need. In such communities, property would be owned collectively while decisions were made democratically. Theirs would be an egalitarian society where class, background, and sex would be meaningless. Central to their ideology was the concept of self-labor. Jewish sweat and work would effect the resurgence and autonomy necessary to bring forth a nation. Toil alone would bestow legitimacy upon Jewish claims to their land. Firing them even more was their perception that they stood at a crossroad of history and by their actions would decide the Jewish future. The following statement of one settler is representative:

It seemed as if an electric current had passed from generation to generation in our long history and had now reached the point where it must be transformed through us into a source of power and of light. We realized that the time had come to take the destiny of our people into our own hands. . . . Against the decadence of society and the degeneration of Jewish life we set the goal of a New Man and a regenerated Jew. We sought for a vision.[23]

Further bolstering this self-conception was "the great interest manifested by world Jewry and the world Jewish press in this handful of Jews in Palestine, every individual conceived himself to be standing at the focus of public interest, his actions under the constant scrutiny of public opinion."[24] It was this hothouse atmosphere of intense attention and idealism which pushed these Jewish men and women to conquer themselves and their environment.[25]

The impetus to Jewish colonization was regained unexpectedly in 1909. Members of the Second *Aliya* organized a strike at the Kinneret settlement to protest their treatment by colony administrators. They rejected the role of menials and hired hands and requested land, equipment, and self-rule. A compromise was reached allowing the more-experienced workers a tract of land which they would farm collectively. Each worker would be paid a wage and the harvested crop would be shared with the Zionist organization. This first collective, *Kibbutz* Degania, was a success and became the progenitor of hundreds of Jewish settlements. The *kibbutz* fulfilled settlers' needs for independence and self-management, a decent standard of living, and the pursuit of their national aims. Often built in a circular pattern for defense, it cultivated a sense of mutuality and self-reliance. Yet, it did not stifle colonists' idealism or shield them from larger goals. In addition, the *kibbutz* became a crucial Zionist channel for dispersing immigrants, providing farming experience, building an agricultural sector for a Jewish society, and gathering land to the end of state building.[26]

Men and women who sought a cooperative agricultural life, but were unable to accommodate to the *kibbutz* regimen, formed in the 1920s *moshavim-ovdim* or workers' cooperatives. In these communities the central role of the family was recognized and homes and land holdings were privately owned. Still, mutual aid, cooperation, and idealism bound the "family of families."[27] The settlers bought supplies and marketed produce as a unit, jointly cultivated certain crops, and shared large equipment. Self-labor was as much a feature of the *moshavim* as the *kibbutzim*. They, too, would serve as effective tools in carrying forth Zionist dreams.[28]

The *kibbutz* and *moshav* concepts were also conducive to Zionism's limited budget. The *chalutzim* arrived with no resources to begin an agricultural life. Their inexperience amid severe conditions, plus the strategic and geopolitical nature of site selection, meant that the settlements would suffer heavy financial losses in a prolonged period of dependency. Settlement of families on separate farms was not only defensively unwise, but beyond Zionist capabilities. "It was," said Arthur Ruppin, "either group settlement or nothing."[29] A variety of organizations existed to provide the subsidization the colonies could not survive without. The Jewish National Fund (JNF), a subsidiary of the World Zionist Organization, acquired the land which the settlers cultivated. It rented tracts to the colonists on a forty-nine-year renewable contract, retaining ownership in perpetuity in the name of the Jewish people. The JNF also extended credits to aid the work of settlement and the purchase of livestock, equipment, and construction materials. The *Keren Hayesod* (Palestine Foundation Fund) granted extensive loans to facilitate the colonization effort. The Palestine Office, superceded after World War I by the Jewish Agency, coordinated colony development and provided additional funds when necessary. The Anglo-Palestine Bank, the *Histadrut* or General Federation of Jewish Labor, and the *kibbutzim* and *moshavim* federations assisted or continued to support the settlement process.[30]

The Jewish colonies in Palestine and later Israel had found the means to ethnic and eventually economic viability. The capital resources of the Zionist organizations gave settlers the opportunity to gradually loosen the shackles of inexperience and poor site location. Their sense of purpose, and even destiny, sustained them when life was difficult and primitive. Self-selection in the migration process, which led to a Palestine destination rather than the United States, guaranteed a core of men and women hardened in their idealism. Persecution and Arab attack at home combined with aid from abroad to increase their determination. In addition, the *kibbutz* and *moshav* support group, its ideology and aims consistent, stiffened resolve and heightened the level of pain and despair that could be endured. The rural settlements were more than a gathering of people, they were a "union of souls."[31] At the same time, few alternatives were sufficiently attractive to tempt colonists from what had become their raison d'etre. The Jewish farmers had internalized the values and goals of a group and a people.

Thus, the Jewish presence on the land increased. In 1914, there were 44 rural settlements of all kinds in Palestine with a population of nearly 12,000 Jews. Thirteen years later, 110 agricultural outposts with 30,000 persons strengthened the Jewish claim to the land. By 1940, 142,000 Jews lived on the soil in 257 colonies of which 79 were *kibbutzim* and 55 *moshavim*. Rural expansion accelerated after independence in 1948. In 1966, government officials counted 230 *kibbutzim* with 80,700 inhabitants and 265 *moshavim* with a combined population of 124,800. The number of rural settlements continues to grow today, their economic health having improved and life having become easier. New agricultural techniques and greater efficiency have increased Israeli farm output for home and foreign markets. The grafting of an industrial sector to *kibbutz* life has, in addition, generated considerable income. The consumer goods once available only in the city are now plentiful on the farm.[32]

Kibbutz Har exemplifies the successful variable interplay that was common in Israeli settlements. Har's achievements also place it and the relationship between the five factors in bold relief because of its resemblance to the Clarion Colony. Har was built in 1938 on a circular pattern in the upper Galilee near the border with Lebanon. Defensive needs rather than economic considerations determined Har's location, for this *kibbutz* was first a military outpost and second a farming settlement. Fifty kilometers from Haifa, a trip which consumed an entire day, it perched atop a mountain range. The soil, like that in Clarion, was rocky and eroded. Water, too, was scarce and the climate inhospitable to crop raising. In addition, hostile Arab bands harassed the settlers and curtailed the time and area devoted to farming. To complicate the situation further, the forty-nine settlers were without agricultural experience and preoccupied with military duties. Harvests under these conditions produced no profits. Diversification was attempted but cheese making, poultry raising, and cattle breeding were all unsuccessful.[33]

The *kibbutzniks* were able to cling to Har's slope for several reasons. Zionist organizations, determined to maintain Har's strategic vantage point, financed the operation. The settlers received their land from the Jewish National Fund. The Jewish Agency, the *Keren Hayesod,* and *kibbutz* federations supported the acquisition of equipment and supplies. "Kibbutz Har," wrote its historian, "would not have been established or been able to survive without the continuing investment of capital from Zionist *Yishuv* [Jewish community in Palestine] and Diaspora institutions."[34] Moreover, Har's citizens perceived themselves as "bridgehead soldiers" on the front line of Jewish defense.[35] The precarious military situation and a common Labor Zionist ideology bridged early divisions between native Hebrew and foreign-born Yiddish speakers. The difficult existence of the first few years was perceived, moreover, "as a necessary, integral stage in the colonization process."[36] After independence, the colonists solved the problem of financial instability. A factory initially built to produce weapon parts was expanded with government aid into an extensive metalworks operation and yielded considerable income. Har increased its acreage when the Israeli government redistributed land left by fleeing Arab farmers. A state-developed irrigation system, the purchase of farm machinery, and continued assistance from Zionist groups brought success in the agricultural sector of the *kibbutz* economy. Clothing and food consumption increased dramatically. The *kibbutz* even found it necessary to compromise upon the main principle of self-labor and hired workers to carry out its economic activities.[37]

Clarion and the Jewish colonies of the United States now are forgotten or, at most, command attention as sites of historical interest. Their imprint upon Jewish America is faint; they do not touch the present or future. The Jewish road took immigrants to the city and their children have grown comfortable in their urban worlds. The small minority who dared to farm are lost or ridiculed. Only in Israel was a farming alternative considered realistic.

This popular conception seems confirmed, for only there did rural settlements retain their ethnic identities and secure the elusive state of financial well-being.

Yet, the road not taken to Clarion and the other doomed colonies needs to be resurveyed and delineated, as it is an essential part of the Jewish-American experience. These farming Jews sensed and acted upon a loyalty to their coreligionists who remained in the eastern ghettos. They defied stereotypes and risked the familiar to effect a restructuring of Jewish society. The Clarions of America, moreover, are intrinsically valuable as models of courage, determination, and discipline against all odds. Their histories speak not merely of achievements by Jews but of Jewish achievements.

The Jewish-American colonies still offer more than a completed past. In their struggles on the land are revealed the keys to colonization success and failure. These colonies fell victim to a negative interaction of variables — experience, morale, capital, environment, and alternatives. The Clarions of America and the *Kibbutz* Hars of Israel thus represent different ends of the same continuum. Is the future of the Jewish settlements of Israel guaranteed? Changes in the variables can lead to slippage, dispersion, and defeat. Ideological commitment can wither with time and routine. The tasks of those who maintain are less dramatic and inspiring than were the acts of creation. The founders' sense of destiny is difficult to sustain as the settlements mature and the world becomes more complex and diverse. Consumerism and the profit motive suggest compromises which threaten to erode basic principles and introduce insidious distinctions. Alternatives can become increasingly attractive, supplementing the forces fraying the ties that bind the community. What would a weakening of its agricultural backbone portend for the state of Israel? Perhaps the lessons so painfully learned in Clarion and the other Jewish agricultural "failures" may highlight the inherent dangers and suggest a choice of directions.

Men and Women of the Clarion Project

Alexander Aarons*
Joseph and Rosa Aberman
Herse and Sonia Airoff
Harry Alimansky
Samuel Alper
Joseph and May Altman
Joseph and Eda Andrews
Max Augert
Morris and Dora Augert
Nathan and Rachel Ayeroff*
David and Fanie Balner
Samuel and Ella Barak*
Samuel and Ida Barak*
Hyman and Ethel Basow*
Abraham and Fannie Bassin*
Morris and Bessie Bassin*
Harry and Rose Bainish*
Harry and Tillie Benskofsky*
Moses Bergan
David and Sara Bernstein*
Aaron and Rose Binder*
Harry Blinderman
Samuel Blinderman
David and Rae Boyarsky*
Morris and Jenny Bordin

Harry and Rebecca Brazin
Solomon Brookman
Benjamin and Clara Brown*
Nathan and Sonya Brown*
Joseph and Pauline Brownstein*
Philip Bubbis
Joseph and Dora Bushell
Samuel Charniak
Samuel and Fannie Chatsky*
Benjamin Cohen*
David and Sophie Cohen*
Louis Cohen
Morris Cohen
Harry and Golda Cooperman
Hyman Dinerstein*
Jacob Dinerstein
Benjamin Druckerman*
Ike Eisenstein*
Aaron Epstein
Benny Epstein
Ele and Wichna Epstein
Morris Epstein
Samuel and Minnie Falitz
Morris and Martha Farbman*
Louis Feldman

Louis Flax
Louis Fox
Morris Frankel
Joseph Fried*
Julus Fried*
Isaac and Mussie Friedlander*
Abraham Friedman
David Friedman*
Isaac Friedman*
Morris and Bessie Friedman
Samuel Friedman*
Joseph and Gussie Furman*
Alexander and Helen Geronemus
Heyman Gesin
Solomon Glasser
Jacob and Bertha Gold
Harry and Minnie Goldberg
Morris and Rebecca Goldberg
Louis Goldimand
Isaac and Esther Gorin*
Harry Gornish
Max and Jennie Greenberg*
Mendel and Shewkee Greenberg
Samuel and Julia Grishkan*
Julius Grossman*
Louis and Celia Yigdoll Hamburger*
Leo Harrison
Isidor Havelock
Isaac and Anna Herbst*
Philip Hoffman
Abraham Horowitz
Berel Horowitz*
Harris Horowitz*
Morris and Rose Hurwitz*
David and Fannie Isakowitz
Isaac and Annie Isgur*
Joseph Jacoby
Abraham Jaffe
Harry Kagel
Nathan Keston
Morris and Anna Koslovsky
Benjamin Krasnick
Hyman and Sara Kreger*
Samuel and Rebecca Kristol*
Isaac Landman
Max and Celia Lapin*

Samuel Lashoff
Max Lattash*
Joshua and Sarah Lerman
Jacob Lerman
Nathan Lerner
Merdehe Letesheff
Meyer and Sarah Levin*
Louis and Dora Levine*
Samuel and Clara Levitsky*
Israel Libow
Samuel and Rose Lieberman*
Sol Magner
Harry Makler
Moshe and Miriam Malamed*
Sidell Mannes
Samuel Markman
Harry and Rebecca Martin*
Isadore and Sarah Mastrow*
Sol Meinwald
Louis Melnikoff
Louis Miller
Joseph Miller*
Charles and Bessie Misler
Max and Fannie Misler
Samuel and Laya Misler
Harry and Gussie Modell*
Labek Nagreki
Samuel and Ida Nelson
Joseph and Eva Nilva*
Louis Okune
Nathan Ostroff
Barnet and Rachel Pally*
Max and Rose Paul
Morris Paul
Benjamin Pearlstein
Eli Peltz
Meyer and Chalyke Peltz*
Jacob and Bertha Pental*
Hyman and Rebecca Perlman
Isidor Peskin
Solomon Peskin
Ike Pittler*
Barnet Piwawer
Benjamin and Bessie Plonsky
Louis Plonsky
Max Plonsky

Mendel and Anna Plonsky*
Philip and Esther Plonsky*
Morris Pomeranz
Joseph and Esther Radding*
Philip Raiva
David and Rachel Reisky*
Louis Roskin
Jack Rouner
Julius Rozen
Samuel Sack*
Morris Salinger*
Louis Salnikoff
Samuel Sammett
Leon Sandratzky
Bennie Schechter
Isaac Schiff
Abraham Schwartz*
Louis Selenkow
Eli and Jennie Sendrow*
David and Minnie Sharry*
Samuel Shatzkin
Abraham and Rose Shein*
David and Pauline Shein
Julius and Kate Shore*
Joseph Siegel
Louis Sigmund
David Silberman
Samuel Silberman*
Abraham Silverman

Barney Silverman*
Samuel Silverman*
Joseph and Leah Simon
Boris Skraly
Barnet and Fanny Slobodin*
Frank Soble
Barney and Mary Sokolov*
Harry Spivak
Morris Spivak
Solomon and Goldie Sternfeld*
Joseph Swetin*
Bennett and Minnie Towbis*
Harry and Sophie Tucker
Morris Udin*
Harry Wadell
Max and Eva Wald
Eli Weisberg
Joseph Weiss
Morris Weissenberg*
Abraham and Fannie Wernick*
Isidor Wise
Samuel and Jennie Yamnitzky
Charles Yarus
Bessie Yigdoll*†
Harry Yigdoll*
Jacob Yourowsky
Harry Zawatovsky
Jacob Zeidel
Louis Zigman*

---

*Utah Colonist
†*Association membership through her brother*

Classification of Occupations by Status Group

I. *High Nonmanual*
   Accountant/Auditor
   Businessman/Store Owner
   College Student
   Contractor
   Draftsman
   Engineer
   Farm Owner
   Floor Manager
   Inspector
   Manufacturer's Agent
   Pharmacist
   Rabbi
   Teacher

II. *Low Nonmanual*
   Agent
   Auctioneer
   Bank Teller
   Bookkeeper
   Cashier
   Collector
   Dispatcher

   Express Messenger
   Foreman
   Head Waiter
   Huckster/Peddler
   Insurance Salesman
   Office Clerk
   Railway Clerk
   Real Estate Salesman
   Sales Clerk
   Salesman
   Shipping and Receiving Clerk
   Stenographer/Secretary
   Telegraph Messenger

III. *Skilled* (Apprentices in IV,
   Self-employed in I)
   Baker
   Blacksmith
   Boilermaker
   Bookbinder
   Brick and Stone Mason
   Butcher
   Cabinetmaker

Carpenter
Cement and Concrete Finisher
Compositor/Printer
Electrician
Engraver
Fireman (locomotive)
Furrier
Glassblower
Jeweler/Watchmaker
Lithographer
Machinist
Mechanic
Millwright
Painter
Plasterer
Plumber
Roofer
Shoemaker (except factory)
Steamfitter
Tailor
Tinsmith
Tool and Die Maker
Upholsterer
Vulcanizer

IV. *Semiskilled and Service*
Apprentice
Attendant

Barber
Brakeman
Chainman
Chauffeur
Conductor (bus or street railroad)
Cook
Cooper
Deliveryman
Driver (car, bus, truck, or tram)
Dyer
Elevator Operator
Factory Operative
Fireman
Guard, Watchman
Heavy Machine Operator
Janitor
Launderer
Meterman
Repairman
Soldier
Switchman (railroad)
Waiter
Welder

V. *Unskilled*
Gardener
Laborer
Porter

Notes

CHAPTER ONE

1. Isaac M. Rubinow, *Economic Condition of the Jews in Russia*, Bulletin of the Bureau of Labor 15: 488; Samuel Joseph, *Jewish Immigration to the United States from 1881 to 1910*, 54-55; Henry J. Tobias, *The Jewish Bund in Russia: From Its Origins to 1905*, 3-5.

2. Michael Davitt, *Within the Pale: The True Story of Anti-Semitic Persecution in Russia*, 12, 37-39; J. H. Adeney, *The Jews of Eastern Europe*, 20-21; Rubinow, *Economic Condition*, 488-94.

3. Lucy S. Dawidowicz, *The Golden Tradition: Jewish Life and Thought in Eastern Europe*, 378.

4. Ibid., 413.

5. Amos Elon, *The Israelis: Founders and Sons*, 43-46; Mary Antin, *The Promised Land*, 4.

6. Tobias, *Jewish Bund*, 1-3.

7. S. M. Dubnow, *History of the Jews in Russia and Poland*, 1: 343, 405-7; 2: 13-26, 30-41, 61, 110, 144; Salo Baron, *The Russian Jew under Tsars and Soviets*, 22, 29-34; Louis Greenberg, *The Jews in Russia*, 1: 29-30.

8. Dubnow, *History of the Jews*, 1: 343-45; 2: 154-72; Baron, *Russian Jew*, 20-22, 39-42; Greenberg, *The Jews*, 1: 41-43, 74-79, 88-97.

9. Alexis Goldenweiser, "Legal Status of Jews in Russia," in Jacob Frumkin, Gregor Aronson, Alexis Goldenweiser, eds., *Russian Jewry*, 85-119.

10. Ilya Trotsky, "Jews in Russian Schools" in Frumkin, et al., *Russian Jewry*, 409-11; Greenberg, *The Jews*, 1: 83, 117-18; Dawidowicz, *Golden Tradition*, 37; Baron, *Russian Jew*, 118.

11. Quoted in Ezra Mendelsohn, *Class Struggle in the Pale: The Formative Years of the Jewish Workers' Movement in Tsarist Russia*, 13.

12. Gerard Israel, *The Jews in Russia*, 18; Baron, *Russian Jew*, 76; Alan M. Kraut, *The Huddled Masses: The Immigrant in American Society, 1880-1921*, 35-36; Greenberg, *The Jews*, 1: 165; 2: 142; Richard Charques, *The Twilight of Imperial Russia*, 36; Mendelsohn, *Class Struggle*, 7-13, 21-22; Rubinow, *Economic Condition*, 525-27, 536, 543; Nora Levin, *While Messiah Tarried: Jewish Socialist Movements, 1871-1917*, 223-36.

13. Quoted in Maldwyn Jones, *Destination America: 1815-1914*, 170.

14. Rubinow, *Economic Condition*, 502, 520, 528-30, 553-56, 568-70; Mendelsohn, *Class Struggle*, 5-6, 14-15, 29; Tobias, *Jewish Bund*, 5-7, 19; Dawidowicz, *Golden Tradition*, 63; Baron, *Russian Jew*, 94-96, 108.

15. I. M. Dijur, "Jews in the Russian Economy," in Frumkin, et al., *Russian Jewry*, 122-25; Rubinow, *Economic Condition*, 506, 508, 513, 518; Baron, *Russian Jew*, 77-79; U.S. Congress, Senate, *Reports of the Immigration Commission, Emigration Conditions in Europe*, 12: 294-95; Tobias, *Jewish Bund*, 5.

16. Quoted in Elon, *The Israelis*, 49.

17. Greenberg, *The Jews*, 2: 19-23; Israel, *Jews in Russia*, 51; Dawidowicz, *Golden Tradition*, 47; Dubnow, *History of the Jews*, 2: 247-57.

18. Quoted in Greenberg, *The Jews*, 2: 24.

19. Dubnow, *History of the Jews*, 2: 243-46, 261-64, 309-12, 340-41, 349-53, 399-406, 427-28; Greenberg, *The Jews*, 2: 23-34; Baron, *Russian Jew*, 44-47.

20. Quoted in Dubnow, *History of the Jews*, 2: 417.

21. Quoted in Joseph, *Jewish Immigration*, 68.

22. Dawidowicz, *Golden Tradition*, 47-48; Greenberg, *The Jews*, 2: 62, 73, 75; Ernest Schwartz and Johan C. TeVelde, "Jewish Agricultural Settlements in Argentina: The ICA Experiment," *Hispanic American Historical Review*, 19: 186-89; Dubnow, *History of the Jews*, 2: 373, 414-21.

23. Quoted in Walter Laqueur, *A History of Zionism*, 67.

24. Greenberg, *The Jews*, 2: 55-58; Levin, *While Messiah Tarried*, 55-61.

25. Gershon Swet, "Russian Jews in Zionism and the Building of Palestine," in Frumkin, et al., *Russian Jewry*, 172-208; Baron, *Russian Jew*, 144-46; Dawidowicz, *Golden Tradition*, 52-54. For more on Zionism see Laqueur, *History of Zionism* and Arthur Hertzberg, ed., *The Zionist Idea: A Historical Analysis and Reader*.

26. Dubnow, *History of the Jews*, 3: 143-45; Levin, *While Messiah Tarried*, 141; Tobias, *Jewish Bund*, 17.

27. Quoted in Mendelsohn, *Class Struggle*, 1.

28. Koppel S. Pinson, "Arkady Kremer, Vladmir Medem, and the Ideology of the Jewish 'Bund'," *Jewish Social Studies*, 7: 233-45, 248-55; Tobias, *Jewish Bund*, 13-15, 50-55, 84, 98-100, 107-9, 161-64, 166, 239, 339-43; Baron, *Russian Jew*, 140-41; Greenberg, *The Jews*, 2: 146-47; Levin, *While Messiah Tarried*, 258-59; Esther Radding, "Journal," 70-71. For pre-Bund Jewish radicalism in Russia, see Mendelsohn, *Class Struggle*.

29. Interview with Al, Joseph, and Samuel Ayeroff, Los Angeles, March 23, 1982.

30. Tobias, *Jewish Bund*, 239; Ayeroff brothers interview.

31. Personal letter, Abraham Bassin, July 28, 1982.

32. Interview with Alex Bassin, Salt Lake City, June 30, 1982; Personal letter, Yetta Bassin Farber, May 3, 1982; Interview with Albert Isgur, Los Angeles, March 22, 1982; Personal letter, Judith Cohen Brodkin, January 8, 1982; Personal letter, Eugene Radding, June 7, 1981; Personal letter, Sarah Sack Bober, August 12, 1982.

33. Pinson, "Arkady Kremer," 259-60; Tobias, *Jewish Bund*, 127, 164, 172-75, 340.

34. Tobias, *Jewish Bund*, 239; C. Bezalel Sherman, "The Beginnings of Labor Zionism in the United States," in Isidore Meyer, ed., *Early History of Zionism in America*, 275-79; Levin, *While Messiah Tarried*, 139-40; Greenberg, *The Jews*, 2: 157-58; Itzchak Ben-Zvi, "Labor Zionism in Russia" in Frumkin, et al., *Russian Jewry*, 209-18; Laqueur, *History of Zionism*, 270-337; Hertzberg, *Zionist Idea*, 329-

96; Interview with Mina Boyarsky Michaelson, Los Angeles, March 26, 1982; Interview with Sivan Hamburger, Los Angeles, March 23, 1982; Interview with Daniel Malamed, Los Angeles, March 22, 1982; Interview with Theresa Herbst Weisberg, Los Angeles, March 24, 1982; Personal letter, Saul Farbman, August 30, 1982; Personal letter, Leon Sternfeld, March 15, 1982; Personal letter, Alice Furman Woll, April 25, 1982; Personal letter, Raymond Sokolov, October 18, 1982.

35. Quoted in Dubnow, *History of the Jews,* 3: 10.

36. Dawidowicz, *Golden Tradition,* 50; Dubnow, *History of the Jews,* 3: 7-10, 14-15, 21, 26-27; Baron, *Russian Jew,* 53-54; Greenberg, *The Jews,* 2: 84-85.

37. Dubnow, *History of the Jews,* 3: 68-75; Baron, *Russian Jew,* 57-61; Greenberg, *The Jews,* 2: 50-52; Davitt, *Within the Pale,* 91-102; Israel, *The Jews in Russia,* 64-67; Kraut, *Huddled Masses,* 38; "From Kishineff to Bialystok: A Table of Pogroms from 1903 to 1906," *American Jewish Year Book,* 6: 34-89.

38. Maurice Warshaw, *Life More Sweet than Bitter,* 26.

39. Ibid., 31.

40. Radding, "Journal," 76.

41. "Table of Pogroms," 34-89; Israel, *The Jews in Russia,* 82-87.

42. Quoted in Tobias, *Jewish Bund,* 249.

43. Ibid., 222.

44. Hamburger interview; Radding, "Journal," 83; "Table of Pogroms," 34-89. Dates of migration were obtained from "Declaration of Intention to Become a Citizen" papers in Utah State Board of Land Commissioners, "Private Sales Files," 2343, 3271, 2317.

45. Greenberg, *The Jews,* 2: 76-81; Personal letter, Judith Cohen Brodkin, January 8, 1982; Personal letter, Alice Furman Woll, April 23, 1982; Personal letter, Leon Sternfeld, March 15, 1982.

46. Bassin interview; Interview with Samuel Chatsky by Ronald N. Goldberg, Miami, Florida, May 18, 1982; Ayeroff brothers interview; Personal letter, Sylvia Grishkam Flinker, March 23, 1983.

47. Mary Antin, *From Plotzk to Boston,* 11-12.

48. Warshaw, *Life,* 50.

49. Malamed interview.

50. Ailon Shiloh, ed., *By Myself I'm a Book!: An Oral History of the Immigrant Jewish Experience in Pittsburgh,* 16-18; Rubinow, *Economic Condition,* 504; Joseph, *Jewish Immigration,* 93, 94, 103, 140-41; U.S. Congress, Senate, *Reports of the Immigration Commission, Abstracts of Reports,* 1: 171, 173; *Emigration Conditions in Europe,* 12: 240; Bernard D. Weinryb, "Jewish Immigration and Accommodation to America: Research, Trends, Problems," *Publications of the American Jewish Historical Society,* 46: 391. Dates of migration were determined from family histories, "Declaration of Intention to Become a Citizen" and Naturalization Papers in Utah State Board of Land Commissioners Records, and U.S. Department of Commerce, Bureau of the Census, "Thirteenth Census of the United States" (Manuscript), 1910. See below, Chapter Two, note 76, for age data.

51. U.S. Department of Commerce and Labor, *Special Consular Reports,* "Emigration to the United States," 30: 106.

52. Warshaw, *Life,* 44-46; Interview with William Brownie and Edith Brownstein Horowitz, Philadelphia, October 30, 1983; Interview with Alex Pally, Ogden, Utah, March 7, 1982; Isgur interview; Personal letter, Ben Kristol, May 12, 1982; Interview with Reeta Silverman Shprintz, Philadelphia, November 1, 1983; Interview with Maia Gregory, New York City, October 24, 1983.

53. Pamela S. Nadell, "The Journey to America by Steam: The Jews of Eastern Europe in Transition," *American Jewish History*, 71: 269-72; Mark Wischnitzer, *To Dwell in Safety: The Story of the Jewish Migration Since 1800*, 68, 113-15; Howe, *World of Our Fathers*, 29-39; Personal letter, Belle Plonsky Rapkin to Benjamin Paul, May 19, 1976; Personal letter, Max Payne to Benjamin Paul, June 17, 1982; Personal letter, Stella Krieger Rosen, September 22, 1982; Shprintz interview; Personal letter, Alice Furman Woll, April 25, 1982. The Plonskys, like David Ben-Gurion and several other Labor Zionists, came from the *shtetl* of Plonsk.

54. *Immigration Commission Reports*, 1: 197; 12: 80-101; Jones, *Destination America*, 44-46; Biographical information from "Declaration of Intention to Become a Citizen" and naturalization papers provided by Sylvia Grishkam Flinker, Sara Binder Steinberg, and Beryl Levitsky Rosenstock.

55. U.S. Congress, Senate, *Reports of the Immigration Commission, Steerage Conditions*, 37: 23.

56. Edward Steiner, *On the Trail of the Immigrant*, 40-41.

57. William A. Heaps, *The Story of Ellis Island*, 24-26, 35-47; David Brownstone, Irene M. Franck, and Douglas L. Brownstone, *Island of Hope, Island of Tears*, 118-30; Warshaw, *Life*, 53-55; Nadell, "Journey to America," 274-78; Kraut, *Huddled Masses*, 49; *Immigration Commission Reports*, 37: 6-12.

58. Jones, *Destination America*, 54-57; Kraut, *Huddled Masses*, 53; Edward Corsi, *In the Shadow of Liberty: The Chronicle of Ellis Island*, 59; Boris D. Bogen, *Jewish Philanthropy: An Exposition of Principles and Methods of Jewish Social Service in the United States*, 91, 96, 98-99.

59. Heaps, *Story of Ellis Island*, 60-71, 74-94; Jones, *Destination America*, 59-64; Brownstone, et al., *Island of Hope*, 153-57; Howe, *World of Our Fathers*, 42-46; Isgur interview; Joseph, *Jewish Immigration*, 195; Ann Novotny, *Strangers at the Door*, 15-19; Miriam Blaustein, ed., *Memoirs of David Blaustein*, 129-30.

CHAPTER TWO

1. Moses Rischin, *The Promised City: New York's Jews, 1870-1914*, 80; Thomas Kessner, *The Golden Door: Italian and Jewish Immigrant Mobility in New York City, 1880-1915*, 155; Edward E. Pratt, *Industrial Causes of Congestion of Population in New York City* (New York, 1911), 34-36; Jeffrey S. Gurock, *When Harlem was Jewish, 1870-1930*, 28-36; Charles S. Bernheimer, ed., *The Russian Jew in the United States*, 43-44. See also, Howe, *World of Our Fathers* and Ronald Sanders, *The Downtown Jews: Portraits of an Immigrant Generation*.

2. 1910 U.S. Manuscript Census.

3. Quoted in Deborah Dwork, "Health Conditions of Immigrant Jews on the Lower East Side of New York: 1880-1914," *Medical History*, 25: 5.

4. Quoted in Abraham J. Karp, *Golden Door to America: The Jewish Immigrant Experience*, 127.

5. Quoted in Rischin, *Promised City*, 84.

6. Robert W. DeForest and Lawrence Veiller, eds., *The Tenement House Problem*, 1: 13.

7. Dwork, "Health Conditions," 8, 10; Roy Lubove, *The Progressives and the Slums: Tenement House Reform in New York City, 1890-1917*, 31, 133-34; Bernheimer, *Russian Jew*, 284-85; Karp, *Golden Door*, 126-27; Rischin, *Promised City*, 82-85; Kraut, *Huddled Masses*, 71; U.S. Industrial Commission, *Reports of the Industrial Commission on Immigration and on Education*, 15: 484-88; New York City, *Tenement House Department, First Report*, 1: 5 (quote), 61-62, 71, 88-89.

8. Quoted in Rischin, *Promised City,* 79.

9. U.S. Congress, Senate, *Reports of the Immigration Commission, Abstracts,* 1: 748, 750; *Immigrants in Cities,* 26: 69, 85, 92, 185, 198; Dwork, "Health Conditions," 8; New York City, Commission on Congestion of Population, *Report,* 6; Kessner, *Golden Door,* 132; Pratt, *Industrial Causes,* 35; Rischin, *Promised City,* 79, DeForest and Veillers, *Tenement House Problem,* 199-204, 217.

10. Maxwell Whiteman, "Philadelphia's Jewish Neighborhoods," in Allen F. Davis and Mark H. Haller, *The Peoples of Philadelphia: A History of Ethnic Groups and Lower Class Life, 1790-1940,* 237-48; Bernheimer, *Russian Jew,* 51-53, 271, 304-7; DeForest and Veillers, *Tenement House Problem,* 134; Lubove, *Progressives and the Slums,* 141. See also, Murray Friedman, ed., *Jewish Life in Philadelphia, 1830-1940.*

11. Rischin, *Promised City,* 61; Kessner, *Golden Door,* 37; Kraut, *Huddled Masses,* 81-82; Bernheimer, *Russian Jew,* 122-24.

12. Dwork, "Health Conditions," 14-15; Bernheimer, *Russian Jew,* 125; Rischin, *Promised City,* 66.

13. Quoted in Karp, *Golden Door,* 168.

14. Pratt, *Industrial Causes,* 119, Appendix II, Tables 1 and 2; U.S. Congress, Senate, *Reports of the Immigration Commission, Immigrants in Industries, Part 6: Clothing Manufacturing,* 11: 383; *Abstracts,* 1: 305, 415, 423; Dwork, "Health Conditions," 22; Interview with Louis Levit by Beryl and Jeffrey Rosenstock, Philadelphia, January 23, 30, 1983.

15. Pauline Newman, "The Rise of the Woman Garment Worker, New York, 1909-10," in Barbara Wertheimer, ed., *We Were There: The Story of Working Women in America,* 294-97; Novotny, *Strangers at the Door,* 141; Quoted in Howe, *World of Our Fathers,* 156.

16. Newman, "Rise of the Woman Garment Worker," 301-2.

17. Ibid., 300-302, 309-10; Kraut, *Huddled Masses,* 94; Karp, *Golden Door,* 165-67; Sanders, *Downtown Jews,* 393-95. For more on working conditions, see New York State, Factory Investigating Commission, *Preliminary Report, 1912,* 1.

18. *Preliminary Report,* 217-18.

19. Dwork, "Health Conditions," 19, 20-22, 25.

20. Levit interview by Rosenstocks.

21. Radding, "Journal," 107.

22. Levit interview by Rosenstocks; Personal letter, Benjamin Paul, February 28, 1982; Personal letter, Beckie Mastrow Pullman, June 29, 1982; Hamburger interview; Radding, "Journal," 107; Interview with Michael Bernstein, Scarsdale, New York, July 28, 1982; Warshaw, *Life,* 79, 95; 1910 U.S. Manuscript Census.

23. Isaac Friedlander, *Virgin Soil,* trans. by Louis C. Zucker, 8.

24. Howe, *World of Our Fathers,* 77-80, 159-68.

25. Quoted in Karp, *Golden Door,* 122-26.

26. Kessner, *Golden Door,* 165, 172, 173. For an in-depth discussion of Jewish and immigrant mobility, see Stephen Thernstrom, *The Other Bostonians: Poverty and Progress in the American Metropolis, 1880-1970,* 135-44, 145-56, 164-65.

27. Howe, *World of Our Fathers,* 183-89; Rischin, *Promised City,* 85, 171-94, 195-209; Kessner, *Golden Door,* 155.

28. Howe, *World of Our Fathers,* 287-324, 357. See also Ira Kipnis, *The American Socialist Movement, 1897-1912;* Arthur Liebman, *Jews and the Left;* David A. Shannon, *The Socialist Party of America.*

29. *Jewish Exponent,* July 5, 1889.

30. Gabriel Davidson, "The Jew in Agriculture in the United States," *American Jewish Year Book*, 37: 134; *Jewish Exponent*, October 1, 1909; Uri D. Herscher, *Jewish Agricultural Utopias in America, 1880-1910*, 23-24; Richard Singer, "The American Jew in Agriculture: Past History and Present Condition," 7-14. Interestingly, Alessandro Mastrovalerio, editor of *La Tribuana Italiana Transatlantica* advocated a similar course for Italian immigrants: "The only means to rebuild the reputation of the Italo-American in general, is the plow." Quoted in Kessner, *Golden Door*, 17.

31. Quoted in Zosa Szajkowski, "The Attitude of American Jews to East European Jewish Immigration, 1881-1893," *Publications of the American Jewish Historical Society*, 40: 226.

32. Ibid., 227.

33. Howe, *World of Our Fathers*, 33; Joseph Brandes, *Immigrants to Freedom: Jewish Communities in Rural New Jersey Since 1882*, 6-7; Quoted in Jones, *Destination America*, 172.

34. Boris Bogen, *Born a Jew*, 70.

35. Wischnitzer, *To Dwell in Safety*, 120-26; Szajkowski, "Attitudes of American Jews," 236-37; Rischin, *Promised City*, 54; The Jewish Agricultural and Industrial Aid Society, *Annual Report*, 1909, 8-10; 1912, 9-10; 1913, 23; 1914, 18. See also, Samuel Joseph, *History of the Baron De Hirsch Fund: The Americanization of the Jewish Immigrant*.

36. Rabbi Joseph Krauskopf, "The Problem of the Ghetto: Not Congestion but Colonization," *Sunday Discourses Before the Reform Congregation Keneseth Israel*, 1903-04, 17: 75.

37. Rabbi Joseph Krauskopf, "What to Do with the Russian Refugee," *Sunday Discourses*, 1905-06, 19: 52.

38. Abraham J. Feldman, "Rabbi Joseph Krauskopf: A Biographical Sketch," *American Jewish Year Book*, 26: 421-22, 441-42; William W. Blood, *Apostle of Reason: A Biography of Joseph Krauskopf*, 7-38, 69-77, 81-89; John F. Sutherland, "Rabbi Joseph Krauskopf of Philadelphia: The Urban Reformer Returns to the Land," *American Jewish Historical Quarterly*, 67: 342, 350-56; Herbert D. Allman, *A Unique Institution: The Story of the National Farm School*, 9, 160-61.

39. Quoted in Abraham Menes, "The Am Oylom Movement," in Joshua A. Fishman, ed., *Studies in Modern Jewish Social History*, 163.

40. Menes, "Am Oylom Movement," 155-62, 171, 178; Helen E. Blumenthal, "The New Odessa Colony of Oregon, 1882-1886," *Western States Jewish Historical Quarterly*, 14: 321-26; Wischnitzer, *To Dwell in Safety*, 61-63; Herscher, *Jewish Agricultural Utopias*, 37-48; Howe, *World of Our Fathers*, 86-87; Levin, *While Messiah Tarried*, 47-50; *Jews in American Agriculture*, 23-25.

41. Quoted in Brandes, *Immigrants to Freedom*, 316.

42. Howe, *World of Our Fathers*, 504-7; Melech Epstein, *Profiles of Eleven*, 298-312; Levin, *While Messiah Tarried*, 176-79; Interview with Nathan Ayeroff by Edward Eisen, Los Angeles, 1972.

43. For a discussion of the American colonies and the Back to the Soil movement see below, Chapter Six.

44. Bernstein interview.

45. *Jews in American Agriculture*, 37; Jewish Agricultural and Industrial Aid Society, *Annual Report*, 1912, 42-43; Bernstein interview; Yaffa Draznin, *It Began with Zade Usher: The History and Record of the Families Bernstein-Loyev, Lewis-*

Mazur, 204-5; Chatsky interview; Hamburger interview; Personal letter, Abraham Bassin, September 6, 1983; Personal letter, Joan Holt, February 17, 1983.

46. *Jewish Exponent,* September 3, 1909.

47. Interview with Lillian Brown Vogel, Los Angeles, June 17, 1983; Interview with Sarah Brown, Phoenix, by Michael and Patricia Walton, November 6, 1982; Benjamin Brown to Rabbi Joseph Krauskopf, July 23, 1907; Krauskopf to Brown, August 12, 1907; Brown to Krauskopf, October 22, 1907, April 22, 1908, Box 1, Rabbi Joseph Krauskopf Papers; *Jewish Exponent,* March 27, 1908; Personal letter Robert Swope to Louis C. Zucker, August 8, 1978.

48. Benjamin Brown, "Far Vus Nit Mir?" ("Why Not We?"), letter in the correspondence section, *Das Naye Lebn* (April 1909), 308.

49. Benjamin Brown, "Memoirs," trans. by Sarah Brown, 1-2.

50. Vogel interview.

51. Interview with Barney Silverman by Ben Kristol, Philadelphia, September 1965.

52. Vogel interview.

53. Vogel interview; Chatsky interview; Interview with Beckie Mastrow Pullman, Glendale, California, June 17, 1982; Radding, "Journal," 161.

54. Brown, "Memoirs," 1.

55. Ibid., 2.

56. Personal letter, Ben Kristol, May 28, 1982; Brown, "Memoirs," 1-2; Barney Silverman, "A Short History of Clarion," 3-5.

57. Silverman interview; Silverman, "Short History," 7.

58. Silverman, "Short History," 17.

59. Friedlander, *Virgin Soil,* 4-5; Silverman, "Short History," 17-18.

60. Personal letter, Paul Lane, April 2, 1982.

61. Silverman, "Short History," 13.

62. Silverman interview.

63. Weisberg interview; Silverman, "Short History," 1-3, 10-12, 14-16; 1910 U.S. Manuscript Census; Shprintz interview; Interview with Steven Davidson, Salt Lake City, April 14, 1982.

64. Silverman interview.

65. Silverman, "Short History," 8-9; Abraham Wernick, "The Clarion Colony: Its Beginnings, Its Life, Its Demise," trans. by Max Rosenfeld, 11-12; Sanpete County, Utah, "Deed of Trust," Book 59, 1912, 123-24.

66. Detailed family histories were compiled for fifty-eight members and revealed the relationships between participants. Political and organizational ties were also ascertained from these histories. Silverman, "Short History," 19-20, 26-30; *Jewish Exponent,* March 3, 1911.

67. Radding, "Journal," 157.

68. Ibid., 126.

69. Ibid., 118-29, 138, 158; Michaelson interview; Isgur interview; Hamburger interview; Clarion biographical data.

70. Interview with Barnet Slobodin by Joseph Slobodin, New York City, August 25, 1974.

71. Pullman interview.

72. Wernick, "Clarion Colony," 7.

73. Ayeroff interview.

74. Silverman interview.

75. Wernick, "Clarion Colony," 6-8; Slobodin interview; Pullman interview; Interview with Louis Levit by Ben Kristol, Merion, Pennsylvania, September 3, 1965; Personal letter, Joseph Levitsky, October 14, 1982; 1910 U.S. Manuscript Census; Brownie and Horowitz interview by author; Personal letter, Abraham Bassin, September 6, 1982; Isgur interview; Gregory interview; Ayeroff interview; Silverman "Short History," 20.

76. Residential and age data were collected from family histories, 1910 U.S. Manuscript Census, "Declaration to Become a Citizen" and Naturalization Papers in Utah State Board of Land Commissioners Records, and city directories. Directories used were: *Baltimore City Directory,* 1910; *Upington's General Directory of the Borough of Brooklyn,* 86: 1909; *New York City Directory,* 1912-13; *Trow's General Directory of the Boroughs of Manhattan and Bronx, City of New York,* 123: 1910; *Boyd's Philadelphia City Directory,* 1908-11.

77. Marital and family data were gathered from family histories, 1910 U.S. Manuscript Census, and Sanpete County, Utah, "Deed of Trust."

78. Occupations given are those related in family histories or listed in 1910 U.S. Manuscript Census and city directories. The socioeconomic classification of occupations employed in this study is a modification of the rankings made by Alba M. Edwards in *A Social-Economic Grouping of the Gainful Workers of the United States: 1930.* Other sources helpful in formulating the occupational classification scheme were Peter Blau and Otis Dudley Duncan, *The American Occupational Structure;* George S. Counts, "The Social Status of Occupations: A Problem in Vocational Guidance," *School Review,* 33: 16-27; Albert J. Reiss, Jr., *Occupations and Social Status;* and Thernstrom, *Other Bostonians.* See Appendix B for a breakdown of status groups by occupation.

CHAPTER THREE

1. Moshe Malamed, "Diary, 1910-1913," trans. by Adah B. Fogel, 3.

2. Malamed, "Diary," 3-4; *Jewish Exponent,* April 7, 1911; Wernick, "Clarion Colony," 14.

3. Silverman, "Short History," 21-24; Silverman interview by Kristol.

4. Silverman interview.

5. Brown, "Memoirs," 6; Silverman, "Short History," 21; *Jewish Exponent,* September 15, 1911; *Salt Lake City Directory,* 1910; "In re Clarion Colony, Utah," 2, Ben Roe Papers, Special Collections, Marriott Library, University of Utah; Hynda Rudd, "Samuel Newhouse: Utah Mining Magnate and Land Developer," *Western States Jewish Historical Quarterly,* 11: 295-99.

6. Everett L. Cooley, "Clarion, Utah – Jewish Colony in 'Zion'," *Gunnison Valley News,* March 12, 1970.

7. Silverman, "Short History," 34.

8. Ibid., 35.

9. *First Successful Jewish Colony in the United States,* 3.

10. Silverman interview.

11. Silverman, "Short History," 34-36; *First Successful Jewish Colony,* 5; Utah State Board of Land Commissioners, "Private Sales Files," 16434-16586; Chatsky interview.

12. Wernick, "Clarion Colony," 15.

13. *Manti Messenger,* January 13, 1911.

14. Brown, "Memoirs," 7.

15. Silverman, "Short History," 34-36; Wernick, "Clarion Colony," 15-16; Brown, "Memoirs," 6-7; Utah National Bank to William J. Lynch, September 2, 1911; Lynch to Benjamin Brown, October 25, 1911; Brown to Lynch, October 30, 1911; Utah State Board of Land Commissioners, Piute Project Correspondence, 1908-1916; *Gunnison Gazette,* August 11, 1911; *Manti Messenger,* August 11, 1911.

16. Wernick, "Clarion Colony," 17-19.

17. Utah State Board of Land Commissioners, "Minute Book," 12, April 4, 1911-March 14, 1913: 205.

18. Slobodin interview.

19. Cooley, "Clarion," *Gunnison Valley News;* Utah State Bureau of Immigration, Labor and Statistics, *Second Biennial Report,* 1913-1914, 27-28; Conrad Frischknecht to Everett L. Cooley, October 3, 1960; Everett Cooley Papers, Special Collections, Marriott Library, University of Utah; C. J. Ullrich, "Report on the Water Supply – Piute Project"; *Gunnison Gazette,* October 14, 1910; Interview with Carl Carpenter, Clarion, May 15, 1982; Interview with Lamont Nielsen, Clarion, June 26, 1982.

20. Silverman, "Short History," 37-38; Wernick, "Clarion Colony," 19-25; *American Jewish Yearbook,* 1912-1913, 155, 179; Brown, "Memoirs," 9.

21. *Gunnison Gazette,* September 1, 1911.

22. U.S. Bureau of the Census, *Thirteenth Census of the United States, 1910; Abstract of the Census with Supplement for Utah,* 575, 590; *Gunnison Gazette,* January 21, April 22, 29, 1910; March 31, 1911; U.S. Bureau of the Census, *Census of Religious Bodies: 1916,* 2: 331.

23. *Gunnison Gazette,* July 1, 1910.

24. *Gunnison Gazette,* January 28, April 1, 8, July 1, November 11, 1910; January 18, June 30, October 6, 1911; *Manti Messenger,* June 30, 1911; Utah State Bureau of Immigration, *Second Biennial Report,* 382-83.

25. Silverman, "Short History," 40.

26. Ibid., 42.

27. Interview with Harry Kimura, Clarion, September 20, 1983.

28. Silverman, "Short History," 44.

29. Silverman, "Short History," 42-44; Chatsky interview; Brownie and Horowitz interview by author; Interview with Allen Frandsen, Clarion, September 20, 1983; Silverman interview; U.S. Department of Agriculture, *Soil Survey of Sanpete Valley Area, Utah,* 1981, 76-77, 80-81.

30. W. Preston Thomas, George T. Blanch, and Edith Haybill, *A Study of Farm Organization by Type of Farm in Sanpete and Sevier Counties,* 9.

31. Friedlander, *Virgin Soil,* 14.

32. *Soil Survey,* 174; Frandsen interview; Utah State Bureau of Immigration, *Second Biennial Report,* 186.

33. National Farm School, *Circular of Information,* 1910-1912, 15.

34. Brown, "Memoirs," 9-10; Wernick, "Clarion Colony," 17-19, 26; Warshaw, *Life,* 108; Interview with Osin Hendrickson, Gunnison, June 26, 1982; Interview with Dean May, Salt Lake City, March 14, 1984; Silverman, "Short History," 41, 45-46; *Gunnison Gazette,* September 15, 1911; Ayeroff interview.

35. Rabbi Charles J. Freund, "Significance of the Jewish Farm Colony at Clarion, Utah," *Improvement Era,* 16: 250.

36. *Jewish Exponent,* September 15, 1911.

37. Ibid.

38. Wernick, "Clarion Colony," 26-28; *Jewish Exponent,* September 15, 1911.

39. Silverman, "Short History," 49.

40. Ibid.

41. Wernick, "Clarion Colony," 37-38; Silverman, "Short History," 49.

42. Friedlander, *Virgin Soil,* 9.

43. Silverman, "Short History," 52.

44. Friedlander, *Virgin Soil,* 13-14.

45. George Reynolds, *Are We of Israel?,* 13.

46. Quoted in Arnold H. Green, "A Survey of Latter-day Saint Proselyting Efforts to the Jewish People," 12.

47. Michael Walton, "The House of Israel in Mormon Theology," 1-3; Green, "Proselyting Efforts," 10-12; Ezra Taft Benson, *A Message to Judah from Joseph,* 6-15; Jan Shipps, "In the Presence of the Past: Continuity and Change in Twentieth Century Mormonism," in Thomas G. Alexander and Jessie L. Embry, eds., *After 150 Years: The Latter-day Saints in Sesquicentennial Perspective,* 27; LeGrand Richards, *The Mormons and the Jewish People,* 2, 7-9. See also Rudolf Glanz, *Jew and Mormon: Historic Group Relations and Religious Outlook.*

48. Benson, *Message,* 3; Shipps, "Presence of the Past," 19, 27; Glanz, *Jew and Mormon,* 110, 116, 130; Leon L. Watters, *The Pioneer Jews of Utah,* Studies in American Jewish History, 2: 11.

49. 3 Nephi 20:29.

50. Green, "Proselyting Efforts," 16.

51. Glanz, *Jew and Mormon,* 116.

52. Green, "Proselyting Efforts," 14-16, 20, 22-23, 28; Richards, *Mormons and the Jewish People,* 16; Glanz, *Jew and Mormon,* 45-47, 79, 103.

53. Ayeroff interview.

54. Friedlander, *Virgin Soil,* 20.

55. *Gunnison Gazette,* February 16, 1912.

56. *First Successful Jewish Colony,* 13.

57. Friedlander, *Virgin Soil,* 19.

58. *Gunnison Gazette,* September 1, 1911.

59. Watters, *Pioneer Jews,* 68, 91; Brownie and Horowitz interview by author; Silverman, "Short History," 53-54; Vogel interview; Chatsky interview; Hamburger interview; Levit interview by Kristol; Malamed interview; *Gunnison Gazette,* January 12, 1912, July 11, 25, 1913; *First Successful Jewish Colony,* 12-13; Rabbi Charles J. Freund to Isaac Landman, October 11, 1912, Box 9, Krauskopf Papers; Redmond First Ward, Salina Stake, "Minutes of Meetings," June 15, 1913; Gunnison Ward, "Minutes of Meetings," July 20, 1912.

60. *Tageblatt,* August 4, 1912.

61. Lieberman interview.

62. Chatsky interview; Lieberman interview; Nielsen interview; Hendrickson interview; Silverman interview.

63. Friedlander, *Virgin Soil,* 10.

64. Silverman, "Short History," 53.

65. *First Successful Jewish Colony,* 16.

66. Friedlander, *Virgin Soil,* 11, 14; Malamed, "Diary," 5-7; Silverman "Short History," 50; Jewish Agricultural and Colonial Association, "Articles of Incorporation," November 28, 1911; Incorporation Record, Sanpete County, Utah, Book Two, 431-39; *Gunnison Gazette,* March 29, 1912.

67. Malamed, "Diary," 7.

68. Silverman, "Short History," 56-56A; Malamed, "Diary," 6-8; Wernick, "Clarion Colony," 32, 36, 38.

69. Silverman, "Short History," 56A-57; *Jewish Exponent,* February 9, March 8, 1912; Friedlander, *Virgin Soil,* 24; Malamed, "Diary," 12; *First Successful Jewish Colony,* 5-6; Wernick, "Clarion Colony," 39, 42, 46 (quote), 47, 51.

70. Silverman, "Short History," 79.

71. Wernick, "Clarion Colony," 43, 52-55, 72; Silverman, "Short History," 77-80.

72. Ayeroff interview.

73. Hendrickson interview; Nielsen interview; Cooley, "Clarion," March 12, 19, 1970.

74. E. A. Crowley to State Board of Land Commissioners, June 15, 1912, in Utah State Board of Land Commissioners, "Minute Book," 12, June 18, 1912: 579.

75. Benjamin Brown to W. D. Candland, May 20, 1912, in "Minute Book," 12, May 22, 1912: 522.

76. Brown to Candland, June 13, 1912, in "Minute Book," 12, June 18, 1912: 579.

77. "Affidavit of Anton Jensen," August 24, 1912, in Board of Land Commissioners, Piute Project Correspondence.

78. Hendrickson interview; Board of Land Commissioners, "Minute Book," 12, May 22, 1912; 522; June 18, 1912, 577-78; Will C. Barnes, "A Miracle-Worker in the Desert," *Breeder's Gazette,* 137; *Gunnison Gazette,* July 5, 1912; Silverman, "Short History," 58; "Jensen Affidavit"; "Petition for Reimbursement," August 21, 1912, in Board of Land Commissioners, Piute Project Correspondence.

79. Henrickson interview.

80. Silverman interview; Nielsen interview; Frandsen interview; Silverman, "Short History," 58.

81. Reform and Orthodox Judaism represent two of the three major groupings of American Jews. Reform Jews, while seeking to preserve their religious identities, have attempted to liberalize Judaism's beliefs and rituals and eliminate those elements which seem anachronistic in modern times. The Orthodox are more traditional in their beliefs and ceremonies, preferring to remain faithful to the religious practices of their fathers. Conservative Judaism, the third branch, occupies a middle ground between the Reform and the Orthodox.

82. Silverman, "Short History," 83-85; Utah Colonization Fund, "Articles of Incorporation," June 11, 1912, Salt Lake County, #9620; Wernick, "Clarion Colony," 34-35, 47-48, 63-65; *Gunnison Gazette,* November 3, 1911; "In re Clarion Colony," 6-8. The sale of bonds to investors to aid settlement was supported by state law and not uncommon. Settlers with insufficient resources, in undeveloped areas, had few other financial options. Brown's plan to use the colony's land and water rights as security for the bonds without having obtained title was, however, unusual.

83. Wernick, "Clarion Colony," 65.

84. Friedlander, *Virgin Soil,* 36.

85. Gunnison Ward, "Minutes," August 18, 1912.

86. Ibid.

87. *First Successful Jewish Colony,* 11.

88. *Gunnison Gazette,* August 16, 23, 1912; Gunnison Ward, "Minutes," August 18, 1912; Salt Lake City *Herald Republican,* August 18, 1912; *First Successful Jewish Colony,* 14-15.

89. Brown, "Memoirs," 12.

90. Board of Land Commissioners, "Minute Book," 12, August 6, 1912: 678; "Jensen Affadavit"; "Petition for Reimbursement"; Silverman, "Short History," 60; *Gunnison Gazette,* September 6, 1912; Isaac Landman to Joseph Krauskopf, August 7, 1912, Box 15, Krauskopf Papers.

CHAPTER FOUR

1. Chatsky interview.

2. David Friedman to Isaac Landman, September 23, 1912, Box 9, Krauskopf Papers; Silverman, "Short History," 69-70; Wernick, "Clarion Colony," 56-58, 59 (quote).

3. Brown, "Memoirs," 6-7.

4. "Deed of Trust," 113-22; Promissory notes of Aaron Binder to Jewish Agricultural and Colonial Association, November 1, December 24, 1912; Interview with George Hunt, Salt Lake City, April 21, 1984; Wernick, "Clarion Colony," 68 (quote).

5. *Gunnison Gazette,* September 13, 20, 1912; Wernick "Clarion Colony," 70; Benjamin Brown to Isaac Landman, October 14, 1912, Box 5, Krauskopf Papers; *First Successful Jewish Colony,* 11.

6. Wernick, "Clarion Colony," 44.

7. Ibid., 106.

8. Brown, "Memoirs," 10.

9. Wernick, "Clarion Colony," 86.

10. Michaelson interview; Isgur interview; Wernick, "Clarion Colony," 40-41, 44-46; Vogel interview; Hamburger interview; Lieberman interview; Moshe Malamed, *A Flash of Joy,* trans. by Miriam Deutsch, 70, 74, 81, 82, 85; Brown, "Memoirs," 10-11, 15; Malamed, "Diary," 11.

11. Personal letter, Saul M. Farbman, August 30, 1982; Ayeroff brothers interview; Brown, "Memoirs," 2-3; Wernick, "Clarion Colony," 106; Friedman to Landman, September 23, 1912, Box 9, Krauskopf Papers.

12. Wernick, "Clarion Colony," 107; Hamburger interview; Michaelson interview; Interview with Esther Wolfe, Oceanside, California, March 25, 1982.

13. Ayeroff interview.

14. Chatsky interview; Brownie and Horowitz interview by author; Lieberman interview; Brownstein interview.

15. Bernstein Family "Memoirs"; Wernick "Clarion Colony," 69, 76-77; Telephone conversation, Alice Furman Woll, New York City, November 4, 1983.

16. *Jewish Exponent,* September 27, 1912.

17. Isaac Landman to Joseph Krauskopf, August 7, 1912, Box 15, Krauskopf Papers.

18. Blood, *Apostle of Reason,* 241; Rudd, "Samuel Newhouse," 305-6.

19. Silverman, "Short History," 63-64; *First Successful Jewish Colony,* 7.

20. Silverman, "Short History," 68.

21. Ibid.; *First Successful Jewish Colony,* 11.

22. Brown, "Memoirs," 13; Wernick, "Clarion Colony," 75; "In re Clarion Colony," 9.

23. *Jews in American Agriculture,* 33-34; J. W. Pincus to Joseph Krauskopf, January 10, 1911, Box 9, Krauskopf Papers; Wernick, "Clarion Colony," 73-74; "In re Clarion Colony," 6, 9 (quote). Unfortunately, the papers of the Jewish Agricultural Society which were housed at the American Jewish Historical Society have been destroyed.

24. Brown, "Memoirs," 14.

25. "In re Clarion Colony," 10.

26. Ibid., 11.

27. Ibid., 9-12; Brown, "Memoirs," 14-15.

28. "In re Clarion Colony," 14.

29. Ibid., 20.

30. Ibid., 12-21; Brown, "Memoirs," 17-18; Henry S. Joseph, "My Visit to Clarion, Utah," *American Hebrew,* October 10, 1913, 664.

31. Silverman, "Short History," 68; "State of Utah in Account with Jewish Association," in Board of Land Commissioners, Piute Project Correspondence.

32. Barnes, "Miracle Worker in the Desert," 137.

33. Wernick, "Clarion Colony," 85-87; Silverman, "Short History," 87-88; Benjamin Brown to W. D. Candland, March 17, 1913, in Board of Land Commissioners, Piute Project Correspondence.

34. Wernick, "Clarion Colony," 87-88; Brownstein interview; *Gunnison Gazette,* May 9, November 14, 1913; Silverman, "Short History," 74-76.

35. *Gunnison Gazette,* September 5, 1913, May 22, 1914; Personal letter, William Brownie, June 3, 1982; "Souvenir Booklet, Clarion School," (n.p., 1913-14).

36. Malamed, "Diary," 14.

37. Ibid., 15.

38. Wernick, "Clarion Colony," 100-105; Chatsky interview; Friedlander, *Virgin Soil,* 31-32.

39. Wernick, "Clarion Colony," 78-79, 83-84, 88, 93-94; Bernstein Family "Memoirs."

40. *Manti Messenger,* July 18, 1913.

41. *Gunnison Gazette,* July 18, 1913.

42. *Jewish Exponent,* August 8, 1913.

43. Brownie and Horowitz interview by author; Bernstein interview; Isgur interview; Personal letter, Paul Lane, April 2, 1982; Pullman interview.

44. Bernstein Family "Memoirs."

45. Personal letter, Alice Furman Woll, May 16, 1982.

46. Bernstein Family "Memoirs"; Brownie letter, June 3, 1982; Ayeroff brothers interview; Pullman interview; Brownie and Horowitz interview by author.

47. Pullman interview.

48. Sanpete County, "Assessment Roll, 1913," Book F, 58-59; Wernick, "Clarion Colony," 90.

49. Wernick, "Clarion Colony," 85.

50. Friedlander, *Virgin Soil,* 29.

51. Wernick, "Clarion Colony," 60-61; Slobodin interview; Friedlander, *Virgin Soil,* 27-29.

52. Ayeroff interview; Board of Land Commissioners, "Minute Book," 13, July 2, 1913: 163; July 16, 1913: 169; Benjamin Brown to Board of Land Commissioners, July 28, 1913; Clarion colonists to Board of Land Commissioners, July 25, 1913, in Piute Project Correspondence; Wernick, "Clarion Colony," 61-62, 80-82, 89-90; "In re Clarion Colony," 15.

53. Friedlander, *Virgin Soil,* 37-38.

54. Silverman, "Short History," 93.

55. Friedlander, *Virgin Soil,* 38.

56. Wernick, "Clarion Colony," 92.

57. *Gunnison Gazette,* August 29, 1913.

58. Wernick, "Clarion Colony," 93.

59. Friedlander, *Virgin Soil*, 42-43.

60. Translated by Michael Walton.

61. *Gunnison Gazette*, August 15, 1913; Friedlander, *Virgin Soil*, 44-45 (quote).

62. Wernick, "Clarion Colony," 91.

63. Lieberman interview; Wernick, "Clarion Colony," 91; Telephone conversation, Miriam Binder, Baltimore, December 22, 1982.

64. *Jewish Daily News*, n.d., in Malamed, "Diary"; Wernick, "Clarion Colony," 85-86, 95-96.

65. Ayeroff interview.

66. Friedlander, *Virgin Soil*, 39.

67. Ibid., 41.

68. Ayeroff interview.

69. Wernick, "Clarion Colony," 95 (quote), 97.

70. Silverman, "Short History," 95; Silverman interview; Ayeroff brothers interview; Brownie and Horowitz interview by author; Woll letter, May 16, 1982; Ayeroff interview.

71. *American Israelite*, February 19, 1914.

72. *Philadelphia Record*, February 15, 1914.

73. *American Israelite*, February 19, 1914.

74. Board of Land Commissioners, "Minute Book," 13, March 4, 1914: 438; Isaac Landman to Leonard Robinson, May 5, 1914; Gabriel Davidson to Landman, n.d.; Landman to William Spry, May 4, 1914; Spry to Landman, June 25, 1914, Box 28, Governor William Spry Correspondence, 1910-1916, Utah State Archives; Wernick, "Clarion Colony," 108; Malamed, "Diary," 20.

CHAPTER FIVE

1. Brown, "Memoirs," 19.

2. Silverman, "Short History," 90-92; Wernick, "Clarion Colony," 113-15, 126; Brown, "Memoirs," 19; *Jewish Exponent*, April 3, 1914.

3. Wernick, "Clarion Colony," 118.

4. Ibid., 119.

5. Ibid.

6. *Jewish Exponent*, April 3, 1914; *Gunnison Gazette*, April 10, 1914; Wernick, "Clarion Colony," 117-20, 125-26; Isgur interview.

7. Wernick, "Clarion Colony," 121.

8. Ibid., 121-23; Sanpete County, "Assessment Rolls, 1914," Book F, 61-64.

9. Wernick, "Clarion Colony," 116.

10. Chatsky interview; Friedlander, *Virgin Soil*, 46-47; Benjamin Brown to William D. Candland, May 28, 1914; July 2, 1914; Brown to William Spry, July 2, 1914, Box 28, Spry Papers; Board of Land Commissioners, "Minute Book," 13, July 7, 1914: 553; September 3, 1914: 601; October 6, 1914: 617; December 1, 1914: 685-86; William J. Lynch to Robert D. Young, April 23, 1914; Benjamin Brown to William D. Candland, July 6, 1914; William J. Lynch to William Spry, July 16, 1914; Robert D. Young, "Report of the Operating for the Piute Canal for the Month of July," August 1, 1914 in Piute Project Correspondence; Bernstein interview; Wernick, "Clarion Colony," 133.

11. Wernick, "Clarion Colony," 124.

12. Ibid., 125.

13. Ibid., 127.

14. Telephone conversation with Dr. Wayne Rose, Salt Lake City, June 8, 1984; Wernick, "Clarion Colony," 124-28.

15. Malamed, "Diary," 18.

16. Wernick, "Clarion Colony," 129-30; Malamed, "Diary," 17-18.

17. Malamed, "Diary," 19.

18. Ibid.

19. Wernick, "Clarion Colony," 131.

20. Ibid., 130-33; Malamed, "Diary," 19-21.

21. Wernick, "Clarion Colony," 138.

22. Ibid., 135-41; Silverman, "Short History," 98-100; Board of Land Commissioners, "Minute Book," 13, August 4, 1914: 576-77; September 3, 1914: 612; January 8, 1915: 724; February 3, 1915: 762-63; "State of Utah in Account with Jewish Association," in Piute Project Correspondence.

23. Wernick, "Clarion Colony," 141.

24. Ibid., 144.

25. *Gunnison Gazette,* January 29, June 18, July 2, September 17, 1915; Wernick, "Clarion Colony," 151-56; Pullman interview; *Jewish Farmer,* October, 1915; Friedlander, *Virgin Soil,* 49-51.

26. Personal letter, William Brownie, June 6, 1982.

27. Silverman, "Short History," 104.

28. *American Israelite,* December 9, 1915.

29. Wernick, "Clarion Colony," 1, 146, 167; Brown, "Memoirs," 20; *Gunnison Gazette,* November 19, 1915; Silverman, "Short History," 102-3.

30. Shprintz interview; Personal letter, Judith Cohen Brodkin, January 8, 1982; Malamed interview; Hamburger interview. In 1937, Labor Zionist Joseph Furman would return to the land by helping to found a cooperative summer retreat in upstate New York called Raananah Park. Its sixty-four acres were held communally while the thirty-nine cottages erected were privately owned. Personal letter, Alice Furman Woll, May 16, 1982.

31. "Information Regarding the Sale of State Land and Water in Sanpete County," January 18, 1916.

32. Board of Land Commissioners, "Minute Book," 14, November 5, 1915: 169.

33. Benjamin Brown to Board of Land Commissioners, December 11, 1916, in Piute Project Correspondence.

34. Wernick, "Clarion Colony," 164; Board of Land Commissioners, "Minute Book," 14, November 5, 1915: 166-69; January 4, 1916: 224-25; January 5, 1916: 228; December 6, 1916: 578, *Gunnison Gazette,* January 7, 21, 1916; "Information Regarding Sale"; Gunnison Ward, "Minutes," January 30, 1916: 122; *Salt Lake City Tribune,* January 20, 1916. In 1921, Bill #130 was introduced into the Utah House of Representatives. It authorized the Board of Land Commissioners to reimburse the Jewish Agricultural and Colonial Association for payments and improvements made during the Clarion project. The state's debt was estimated to be approximately $11,000. The bill was tabled after a second reading. Salt Lake City *Deseret News,* February 14, 1921; Utah Legislature, House, *Journal,* 14th sess., 1921, 260, 565.

35. Telephone conversation, anonymous, Salt Lake City, March 1, 1982; Lieberman interview; Personal letter, Ben Kristol, February 12, 1982; Personal letters, Benjamin Paul, February 11, 28, 1982; Slobodin interview; Pally interview; Personal letter, Joseph Pally, March 10, 1982; Pullman interview.

36. Marinoff interview.

37. Pally interview.

38. Silverman, "Short History," 103; Brownie and Horowitz interview by author; Marinoff interview; Pally interview; Brownstein interview.

39. Brown, "Memoirs," 22.

40. John S. H. Smith, "Localized Aspects of the Urban-Rural Conflict in the United States: Sanpete County, Utah, 1919-1929," 43-44; Vogel interview; Albert C. T. Antrei, ed., *The Other Forty-Niners: A Topical History of Sanpete County, Utah, 1849-1983*, 293; Brown interview; Quoted in Warshaw, *Life*, 114.

41. Baron, *Russian Jew*, 194.

42. Chimen Abramsky, "The Biro-Bidzhan Project, 1927-1959," in Lionel Kochan, ed., *The Jews in Soviet Russia Since 1917*, 62-75; Israel, *Jews in Russia*, 160-63; Baron, *Russian Jew*, 194-97, 292-93; Solomon Schwarz, "Birobidzhan: An Experiment in Jewish Colonization," in Aronson, et al., *Russian Jewry*, 356-69, 381-94; Weisberg interview; Brown interview.

43. Quoted in Warshaw, *Life*, 113.

44. Edwin Rosskam, *Roosevelt, New Jersey: Big Dreams in a Small Town and What Time Did to Them*, 17-21; Ralph F. Armstrong, "Four-Million-Dollar Village," *Saturday Evening Post* 210: 5-7, 34, 36, 38; Brown interview.

45. Brown interview; Armstrong, "Village," 38-39; Lisa Belkin, "Reunion: Commune Is Recalled," *New York Times*, June 4, 1984, B2; *Deseret News*, February 13, 1939.

46. Wernick, "Clarion Colony," 2.

47. Levit interview by Rosenstocks; Shprintz interview; Lieberman interview; Wolfe interview; Ayeroff interview; Bassin interview; Malamed interview; Bernstein interview; Davidson interview; Isgur interview; Michaelson interview; Pally interview; Vogel interview; Personal letter, Benjamin Paul, May 11, 1982; Pullman interview.

48. Radding, "Journal," 171.

49. Ibid., 171-72; Ayeroff brothers interview; Hamburger interview.

50. Clarion Ward, "Minutes," 1916-1928; Nielsen interview; Frandsen interview; Kimura interview; Hendrickson interview; Cooley, "Clarion," *Gunnison Valley News;* Lamont Nielsen, "The Tragedy of Poverty Flats."

CHAPTER SIX

1. Leo Shpall, "Jewish Agricultural Colonies in the United States," *Agricultural History*, 24: 120-21; *Jews in American Agriculture*, 16; Darwin S. Levine, "A Brief Survey of the Activities of Jews in American Agriculture," 26-33; Singer, "American Jew," 28-30; Herscher, *Jewish Agricultural Utopias*, 29-30.

2. Levine, "Brief Survey," 40-41; Singer, "American Jew," 96-105.

3. Herscher, *Jewish Agricultural Utopias*, 32-37, 48-52; Levine, "Brief Survey," 42-48, 60-61; Singer, "American Jew," 439-41; Shpall, "Jewish Agricultural Colonies," 129-33; Violet and Orlando Goering, "Jewish Farmers in South Dakota—The Am Olam," *South Dakota History*, 12: 232-46.

4. Singer, "American Jew," 409-19; W. Gunther Plaut, "Jewish Colonies at Painted Woods and Devils Lake," *North Dakota History*, 32: 61-64; Lois Schwartz, "Early Jewish Agricultural Colonies in North Dakota," *North Dakota History*, 32: 229-31.

5. *American Israelite*, January 9, 1883.

6. Elbert L. Sapinsley, "Jewish Agricultural Colonies in the West: The Kansas Example," *Western States Jewish Historical Quarterly,* 3: 159; Singer, "American Jew," 453-70, 473-86; Levine, "Brief Survey," 48-51, 56-59; Lipman G. Feld, "New Light on the Lost Jewish Colony of Beersheba, Kansas, 1882-1886," *American Jewish Historical Quarterly,* 60: 159-63; A. James Rudin, "Beersheba, Kansas," *Kansas Historical Quarterly,* 34: 296-97.

7. Quoted in Dorothy Roberts, "The Jewish Colony at Cotopaxi," *Colorado Magazine,* 18: 127.

8. Levine, "Brief Survey," 64; Herscher, *Jewish Agricultural Utopias,* 55-60; Roberts, "Cotopaxi," 124-29.

9. Herscher, *Jewish Agricultural Utopias,* 61-70; Gabriel Davidson, "The Palestine Colony in Michigan: An Adventure in Colonization," *Publications of the American Jewish Historical Society* 29: 61-74; A. James Rudin, "Bad Axe, Michigan: An Experiment in Jewish Agricultural Settlement," *Michigan History,* 56: 120-24, 127, 130.

10. Singer, "American Jew," 391.

11. Levin, *While Messiah Tarried,* 73-75; Singer, "American Jew," 379-94; Louis J. Swichkow, "The Jewish Agricultural Colony of Arpin, Wisconsin," *American Jewish Historical Quarterly,* 54: 84-90.

12. Brandes, *Immigrants to Freedom,* 7.

13. Ibid., 8.

14. Herscher, *Jewish Agricultural Utopias,* 31, 109-12; Shpall, "Jewish Agricultural Colonies," 146; Brandes, *Immigrants to Freedom,* 49, 60-68; Singer, "American Jew," 283-310.

15. Levine, "Brief Survey," 82-83; Shpall, "Jewish Agricultural Colonies," 141-43; Herscher, *Jewish Agricultural Utopias,* 73-83; Brandes, *Immigrants to Freedom,* 55-58; Philip R. Goldstein, *Social Aspects of the Jewish Colonies of South Jersey,* 13-16; Singer, "American Jew," 261-79.

16. Goldstein, *Social Aspects,* 29-31; Brandes, *Immigrants to Freedom,* 93.

17. Quoted in Henrik Infield, *Cooperative Living in Palestine,* 38-39.

18. Arthur Ruppin, "Agricultural Achievements in Palestine," *Contemporary Jewish Record* 5: 270.

19. Wischnitzer, *Dwell in Safety,* 52, 57-60; Levin, *While Messiah Tarried,* 47-50, 389 (quote) 390; Ruppin, "Agricultural Achievements," 268-70; D. Weintraub, M. Lissak, and Y. Azmon, *Moshava, Kibbutz, and Moshav: Patterns of Jewish Rural Settlement and Development in Palestine,* 3-4; Alex Bein, *The Return to the Soil: A History of Jewish Settlement in Israel,* 5-10.

20. Ruppin, "Agricultural Achievements," 270-71; Bein, *Return,* 31; Dan Giladi, "The Agronomic Development of the Old Colonies in Palestine (1882-1914)," in Moshe Ma'oz, ed., *Studies on Palestine During the Ottoman Period,* 178-79; Weintraub, et al., *Moshava,* 4-5.

21. Arthur Ruppin, *The Agricultural Colonisation of the Zionist Organization in Palestine,* 5.

22. Ruppin, *Agricultural Colonisation,* 5; Arthur Ruppin, *Three Decades of Palestine: Speeches and Papers on the Upbuilding of the Jewish National Home,* 49-50; Eliyahu Kanovsky, *The Economy of the Israeli Kibbutz,* 12; Quoted in Levin, *While Messiah Tarried,* 441-42.

23. Avraham Ben-Shalom, *Deep Furrows: Pioneer Life in the Collective in Palestine,* 22.

24. Ruppin, *Three Decades,* 68.

25. Weintraub, et al., *Moshava*, 8; Levin, *While Messiah Tarried*, 377-406; Melford E. Spiro, *Kibbutz: Venture in Utopia*, 32-36; Yosef Criden and Saadia Gelb, *The Kibbutz Experience, Dialogue in Kfar Blum* 7-8; Infield, *Cooperative Living*, 35-36, 42; Kanovsky, *Economy*, 3-4, 25, 31-32; Samuel Kurland, *Cooperative Palestine: The Story of the Histadrut*, 8-11; Paula Rayman, *The Kibbutz Community and Nation Building*, 11-16.

26. Bein, *Return*, 61-62; Kanovsky, *Economy*, 16, 126; Ruppin, *Agricultural Colonisation*, 132-33.

27. Weintraub, et al., *Moshava*, 128.

28. Ibid., 10-11, 125-32; Harry Viteles, *Co-Operative Smallholders Settlements (The Moshav Movement)*, 4: 4, 23, *The Evolution of the Co-Operative Movement*, 1: 33, of *A History of the Co-Operative Movement in Israel;* Kanovsky, *Economy*, 7-9.

29. Ruppin, *Three Decades*, 136.

30. Kanovsky, *Economy*, 47; Ruppin, *Agricultural Colonisation*, 68, 98-99; Weintraub, et al., *Moshava*, 6-7, 12, 185-227; Ruppin, *Three Decades*, 131-32.

31. Ruppin, *Agricultural Colonisation*, 42.

32. Ruppin, "Agricultural Achievements," 278-79; Kanovsky, *Economy*, 8-9, 18-21; Criden and Gelb, *Kibbutz Experience*, 13-19; Viteles, *Smallholder Settlements*, 397.

33. Rayman, *Kibbutz Community*, 28-30, 64-68, 80.

34. Ibid., 74.

35. Ibid., 80.

36. Ibid., 69.

37. Ibid., 46-47, 61, 70, 75-84, 91-100, 109, 253-54.

Bibliography

PRIMARY SOURCES

Manuscript Collections:

Adler, Sophie, Papers. Yivo Institute for Jewish Research.

Baron de Hirsch Fund, Papers. American Jewish Historical Society.

Cooley, Everett L., Papers. Special Collections, Marriott Library, University of Utah.

Jewish Archives, Papers. Special Collections, Marriott Library, University of Utah.

Krauskopf, Rabbi Joseph, Papers. Urban Archives Center, Temple University.

Roe, Ben M., Papers. Special Collections, Marriott Library, University of Utah.

Spry, William, Papers. Utah State Archives.

Spry, William, Papers. Utah State Historical Society.

Zucker, Louis C., Papers. In the author's possession.

Clarion Materials:

Bernstein Family "Memoirs" (unpublished), 1984.

Brown, Benjamin. "Memoirs" (unpublished), n.d.

First Successful Jewish Colony in the United States.

Friedlander, Isaac. *Virgin Soil.* Los Angeles, 1949.

Jensen, Bert. "Clarion" (unpublished), n.d.

Malamed, Moshe. "Diary" (unpublished), 1910-1913.

_____. *A Flash of Joy.* Philadelphia, 1924.

Nielsen, Lamont. "The Tragedy of Poverty Flats" (unpublished), 1982.

Radding, Esther. "Journal" (unpublished), 1962.

Silverman, Barney. "A Short History of Clarion" (unpublished), 1967.

Souvenir Booklet, Clarion School. N.p., 1914.

Warshaw, Maurice. *Life More Sweet than Bitter.* Salt Lake City, 1975.
Wernick, Abraham. "The Clarion Colony: Its Beginnings, Its Life, Its Demise" (unpublished), n.d.

Interviews and Telephone Conversations:
Ayeroff, Al, Joseph, and Sam. Los Angeles, March 23, 1982.
Ayeroff, Nathan, by Edward Eisen. Los Angeles, 1972.
Barak, Henry, telephone conversation. February 21, 1982.
Bassin, Alex. Salt Lake City, June 30, 1982.
Bernstein, Michael. New York, July 28, 1982.
Brown, Sarah, by Michael and Patricia Walton. Phoenix, November 6, 1982.
Brownie, William and Edith Brownstein Horowitz, by author. Philadelphia, October 30, 1983.
Brownie, William and Edith Brownstein Horowitz, by Ben Kristol. Philadelphia, June 17, 1982.
Brownstein, Joseph, by Ben Kristol. Philadelphia, June 1965.
Carpenter, Carl. Clarion, May 15, 1982.
Chatsky, Samuel, by Ronald N. Goldberg. Miami, May 18, 1982.
Davidson, Steven. Salt Lake City, April 14, 1982.
Feldstein, Joshua, telephone conversation. February 23, 1983.
Frandsen, Allen. Clarion, September 20, 1983.
Gorin, Abner. Los Angeles, March 23, 1982.
Gregory, Maia. New York, October 24, 1983.
Hamburger, Sivan. Los Angeles, March 23, 1982.
Hendrickson, Osin. Gunnison, June 26, 1982.
Hunt, George. Salt Lake City, April 21, 1984.
Isgur, Albert. Los Angeles, March 22, 1982.
Kimura, Harry. Clarion, September 20, 1983.
Levit, Louis, by Ben Kristol. Philadelphia, September 3, 1968.
Levit, Louis, by Beryl and Jeffrey Rosenstock. Philadelphia, January 23, 30, 1983.
Lieberman, Herman. Los Angeles, June 17, 1983.
Malamed, Daniel. Los Angeles, March 22, 1982.
Marinoff, Lena Brown. Los Angeles, March 24, 1982.
May, Dean. Salt Lake City, March 14, 1984.
Michaelson, Mina Boyarsky. Los Angeles, March 26, 1982.
Nielson, Lamont. Clarion, June 26, 1982.
Pally, Alex. Ogden, March 7, 1982.
Paul, Benjamin. Salt Lake City, December 2, 1982.
Pullman, Bessie Mastrow. Los Angeles, June 17, 1983.
Rose, Wayne, telephone conversation. June 8, 1984.
Shprintz, Reeta Silverman. Philadelphia, November 2, 1983.
Silverman, Barney, by Ben Kristol. Philadelphia, September 1965.
Slobodin, Barnet, by Joseph Slobodin. New York, August 25, 1974.
Slobodin, Joseph, telephone conversation. March 14, 1982.

Vogel, Lillian Brown. Los Angeles, June 17, 1983.
Weiner, Sara, telephone conversation. September 15, 1983.
Weisberg, Theresa Herbst. Los Angeles, March 24, 1982.
Wolfe, Esther. Oceanside, California, March 25, 1982.
Woll, Alice Furman, telephone conversation. November 4, 1983.
Telephone conversation. March 1, 1982.

Correspondence:
Bassin, Abraham
Bassin, Alex
Bernstein, Harry
Bernstein, Michael
Binder, Miriam
Bober, Sara Sack
Brodkin, Judith Cohen
Brookman, Albert
Brownie, William
Dolowitz, David A.
Farber, Yetta Bassin
Farbman, Saul
Flinker, Sylvia Grishkam
Geronemus, Clement
Hamburger, Sivan
Hausen, Rabbi Max
Holt, Joan
Isgur, Albert
Kristol, Ben
Lane, Paul
Levit, Louis
Levitsky, Joseph
Lieberman, Herman
Malamed, Daniel
Michaelson, Mina Boyarsky
Misler, Eva
Nilva, Daniel
Pally, Joseph
Paul, Benjamin
Payne, Allan S.
Payne, Max
Pearlman, Beatrice
Pullman, Beckie Mastrow
Radding, Eugene
Rapkin, Belle
Rosen, Stella Kreger
Rosenstock, Beryl Levitsky

Shprintz, Reeta Silverman
Smith, Carol
Sokolov, Raymond
Steinberg, Sara Binder
Sternfeld, Leon
Warshaw, Keith
Weiner, Sara
Weisberg, Theresa Herbst
Woll, Alice Furman
Yavil, Isabella Shore
Zigoures, Mollie Yigdoll
Zuckerman, Fannie P.

Public Documents:
  United States:
Department of Agriculture. *Soil Survey of Sanpete Valley Area, Utah.* 1981.
Department of Commerce and Labor. Isaac M. Rubinow. *Economic Condition of the Jews in Russia.* Bulletin of the Bureau of Labor, No. 72, Vol. 15 (September 1907).
_____. Bureau of the Census. *Thirteenth Census of the United States, 1910.* Reports on Population, Manufactures, and Utah.
_____. Census (Manuscript) for New York City and Philadelphia, 1910.
_____. *Census of Religious Bodies: 1916.*
_____. Special Consular Reports. *Emigration to the United States, 1904,* Vol. 30.
Congress, Senate. *Reports of the Immigration Commission,* 1911. Vols. 1, 2, 11, 12, 15, 22, 26, 37.
Industrial Commission. *Reports of the Industrial Commission on Immigration and on Education, 1901.* Vol. 15.

  New York:
New York City. Commission on Congestion of Population. *Report.* New York, 1911.
_____. Tenement House Department. *First Report, 1902-1903.* New York, 1903.
New York State. Factory Investigating Commission. *Preliminary Report, 1912.* Albany, 1912.

  Utah:
Board of Land Commissioners. *Annual Reports.* 1913-1914.
_____. "Certificates of Sale," 1911-1917.
_____. "Information Regarding the Sale of State Lands and Water in Sanpete County, Utah." 1916.
_____. "Minute Book." Vols. 11-14, 1909-1917.

_____. "Piute Project Correspondence." 1908-1916.

_____. "Private Sales Files." Nos. 2877-3000, 3299, 3300, 3754-3763, 3839, 3924.

Bureau of Immigration, Labor and Statistics. *Second Biennial Report, 1913-1914.* 1915.

Utah State Legislature. *House Journals.* 10th, 11th, 14th sess. Salt Lake City, 1913, 1915, 1921.

_____. *Senate Journals.* 10th, 11th, 14th sess. Salt Lake City, 1913, 1915, 1921.

Legal Documents:

Articles of Incorporation, Jewish Agricultural and Colonial Association, 259-5. State of Delaware, 1910.

Articles of Incorporation, Jewish Agricultural and Colonial Association, Incorporation Record, Book 2, 1911. County of Sanpete, 431-40.

Articles of Incorporation, Jewish Agricultural and Colonial Association, 9318. County of Salt Lake, 1912.

Articles of Incorporation, Utah Colonization Fund, Inc. 9620. County of Salt Lake, 1912.

Assessment Rolls, Book "F," 1913-1915. County of Sanpete.

Deed of Trust, Book 59, 1912. County of Sanpete, 113-24.

Jewish Agricultural and Colonial Association, a Corporation v. Louis Hamburger, 1040. County of Sanpete District Court, 1914.

West View Irrigation Company, a Corporation v. the Jewish Agricultural and Colonial Association, 999. County of Sanpete District Court, 1913.

Newspapers:

American Hebrew (New York)

American Israelite (Cincinnati)

Deseret Evening News (Salt Lake City)

Gunnison Gazette

Herald Republican (Salt Lake City)

Jewish Exponent (Philadelphia)

Jewish Farmer (New York)

Manti Messenger

New York Times

Philadelphia Record

Richfield Reaper

Salt Lake Telegram

Salt Lake Tribune

Minutes, Sermons, and Yearbooks:

Church of Jesus Christ of Latter-day Saints. General Minutes of the Axtell Ward. 1912-1916.

_____. General Minutes of the Centerfield Ward. 1910-1916.

_____. General Minutes of the Clarion Ward. 1916-1928.

_____. General Minutes of the Gunnison Ward. 1910-1916, 1924-1925.

_____. General Minutes of the Redmond First Ward. 1910-1916.

_____. General Minutes of the Salina First and Second Wards. 1911-1916.

Jewish Agricultural and Industrial Aid Society. *Annual Reports.* N.p., 1902-1916.

Krauskopf, Rabbi Joseph. *Sunday Discourses Before the Reform Congregation Keneseth Israel.* Philadelphia, 1904-1906.

National Farm School. *Circular of Information.* N.p., 1910-1912.

City Directories:
Baltimore City Directory (1910).
Boyd's Philadelphia City Directory (1907-11).
New York City Directory (1912).
Trow's General Directory of the Boroughs of Manhattan and Bronx, City of New York (1910).
Upington's General Directory of the Borough of Brooklyn (1909).

SECONDARY SOURCES

Books:
Adeney, J. H. *The Jews of Eastern Europe.* London, 1921.

Alexinsky, Gregor. *Modern Russia.* New York, 1913.

Allman, Herbert D. *A Unique Institution: The Story of the National Farm School.* Philadelphia, 1935.

Anderson, Nels. *Desert Saints: The Mormon Frontier in Utah.* Chicago, 1942.

Antin, Mary. *From Plotzk to Boston.* Boston, 1899.

_____. *The Promised Land.* Boston, 1912.

Antrei, Albert C. T., ed. *The Other Forty-Niners: A Topical History of Sanpete County, Utah, 1849-1983.* Salt Lake City, 1982.

Baron, Salo. *The Russian Jew under Tsars and Soviets.* New York, 1964.

Bein, Alex. *The Return to the Soil: A History of Jewish Settlement in Israel.* Jerusalem, 1952.

Belkin, Simon. *Through Narrow Gates: A Review of Jewish Immigration, Colonization and Immigrant Aid Work in Canada (1840-1940).* Montreal, 1966.

Ben-Gurion, David. *Memoirs.* New York, 1970.

Ben-Shalom, Avraham. *Deep Furrows: Pioneer Life in the Collective in Palestine.* New York, 1937.

Benson, Ezra Taft. *A Message to Judah from Joseph.* Salt Lake City, 1978.

Bernheimer, Charles S., ed. *The Russian Jew in the United States.* Philadelphia, 1905.

Best, Gary. *To Free a People: American Jewish Leaders and the Jewish Problem in Eastern Europe, 1890-1914.* Westport, Conn., 1981.

Billington, James. *The Icon and the Axe.* New York, 1966.

Blau, Peter, and Duncan, Otis Dudley. *The American Occupational Structure.* New York, 1967.

Blaustein, Miriam, ed., *Memoirs of David Blaustein.* New York, 1913.

Blood, William W. *Apostle of Reason: A Biography of Joseph Krauskopf.* Philadelphia, 1973.

Blum, Isidor. *The Jews of Baltimore.* Baltimore, 1910.

Bogen, Boris D. *Born a Jew.* New York, 1930.

Book of Mormon. Salt Lake City, 1977.

Brandes, Joseph. *Immigrants to Freedom: Jewish Communities in Rural New Jersey Since 1881.* Philadelphia, 1971.

Brooks, Juanita. *History of the Jews in Utah and Idaho.* Salt Lake City, 1973.

Brownstone, David; Franck, Irene M; and Brownstone, Douglas L. *Island of Hope, Island of Tears.* New York, 1979.

Cahan, Abraham. *The Education of Abraham Cahan.* Philadelphia, 1969.

Charnofsky, Michael. *Jewish Life in the Ukraine.* New York, 1965.

Charques, Richard. *The Twilight of Imperial Russia.* New York, 1958.

Corsi, Edward. *In the Shadow of Liberty: The Chronicle of Ellis Island.* New York, 1935.

Criden, Yosef, and Gelb, Saadia. *The Kibbutz Experience: Dialogue in Kfar Blum.* New York, 1974.

Davidson, Gabriel. *Our Jewish Farmers and the Story of the Jewish Agricultural Society.* New York, 1943.

Davitt, Michael. *Within the Pale: The True Story of Anti-Semitic Persecution in Russia.* New York, 1903.

Dawidowicz, Lucy S. *The Golden Tradition: Jewish Life and Thought in Eastern Europe.* New York, 1967.

DeForest, Robert W., and Veiller, Lawrence, eds. *The Tenement House Problem.* 2 vols. New York, 1903.

Draznin, Yaffa. *It Began with Zade Usher: The History and Record of the Families Bernstein-Loyev, Lewis-Mazur.* Los Angeles, 1972.

Dubnow, S.M. *History of the Jews in Russia and Poland.* 3 vols. Philadelphia, 1916-1920.

Edwards, Alba M. *A Social-Economic Grouping of the Gainful Workers of the United States: 1930.* Washington, D.C., 1938.

Elon, Amos. *The Israelis: Founders and Sons.* New York, 1971.

Epstein, Melech. *Profiles of Eleven.* Detroit, 1965.

Feitelberg, Lionel. *Afikim: The Story of a Kibbutz.* Tel Aviv, 1947.

Feldstein, Stanley. *The Land That I Show You: Three Centuries of Jewish Life in America.* Garden City, New York, 1978.

Fishberg, Maurice. *The Jews: A Study of Race and Environment.* London, 1911.

Friedman, Murray, ed. *Jewish Life in Philadelphia, 1830-1940.* Philadelphia, 1983.

Frumkin, Jacob; Aronson, Gregor; and Goldenweiser, Alexis, eds. *Russian Jewry.* New York, 1966.

Gardner, Hugh. *The Children of Prosperity: Thirteen Modern American Communes.* New York, 1978.

Glanz, Rudolf, *Jew and Mormon: Historic Group Relations and Religious Outlook.* New York, 1963.

Goldstein, Philip R. *Social Aspects of the Jewish Colonies of South Jersey.* New York, 1921.

Goren, Arthur A. *New York Jews and the Quest for Community: The Kehillah Experiment, 1908-1922.* New York, 1970.

Gottesfeld, Chune. *Tales of the Old World and the New.* New York, 1964.

Granovsky, A. *Land Problems in Palestine.* London, 1926.

Green, James R. *Grass-Roots Socialism: Radical Movements in the Southwest, 1895-1943.* Baton Rouge, La., 1978.

Greenberg, Louis. *The Jews in Russia.* 2 vols. New Haven, 1944-1951.

Gunnison Valley's Centennial Memory Book, 1859-1959. N.p., 1966.

Gurock, Jeffrey S. *When Harlem Was Jewish, 1870-1930.* New York, 1979.

Handlin, Oscar. *The Uprooted.* Boston, 1951.

Hapgood, Hutchins. *Spirit of the Ghetto.* New York, 1902.

Heaps, Willard A. *The Story of Ellis Island.* New York, 1967.

Herscher, Uri D. *Jewish Agricultural Utopias in America, 1880-1910.* Detroit, 1981.

Hertzberg, Arthur, ed. *The Zionist Idea: A Historical Analysis and Reader.* Westport, Conn., 1959.

Howe, Irving. *World of Our Fathers.* New York, 1976.

Hurwitz, Maximilian. *The Workman's Circle: Its History, Ideals, Organization and Institutions.* New York, 1936.

Infield, Henrik. *Cooperative Living in Palestine.* New York, 1944.

Israel, Gerard. *The Jews in Russia.* New York, 1975.

Israelsen, Orson W. *Irrigation Science: The Foundation of Permanent Agriculture in Arid Regions.* Logan, Utah, 1943.

Jackson, Richard H., ed. *The Mormon Role in the Settlement of the West.* Provo, Utah, 1978.

Jews in American Agriculture. New York, 1954.

Jones, Maldwyn. *American Immigration.* Chicago, 1960.

_____. *Destination America.* New York, 1976.

Joseph, Samuel. *History of the Baron de Hirsch Fund: The Americanization of the Jewish Immigrant.* Philadelphia, 1935.

_____. *Jewish Immigration to the United States from 1881 to 1910.* New York, 1914.

Kanovsky, Eliyahu. *The Economy of the Israeli Kibbutz.* Cambridge, Mass., 1966.

Karp, Abraham J. *Golden Door to America: The Jewish Immigrant Experience.* New York, 1976.

Kephert, William M. *Extraordinary Groups: The Sociology of Unconventional Life-Styles.* New York, 1976.

Kessner, Thomas. *The Golden Door: Italian and Jewish Immigrant Mobility in New York City, 1880-1915.* New York, 1977.

Kipnis, Ira. *The American Socialist Movement, 1897-1912.* New York, 1952.

Klein, Moses. *Migdal Zophim (The Watch Tower): The Jewish Problem and Agriculture as its Solution.* Philadelphia, 1889.

Kraut, Alan M. *The Huddled Masses: The Immigrant in American Society, 1880-1921.* Arlington Heights, Ill., 1982.

Kurland, Samuel. *Cooperative Palestine: The Story of the Histadrut.* New York, 1947.

Laqueur, Walter. *A History of Zionism.* New York, 1972.

Levin, Nora. *While Messiah Tarried: Jewish Socialist Movements, 1871-1917.* New York, 1977.

Lieblich, Amia. *Kibbutz Makom: Report from an Israeli Kibbutz.* New York, 1981.

Liebman, Arthur. *Jews and the Left.* New York, 1979.

Linfield, Harry. *Statistics of Jews and Jewish Organizations.* New York, 1939.

Litvinoff, Barnet. *Ben-Gurion of Israel.* New York, 1954.

Lubove, Roy. *The Progressives and the Slums: Tenement House Reform in New York City, 1890-1917.* Pittsburgh, 1962.

Mendelsohn, Ezra. *Class Struggle in the Pale: The Formative Years of the Jewish Workers' Movement in Tsarist Russia.* Cambridge, England, 1970.

Metzker, Isaac. ed., *A Bintel Brief: Sixty Years of Letters from the Lower East Side to the Jewish Daily Forward.* Garden City, New York, 1971.

Morris, Yaacov. *On the Soil of Israel: Americans and Canadians in Agriculture.* Tel Aviv, 1965.

Morrissey, Evelyn. *Jewish Workers and Farmers in the Crimea and Ukraine.* New York, 1937.

Novotny, Ann. *Strangers at the Door.* New York, 1971.

O'Dea, Thomas F. *The Mormons.* Chicago, 1957.

Nelson, Lowry. *The Mormon Village: A Pattern and Technique of Land Settlement.* Salt Lake City, 1952.

Pratt, Alan R., and Callaghan, Eugene. *Land and Mineral Resources of Sanpete County, Utah.* Salt Lake City, 1970.

Pratt, Edward E. *Industrial Causes of Congestion of Population in New York City.* New York, 1911.

Rayman, Paula. *The Kibbutz Community and Nation Building.* Princeton, 1981.

Rees, Albert. *Real Wages in Manufacturing, 1890-1914.* Princeton, 1961.

Reiss, Albert J., Jr., *Occupations and Social Status.* New York, 1961.

Reynolds, George. *Are We of Israel?* Salt Lake City, 1916.

Richards, LeGrand. *The Mormons and the Jewish People.* Salt Lake City, n.d.

Riis, Jacob A. *How the Other Half Lives: Studies Among the Tenements of New York.* New York, 1904.

Rischin, Moses. *The Promised City: New York's Jews, 1870-1914.* New York, 1962.

Roberts, B. H. *Rasha — The Jew: A Message to all Jews.* Salt Lake City, 1932.

Robinson, Geroid T. *Rural Russia Under the Old Regime.* New York, 1932.

Roper, William Len, and Arrington, Leonard J. *William Spry, Man of Firmness, Governor of Utah.* Salt Lake City, 1975.

Rose, Peter I. *Strangers in their Midst: Small-town Jews and Their Neighbors.* New York, 1977.

Rosskam, Edwin. *Roosevelt, New Jersey: Big Dreams in a Small Town and What Time Did to Them.* New York, 1972.

Rottenberg, Dan. *Finding Our Fathers.* New York, 1977.

Ruppin, Arthur. *The Agricultural Colonisation of the Zionist Organization in Palestine.* London, 1926.

_____. *Three Decades of Palestine: Speeches and Papers on the Upbuilding of the Jewish National Home.* Jerusalem, 1936.

Sanders, Ronald. *The Downtown Jews: Portraits of an Immigrant Generation.* New York, 1969.

Schmitt, Peter. *Back to Nature: The Arcadian Myth in Urban America, 1900-1930.* New York, 1969.

Shannon, David A. *The Socialist Party of America.* New York, 1955.

Shapiro, Judah J. *The Friendly Society: A History of the Workmen's Circle.* New York, 1970.

Shiloh, Ailon, ed. *By Myself I'm a Book!: An Oral History of the Immigrant Jewish Experience in Pittsburgh.* Waltham, Mass., 1972.

Shur, Shimon; Beit-Hallahmi, Benjamin; Blasi, Joseph Raphael; and Rabin, Albert I. *The Kibbutz: A Bibliography of Scientific and Professional Publications in English.* Darby, Penn., 1982.

Singer, S. *The Return of the Jews to an Agricultural Life.* London, 1889.

Spiro, Melford E. *Kibbutz: Venture in Utopia.* New York, 1970.

Steiner, Edward. *On the Trail of the Immigrant.* New York, 1906.

Stegner, Wallace. *Mormon Country.* New York, 1942.

Thernstrom, Stephen. *The Other Bostonians: Poverty and Progress in the American Metropolis, 1880-1970.* Cambridge, Mass., 1973.

These . . . Our Fathers: A Centennial History of Sanpete County, 1849 to 1947. Springville, Utah, 1947.

Thomas, W. Preston; Blanch, George T.; and Haybill, Edith. *A Study of Farm Organization by Type of Farm in Sanpete and Sevier Counties.* Logan, Utah, 1941.

Thorne, D. Wynne. *The Desert Shall Blossom as the Rose.* Logan, Utah, 1951.

Tobias, Henry J. *The Jewish Bund in Russia: From Its Origins to 1905.* Stanford, Calif., 1972.

Troyat, Henri. *Daily Life in Russia Under the Last Tsar.* New York, 1962.

Viteles, Harry. *A History of the Co-Operative Movement in Israel.* 7 vols. London, 1966.

Watters, Leon L. *The Pioneer Jews of Utah.* Studies in American Jewish History, Vol. II. New York, 1952.

Weintraub, D.; Lissak, M.; and Azmon, Y. *Moshava, Kibbutz, and Moshav: Patterns of Jewish Rural Settlement in Palestine.* Ithaca, New York, 1969.

Wischnitzer, Mark. *To Dwell in Safety: The Story of the Jewish Migration Since 1800.* Philadelphia, 1948.

Zborowski, Mark and Herzog, Elizabeth. *Life Is with People: The Jewish Little-Town of Eastern Europe.* New York, 1952.

Zucker, Louis C. *Mormon and Jew: A Meeting on the American Frontier.* Salt Lake City, 1959.

Articles:

"A Colony in Kansas—1882." *American Jewish Archives* 17 (November 1965): 114-39.

Abramsky, Chimen. "The Biro-Bidzhan Project, 1927-1959." In *The Jews in Soviet Russia Since 1917,* edited by Lionel Kochan. London, 1972.

Armstrong, Ralph F. "Four-Million-Dollar Village." *Saturday Evening Post* 210 (February 5, 1938): 5-7, 34, 36, 38-39.

Aronson, Gregor. "Soviet Russia." In *The Jewish People Past and Present,* Vol. 2. New York, 1948.

Barnes, Will C. "A Miracle-Worker in the Desert." *Breeder's Gazette* (July 22, 1920): 136-37.

Belkin, Lisa. "Reunion: Commune Is Recalled." *New York Times,* June 4, 1984, B2.

Bloom, Bernard H. "Yiddish Speaking Socialists in America: 1892-1905." *American Jewish Archives* 12 (April 1960): 34-69.

Blumenthal, Helen E. "The New Odessa Colony of Oregon, 1882-1886." *Western States Jewish Historical Quarterly* 14 (July 1982): 321-32.

Bronstein, Zelder and Kann, Kenneth. "Basha Singerman: Comrade of Petaluma." *California Historical Quarterly* 56 (Spring 1977): 20-23.

"Colonies, Agricultural." *Universal Jewish Encyclopedia,* Vol. 3. 1941.

Cooley, Everett L. "Clarion, Utah—Jewish Colony in 'Zion'." *Gunnison Valley News,* March 12, 19, 1970.

_____. "Clarion, Utah: Jewish Colony in Zion." *Utah Historical Quarterly* 30 (Spring 1968): 113-31.

Counts, George S. "The Social Status of Occupations: A Problem in Vocational Guidance." *School Review* 33 (January 1925): 16-27.

Davidson, Gabriel. "The Jew in Agriculture in the United States." *American Jewish Year Book* 37 (1935-1936): 99-134.

_____. "The Palestine Colony in Michigan: An Adventure in Colonization." *Publications of the American Jewish Historical Society* 29 (1925): 61-74.

Dwork, Deborah. "Health Conditions of Immigrant Jews on the Lower East Side of New York: 1880-1914." *Medical History* 25 (1981): 1-40.

"Eastern European Immigrant Jew in America (1881-1981)." *American Jewish Archives* 33 (April 1981): 1-140.

Eaton, Joseph W. "Jewish Agricultural Colonization in Palestine." *Rural Soci-*

ology 5 (September 1940): 327-44.

Elazar, Daniel J. "Jewish Frontier Experiences in the Southern Hemisphere: The Cases of Argentina, Australia and South Africa." *Modern Judaism* 3 (May 1982): 129-46.

Feld, Lipman G. "New Light on the Lost Jewish Colony of Beersheba, Kansas, 1882-1886." *American Jewish Historical Quarterly* 60 (December 1970): 159-69.

Feldman, Abraham J. "Rabbi Joseph Krauskopf: A Biographical Sketch." *American Jewish Year Book* 26 (1924-1925): 420-47.

Frank, H. "Jewish Farming in the United States." In *The Jewish People Past and Present,* Vol. 2. New York, 1948.

Freund, Rabbi Charles J. "Significance of the Jewish Farm Colony at Clarion, Utah." *Improvement Era* 16 (December 1912): 106-11; (January, 1913): 248-53.

"From Kishineff to Bialystok: A Table of Pogroms from 1903 to 1906." *American Jewish Year Book* 6 (1906-1907): 34-89.

Geffen, Joel S. "Jewish Agricultural Colonies as Reported in the Pages of the Russian Hebrew Press *Ha-Melitz* and *Ha-Yom.*" *American Jewish Historical Quarterly* 60 (June 1971): 355-82.

Giladi, Dan. "The Agronomic Development of the Old Colonies in Palestine (1882-1914)." In *Studies on Palestine During the Ottoman Period,* edited by Moshe Ma'oz. Jerusalem, 1975.

Goering, Violet and Orlando. "Jewish Farmers in South Dakota—The Am Olam." *South Dakota History* 12 (Winter 1982): 232-47.

Gold, David M. "Jewish Agriculture in the Catskills, 1900-1920." *Agricultural History* 55 (January 1981): 31-49.

Goodman, Jack. "Jews in Zion." In *The Peoples of Utah,* edited by Helen Z. Papanikolas. Salt Lake City, 1976.

Harris, Franklin S. "A Day in a Jewish Village in Russia." *Relief Society Magazine* 16 (December 1929): 633-39.

"Jewish Immigrant Life in Philadelphia." *American Jewish Archives* 9 (April 1957): 32-41.

Joseph, Henry S. "My Visit to Clarion, Utah." *American Hebrew,* October 10, 1913, 664.

Lestschinsky, Jacob. "Economic and Social Development of the Jews." In *Jewish People Past and Present,* Vol. 4. New York, 1955.

Liebman, Arthur. "The Ties that Bind: The Jewish Support for the Left in the United States." *American Jewish Historical Quarterly* 66 (December 1976): 285-321.

Lifschutz, Ezekiel. "Jacob Gordin's Proposal to Establish an Agricultural Colony." *American Jewish Historical Quarterly* 56 (December 1966): 151-62.

Lindenthal, Jacob Jay. "Abi Gezunt: Health and the Eastern European Jewish Immigrant." *American Jewish Historical Quarterly* 70 (June 1981): 442-61.

Menes, Abraham. "The Am Oylom Movement." In *Studies in Modern Jewish Social History,* edited by Joshua A. Fishman. New York, 1972.

Nadell, Pamela S. "The Journey to America by Steam: The Jews of Eastern Europe in Transition." *American Jewish History* 71 (December 1981): 269-84.

Newman, Pauline. "The Rise of the Woman Garment Worker: New York, 1909-1910." In *We Were There: The Story of Working Women in America,* edited by Barbara Wertheimer. New York, 1977.

Plaut, W. Gunther. "Jewish Colonies at Painted Woods and Devils Lake." *North Dakota History* 32 (January 1965): 59-70.

Price, George M. "The Russian Jews in America: Jewish Agricultural Colonies in America." *Publications of the American Jewish Historical Society* 48 (December 1958): 78-133.

Reizenstein, Milton. "Agricultural Colonies in the United States." *Jewish Encyclopedia,* Vol. 1. 1901.

Peterson, Charles S. "Imprint of Agricultural Systems on the Utah Landscape." In *The Mormon Role in the Settlement of the West,* edited by Richard H. Jackson. Provo, Utah, 1978.

Pinson, Kopel S. "Arkady Kremer, Vladmir Medem, and the Ideology of the Jewish 'Bund'." *Jewish Social Studies* 7 (July 1945): 233-64.

Rischin, Moses. "The Jewish Labor Movement in America: A Social Interpretation." *Labor History* 4 (Fall 1963): 227-47.

Roberts, Dorothy. "The Jewish Colony at Cotopaxi." *Colorado Magazine* 18 (July 1941): 124-31.

Robinson, Leonard G. "Agricultural Activities of the Jews in America." *American Jewish Year Book* 14 (1912-1913): 21-115.

Rosenthal, Herman. "Agricultural Colonies in Palestine." *Jewish Encyclopedia,* Vol. 1. 1901.

_____. "Agricultural Colonies in Russia." *Jewish Encyclopedia,* Vol. 1. 1901.

Rubinow, Isaac Max. "The Jewish Question in New York City [1902-1903]." *Publications of the American Jewish Historical Society* 49 (December 1959): 90-136.

Rudd, Hynda. "Samuel Newhouse: Utah Mining Magnate and Land Developer." *Western States Jewish Historical Quarterly* 11 (July 1979): 291-307.

Rudin, A. James. "Bad Axe, Michigan: An Experiment in Jewish Agricultural Settlement." *Michigan History* 56 (Summer 1972): 119-30.

_____. "Beersheba, Kansas." *Kansas Historical Quarterly* 34 (Autumn 1968): 282-98.

Ruppin, Arthur. "Agricultural Achievements in Palestine." *Contemporary Jewish Record* 5 (June 1942): 269-81.

Sapinsley, Elbert L. "Jewish Agricultural Colonies in the West: The Kansas Example." *Western States Jewish Historical Quarterly* 3 (April 1971): 157-69.

Schwartz, Ernest and TeVelde, Johan C. "Jewish Agricultural Settlements in Argentina: The ICA Experiment." *Hispanic American Historical Review* 19 (May 1939): 185-203.

Schwartz, Lois Fields. "Early Jewish Agricultural Colonies in North Dakota." *North Dakota History* 32 (October 1965): 217-32.

Schwarz, Solomon. "Birobidzhan: An Experiment in Jewish Colonization." In *Russian Jewry, 1917-1967*, edited by Gregor Aronson, Jacob Frumkin, Alexis Goldenweiser, and Joseph Lewitan. New York, 1969.

Shankman, Arnold. "Happyville, the Forgotten Colony." *American Jewish Archives* 30 (April 1978): 3-19.

Sherman, C. Bezalel. "The Beginnings of Labor Zionism in the United States." In *Early History of Zionism in America*, edited by Isidore Meyer. New York, 1958.

Shipps, Jan. "In the Presence of the Past: Continuity and Change in Twentieth Century Mormonism." In *After 150 Years: The Latter-day Saints in Sesquicentennial Perspective*, edited by Thomas G. Alexander and Jessie L. Embry. Provo, Utah, 1983.

Shpall, Leo. "A Jewish Agricultural Colony in Louisiana." *Louisiana Historical Quarterly* 20 (July 1937): 821-31.

_____. "Jewish Agricultural Colonies in the United States." *Agricultural History* 24 (July 1950): 120-46.

_____. "The Memoir of Doctor George M. Price." *Publications of the American Jewish Historical Society* 47 (December 1957): 101-10.

Spencer, Joseph Earle. "The Development of Agricultural Villages in Southern Utah." *Agricultural History* 14 (October 1940): 181-89.

Stern, Norton B. "The Jewish Dairyman of San Francisco." *Western States Jewish Historical Quarterly* 14 (January 1982): 167-74.

_____. "The Orangeville and Porterville, California Jewish Farm Colonies." *Western States Jewish Historical Quarterly* 10 (January 1976): 159-67.

Stern, Norton B., and Kramer, William M. "An American Zion in Nevada: The Rise and Fall of an Agricultural Colony." *Western States Jewish Historical Quarterly* 12 (January 1981): 130-35.

Sulzberger, David. "The Beginnings of the Russo-Jewish Immigration to Philadelphia." *Publications of the American Jewish Historical Society,* 19 (1910): 125-50.

Sutherland, John F. "Rabbi Joseph Krauskopf of Philadelphia: The Urban Reformer Returns to the Land." *American Jewish Historical Society* 67 (June 1978): 342-62.

Swichkow, Louis J. "The Jewish Agricultural Colony of Arpin, Wisconsin." *American Jewish Historical Quarterly* 54 (September 1964): 82-91.

Szajkowski, Zosa. "The Attitude of American Jews to East European Jewish Immigration, 1881-1893." *Publications of the American Jewish Historical Society* 40 (March 1951): 221-80.

_____. "How the Mass Migration Began." *Jewish Social Studies* 4 (1942): 291-310.

Szold, Henrietta. "Recent Jewish Progress in Palestine." *American Jewish Year Book* 17 (1915-1916): 24-158.

Tcherikower, Elias. "Jewish Immigrants to the United States, 1881-1900." *Yivo Annual of Jewish Social Studies* 6 (1951): 157-76.

Weinryb, Bernard D. "Jewish Immigration and Accommodation to America: Research, Trends, Problems." *Publications of the American Jewish Historical Society* 46 (March 1957): 366-403.

Whiteman, Maxwell. "Philadelphia's Jewish Neighborhoods." In *The Peoples of Philadelphia: A History of Ethnic Groups and Lower-Class Life, 1790-1940,* edited by Allen F. Davis and Mark H. Haller. Philadelphia, 1973.

_____. "Zionism Comes to Philadelphia." In *Early History of Zionism in America,* edited by Isidore S. Meyer. New York, 1958.

Unpublished Materials:

Green, Arnold H. "A Survey of Latter-day Saint Proselyting Efforts to the Jewish People." Master's thesis, Brigham Young University, 1967.

Levine, Darwin S. "A Brief Survey of the Activities of Jews in American Agriculture." Master's thesis, Columbia University, 1928.

Morn, Frank T. "Simon Bamberger: A Jew in a Mormon Commonwealth." Master's thesis, Brigham Young University, 1966.

Satt, Flora Jane. "The Cotopaxi Colony." Master's thesis, University of Colorado, 1950.

Singer, Richard. "The American Jew in Agriculture: Past History and Present Condition." Prize essay, Hebrew Union College, 1941.

Smith, John S. H. "Localized Aspects of the Urban-Rural Conflict in the United States: Sanpete County, Utah, 1919-1929." Master's thesis, University of Utah, 1972.

Ullrich, C. J. "Report on the Water Supply – Piute Project." Manuscript, 1917.

Vogel, Barbara. "Clarion's Call." Manuscript, 1962.

Walton, Michael. "The House of Israel in Mormon Theology." Manuscript, 1984.

Index